Secret
Ritual and
Manhood
in Victorian
America

Secret Ritual and Manhood in Victorian America

❖ MARK C. CARNES ❖

Yale University Press ❖ *New Haven & London*

Illustrations from The New York Public Library are reproduced courtesy of the
General Research Division; The New York Public Library; Astor, Lenox, and
Tilden foundations.

Designed by Richard Hendel
and set in Ehrhardt type by
Tseng Information Systems, Inc., Durham, North Carolina
Printed in the United States of America by
Vail-Ballou Press, Binghamton, New York

Library of Congress Cataloging-in-Publication Data
Carnes, Mark C. (Mark Christopher), 1950–
Secret ritual and manhood in Victorian America / Mark C. Carnes.
p. cm.
Bibliography: p.
Includes index.
ISBN 0–300–04424–0 (cloth)
0-300-05146-8 (pbk.)
1. Secret societies—History—19th century. 2. Initiations
(into trades, societies, etc.)—History—19th century. 3. Men—
United States—Attitudes—History—19th century. I. Title.
HS204.C37 1989
366'.0973'09034—dc 20 89–8947
CIP

The paper in this book meets the guidelines for permanence and durability of the
Committee on Production Guidelines for Book Longevity of the Council on Library
Resources.

10 9 8 7 6 5 4 3 2

TO MEK

❖ CONTENTS ❖

❖ PREFACE ❖

This is a book about passages. On the simplest level, it examines the cru-
sades, pilgrimages, and assorted peripatetic adventures that millions of men
experienced during secret fraternal rituals. The central argument is that
these long and "perilous" initiatory journeys facilitated the young man's
transition to, and acceptance of, a remote and problematic conception of
manhood in Victorian America.

The researching and writing of this book has been something of a personal odyssey as well. As the secrets of the rituals gradually unfolded, I was
confronted with the more elusive mystery of determining what they meant to
the people who created and performed them. Of necessity I have embarked
on excursions into the fields of religious history and theology, child rearing and developmental psychology, women's history and gender studies, and
structural and cultural anthropology.

My initial foray was supported by a Whiting fellowship. The final push was
aided by a timely year-long research fellowship from the American Council
of Learned Societies and the Barnard College faculty grants committee.

Along the way, many friends and colleagues read sections of the manuscript, or indeed all of it, and consistently provided wise guidance. In addition to those whose assistance is identified in the notes, I especially thank
Sigmund Diamond, Clyde Griffen, Kenneth Jackson, Morton Klass, Robert
McCaughey, William McNeil, and Rosalind Rosenberg. That I sometimes
may have gone astray is no fault of theirs.

I received considerable assistance from the staffs of the New York Public Library, the National Archives, the Columbia University libraries, the
Rush Rhees Library at the University of Rochester, the Newburgh Free
Library, the Wheaton College (Illinois) library, and the Masonic libraries of
the Supreme Council of Scottish Rite of Freemasonry in Washington, D.C.,
and of the Grand Lodge of New York City. I also appreciate the bibliographical help of Susi Pichler. Mary Ellen and Jim Collinge in Rochester,
New York, and Betsy and George Parman in Washington, D.C., were kind
and indulgent hosts during my research trips to their communities.

At the Yale University Press, Charles Grench reassured me repeatedly
that the journey was worth the trouble, and Cynthia Wells labored to make
the voyage less difficult for readers.

I was taught the navigational tools of the historical profession by a master
of the trade, John A. Garraty. For indulging my intellectual peregrinations
but not my wayward logic or prose, I thank him. Simple decency requires

that I describe my debt more fully, but his loathing of adverbs nearly surpasses his aversion to wordiness.

My lodestar for many years has been the extraordinary support, love, and example of my parents, and my voyage was amply provisioned with smiles and hugs from my daughter, Stephanie, who repeatedly braved the trip up to the attic study.

As I groped through the dark and labyrinthine passageways of this endeavor, time and again I was raised to light and to life by the person to whom this book is dedicated. Without her, I would have become lost.

Secret
Ritual and
Manhood
in Victorian
America

❖ P R O L O G U E ❖

Slowly the young man walks toward the sacred campfire. He hesitates, and glances back at the tribal elders, who urge him forward. Thunder rumbles in the distance and lightning pierces the darkness, revealing tribesmen seemingly asleep by a teepee. As the youth approaches, the tribesmen leap to their feet, bind him with a rope, and carry him into the bushes. There they give him a ritual loincloth and moccasins and smear dyes on his face. Several nights later he is brought back to the camp and bound to a log, his bare arms and legs glistening in the light of the campfire. As the fire grows brighter, the prayers and incantations reach a climax. Suddenly an elder, knife in hand, rushes toward the bound figure and subjects him to an ordeal. The tribesmen and elders then gather round, eager to embrace the newest member of their secret society.

Such initiations are common in primitive societies. But this one was, perhaps, different. The tribesmen and elders were members of the Improved Order of Red Men; probably they were friends or business associates of the initiate. The teepee was located in the center of the lodge room. The lightning was provided by lamps or gaslights, the thunder by a gong. And the ritual, which lasted nearly an hour, had been created in the 1860s by a committee in Baltimore.

❖

In 1897 W. S. Harwood, writing for the *North American Review*, described the last third of the nineteenth century as the "Golden Age of Fraternity." A total adult male population of nineteen million in 1896 provided five and a half million members for fraternal groups such as the Odd Fellows (810,000 members), Freemasons (750,000), Knights of Pythias (475,000), Red Men (165,000), and hundreds of smaller orders. Because many men joined more than one order, Harwood estimated that every fifth, or perhaps eighth, man belonged to at least one of the nation's 70,000 fraternal lodges. Millions more belonged to the Grand Army of the Republic (GAR), the Knights of Labor, the Grange, mutual insurance societies, and other organizations that similarly stressed elaborate initiations.[1]

Why, Harwood wondered, did so many men join? He noted that the orders did not promote friendship, for so much time was spent on initiation ceremonies that members never got a chance to know each other. He also rejected the claim that membership was good for business. Members intent on "gratifying their desire" to accumulate initiatory degrees neglected work and wasted huge sums of money. He concluded that men joined the orders and attended the lodges because they felt a "strange and powerful attraction" to the ritual. He explained, "There is a peculiar fascination in the unreality of the initiation, an allurement about fine 'team' work, a charm of deep potency in the unrestricted, out-of-the-world atmosphere which surrounds the scenes where men are knit together by the closest ties, [and] bound by the most solemn obligations to maintain secrecy." [2] Another observer, writing in the same year, proposed an inquiry into the cause of this mysterious attraction, adding that it raised the question of "whether the mystical side of our natures has not expanded relatively more rapidly than that which looks mainly to material comfort." [3]

It is hard not to smile at such nonsense. Scholars have understandably dismissed the notion that on the eve of the twentieth century between 15 and 40 percent of American men, including a majority of those categorized as middle-class, were transfixed by this hokum. They have assumed instead that men joined the orders for much the same reason that men joined other voluntary associations, an American phenomenon Tocqueville had explained long ago: In a nation devoid of established hierarchies and traditional protections, the "independent and feeble" citizens sought strength through association.[4] A century after Tocqueville, Arthur M. Schlesinger, Sr., remarked that America had matured into a "nation of joiners," as evidenced by the growth of business and professional associations, farmers' and laborers' cooperatives, reform societies—and secret fraternal orders. He scoffed at the latter's ritualism: "The plain citizen sometimes wearied of his plainness and, wanting rites as well as rights, hankered for the ceremonials, grandiloquent titles, and exotic costumes of a mystic brotherhood." [5]

Other historians have noted, contrary to Harwood's arguments, that membership carried tangible benefits. Businessmen made contacts, cultivated credit sources, and gained access to a nationwide network of lodges. Ambitious young men could socialize with their bosses. Moreover, fraternal life insurance and death benefits, and even lodge charity, were strong inducements to join at a time when governmental assistance was nonexistent, and industrial accidents all too common. Historians of urbanization and industrialization have suggested further that the sociological benefits of membership outweighed the economic. In an impersonal and bewildering urban environment, the orders provided cohesive social networks. Men who had recently arrived in the city could re-create the face-to-face relationships and values formerly associated with family and community. The orders became a source of stability amidst the social chaos of modern life.[6]

These arguments satisfactorily explain why men joined volunteer fire companies, friendly societies, businessmen's and professional associations, and social clubs. But they do not explain why men joined organizations whose chief, and in some cases only, ostensible purpose was the performance of elaborate successions of initiatory rituals.

In the first scholarly history of a nineteenth-century order, Lynn Dumenil argued that the rituals of Victorian Freemasonry contributed to its sociological function. She agreed that the lodges served as a "spiritual oasis" and "sacred asylum" in a rapidly changing and increasingly heterogeneous world. But where previous scholars had ignored the rituals, she recognized their centrality to the fraternal experience. They were part of a process for separating men from the outside world and placing them securely amongst the brothers of the lodge. The solemn setting intensified the bonds of friendship, and the eclectic religious motifs underscored the values common to all members. She added that the ceremonies articulated prevailing middle-class norms, thereby conferring respectability and legitimacy upon the enterprise.[7]

Dumenil's refinement represents a major advance in the sociological interpretation, but the argument rests on a paradox: It holds that Masons who sought to become part of a "psychic community" nonetheless repeatedly performed long rituals that left little time for members to get to know each other. Why members who desired brotherhood would settle for its ritualistic surrogate is unclear. Indeed, Dumenil cites evidence that Masons in the twentieth century eliminated or abbreviated the rituals precisely because they stood in the way of social activities.[8]

Other important questions remain unanswered: If men already shared a common religious experience, why did they need to have it replicated in the lodge? And if the rituals reaffirmed the values of Victorian America, why did the orders take pains to keep them secret? Before trying to answer these questions, we should establish, first, what the members had in common and, second, what was encompassed in the rituals themselves.

Historians consistently have assumed that the fraternal movement was an urban middle-class phenomenon, and this judgment has been confirmed by recent studies. Occupational analyses show that the majority of members in most Masonic lodges held professional or white-collar occupations.[9] Even the less prestigious orders in cities with disproportionately high immigrant and working-class populations included substantial numbers of middle-class members.[10]

Perhaps more important than the occupational profile of the lodge was the extent to which members identified with the middle classes and enshrined bourgeois sensibilities. Theodore Ross, a nineteenth-century historian of the Odd Fellows, described the membership as derived "almost exclusively" from the "great middle, industrial classes." For Ross, as for most officers of fraternal orders, class did not refer to occupational or economic distinctions, but to cultural and ideological predispositions.[11]

Purely economic considerations, however, made it difficult, if not impossible, for many workers to join fraternal groups. In 1897, a time when factory workers earned four hundred to five hundred dollars a year, the *North American Review* estimated that the average lodge member spent fifty dollars annually on dues and insurance, and two hundred dollars on initiation fees, ritualistic paraphernalia, uniforms, gifts for retiring officers, banquets, and travel. The expectation of having to spend even a fraction of this probably high estimate would have dissuaded most workers from joining.[12]

Relatively few Catholics belonged to the orders, which were repeatedly proscribed by papal edicts during the eighteenth and nineteenth centuries. Parish priests were instructed to urge lodge members to quit their orders; Catholics who persisted in error were to be excommunicated. When the wealthy Catholic businessman Stephen Girard died in 1831, merchants closed their shops and his funeral procession numbered in the thousands. Yet this failed to influence his priest, who, noting Girard's Masonic affiliation, refused to conduct burial rites.[13] Few Catholics were willing similarly to jeopardize their access to the sacraments.

The orders were significant because millions of middle-class Protestant men belonged to them. Their rituals warrant study because they were the main, and often the only, activity on lodge nights. Historians have followed Schlesinger's lead in assuming that fraternal rituals were similar to fraternity initiations, which were used once a year and then forgotten. But fraternal rituals were long and complex; nearly all required well over an hour to perform. Moreover, all of the orders, and the GAR and insurance societies as well, offered elaborate successions of initiatory degrees. When, for example, at an evening meeting an order initiated a member into its third degree, it formally closed the lodge, asked all members who had not attained that degree to leave, and then reopened the lodge and performed the ceremony. Later in the evening it would repeat the procedure for the fourth degree. As the number of degrees increased, meetings often extended well past midnight. This cumbersome arrangement eventually was circumvented by establishing higher-degree lodges, which met on a separate schedule.

In addition to the first three degrees of Freemasonry (termed Blue Lodge Masonry), American Masons could belong to many different degree-granting lodges, which by the mid-nineteenth century had been grouped into two different sets of degrees (or rituals) above the Blue Lodge rites: York (or American) Rite Freemasonry, with ten additional degrees conferred by three separate organizations (lodges affiliated with the Royal Arch, Royal and Select Master, and Knights Templar degree sequences); and Scottish Rite Masonry, with twenty-nine degrees conferred by the Ancient and Accepted Scottish Rite. Odd Fellowship had eight separate major degrees and several minor and honorary ones. (See Appendix B.)

During the last third of the nineteenth century millions of members underwent repeated initiations. Among the nearly one million American Rite Masons in 1903, more than 750,000 had experienced all three Blue Lodge degrees. Of these, 330,000 were members of Royal Arch lodges, which offered four additional rituals. Another 163,000 belonged to the Knights Templars, which conferred degrees eleven through thirteen of the American Rite. Statistics are more difficult to compile for the Scottish Rite, which suffered from jurisdictional disputes. But in the Northern branch alone, about a quarter of the 100,000 members had submitted to all thirty-two initiations. It is not known how many of the 800,000 Odd Fellows had completed all six degrees of the subordinate lodges, but this was a prerequisite for membership in the Encampment branch of the order (degrees seven through nine), which had 130,000 members in 1896.[14]

Members spent huge sums on initiation fees, annual dues, mutual assessment funds, and ritualistic paraphernalia. During the last half of the nineteenth century the revenues of the Odd Fellows exceeded $175 million. The income of the various Masonic bodies was many times this figure. Another $650 million had been spent on insurance payments for the beneficiary orders.[15]

Because such large sums were involved, the writing of rituals was a major growth industry. Self-styled ritualists combed the Bible, ancient mythology, and even contemporary fiction for materials. A group of insurance men approached Lew Wallace in 1893 with a scheme for establishing a secret mutual assessment society with rituals based on his best-selling novel, *Ben-Hur*. They proposed to name the society the Knights of Ben-Hur, knights being a staple of the fraternalists' metaphorical diet, but Wallace, who pointed out that ancient Rome preceded the Middle Ages, insisted upon historical accuracy. Within months an inspired ritual for the Supreme Tribe of Ben-Hur was forthcoming. Soon tens of thousands of men were joining the order, paying dues and assessments, and reenacting the famous chariot race.[16]

Unbeknownst to prospective members, many orders plagiarized the most successful rituals of their competitors. To protect themselves from unscrupulous rivals, some "secret" societies copyrighted their rituals. Freemasons, the most frequent victims of ritual piracy, warned potential members against being inveigled into taking illegitimate degrees, "for the clandestine Masonry hawked about in the marketplaces, however sweet it may seem in the taking, will be sure to disgust in the end." Masons who knowingly accepted unauthorized higher degrees were to be drummed out of their regular lodges, while those who unwittingly became initiated into false degrees were to be "healed" through a special rite of purification.[17] One official observed that these measures failed to restrain younger men, who often were "so in love with mysteries" that they did not care where they came from.[18] Why that was, he did not say.

❖

Young Protestant middle-class men sought their rituals not only in the fraternal and beneficiary lodges, but also in scores of voluntary associations with primarily religious, reform, political, or economic objectives. College fraternities are an obvious example, but they involved few men and their initiations were brief and undeveloped.[19] Fraternal initiation was more important in Mormonism, temperance societies, the Know-Nothings and the Knights of the Golden Circle, the Grange, labor and veterans' organizations, and the life insurance industry. Historians of each of these subjects have commented on the peculiar role of initiation, which they generally have attributed to special functional requirements: Labor organizers employed secrecy to shield members from blacklisting, and fraternal life insurance firms used ritual to remind members to pay premiums. What is less well appreciated is the extent to which founders and members regarded ritual as important in and of itself. Some illustrations are in order.

Mormonism. On May 4, 1842, six weeks after he had been raised to the "sublime degree" in Freemasonry, Joseph Smith, the founder of the Mormon Church, instituted secret rites for bringing men into the priesthood of the Mormon Temple.[20] He told the church elders that God had given King Solomon the secrets of a holy priesthood, but that over the years these rituals—known as Freemasonry—had been corrupted. The new rites of the Mormon Temple were actually the perfected rituals as Solomon had received them.[21] During the temple rites elders wore quasi-Masonic aprons depicting Old Testament characters and employed Masonic language, grips, passwords, oaths, and symbols; candidates for the priesthood wore sacred undergarments bearing the square and compass. Whether Smith stole the temple rites from Freemasonry, as the Masons claim, or received them as revelation from God is ultimately a question of faith. What cannot be disputed is that quasi-Masonic ritual figured prominently in the lives of most Mormon men.[22]

Temperance societies. With the decline of the temperance campaign by reformed drunkards in the Washington movement during the 1840s, a new temperance organization, the Sons of Temperance (1842), was created. It modeled its constitution on those of the Freemasons and Odd Fellows and established simple initiation ceremonies.[23] In the 1850s and 1860s a host of rival temperance societies emerged, all of which proposed more impressive rituals. The Sons of Honor offered six initiatory rituals based on the higher degrees of Masonry and Odd Fellowship. Early meetings of the Independent Order of Good Templars, founded in 1851, were almost entirely occupied with debates over ritual.[24]

Nativism. In 1844 six men, including three Freemasons, held discussions in Philadelphia that led to the creation on July 4, 1845, of the United American Mechanics, Jr., the first fraternal society with nativist aims. Within a month it adopted secret rituals derived from Freemasonry and established a sickness and death benefits fund resembling that of the Odd Fellows.[25] By 1855 its membership approached 50,000, but the members, preoccupied with social and ritualistic activities, had little time for a political program.[26] The order was soon overshadowed by a far more powerful nativist organization.

Know-Nothings. Charles B. Allen founded the Order of the Star-Spangled Banner in New York in 1849. Eventually called the "Know-Nothings," a phrase taken from the group's first-degree ritual, the order spread rapidly and soon nominated candidates for public office under the designation of the American Party. In 1854 the Know-Nothings managed to elect nearly seventy-five Congressmen. The following year they carried statewide elections in Rhode Island, New Hampshire, Connecticut, Maryland, and Kentucky. Their candidate for president of the United States in 1856, ex-President Millard Fillmore, received 875,000 votes. The meteoric rise of the Know-Nothings was largely due to the disintegration of the Whigs and divisions in the Democratic Party over slavery. But scholars have observed that the secret rituals lured thousands of men into the organization and were a major reason for the political movement's ability to attract and hold members.[27]

Copperhead societies. In early 1861 George Bickley, a member of the Know-Nothings, blended Masonic imagery with nativist rhetoric to create his own society, the Knights of the Golden Circle, which featured three initiatory degrees.[28] There was no mention of slavery or states' rights. Bickley organized "castles" by mail, sending interested individuals coded copies of the rituals and their keys for a fee of five dollars.[29] After the firing on Fort Sumter, he changed the rituals. Anagrams of the name Calhoun now served as passwords, and Knights swore to support a states' rights platform. During the Civil War the lodges of the Knights served as gathering places for Copperheads, northerners who sympathized with the South, and at its peak the organization had some 200,000 members who had experienced the three initiations.[30] Although Thaddeus Stevens and other Radical Republicans insisted that the Knights were bent on sedition,[31] historians since have dismissed such claims. The Knights apparently paid little attention to the rhetoric of their leaders. As one historian commented, members attended the meetings because they were "dazzled by the elements of secrecy."[32]

Veterans' organizations. After the Civil War, soldiers from the Union and Confederate armies established veterans' organizations. What distinguished the Military Order of the Loyal Legion (1865), the Grand Army of the Republic, or GAR (1866), the Union Veterans' Legion (1884), and the United Confederate Veterans (1889) from veterans' organizations before and since was their emphasis on ritual. Of these organizations, the GAR, with 400,000 members in the 1880s, was the most important.

Ku Klux Klan. The Ku Klux Klan was organized in 1866 at Pulaski, Tennessee, by young men who were apparently familiar with the ceremonies of a fraternal order called the Sons of Malta, as those ceremonies closely resembled the Klan's initiations.[33] Dissolved by federal troops in 1869, the Klan was of limited significance during the nineteenth century. One historian observed that initiation was the order's "principal object."[34]

Grangers. The Order of the Patrons of Husbandry was the brainchild of Oliver H. Kelley, a clerk for the U.S. Department of Agriculture.[35] In 1866 Kelley drafted rituals for the order and read them to fellow bureaucrats within the Department of Agriculture, many of whom happened to be Masons. He told them that his rituals would "lend an interest and a peculiar fascination, while the material for manufacturing new degrees to keep up interest" would be "inexhaustible." Kelley quit his job, packed his coded ritual books, and headed west to organize farmers' lodges. By 1876 membership in the organization, commonly known as the Grange, approached 800,000.[36] Subsequent farmers' organizers included similar ceremonies, and even the National Farmers' Alliance, organized in 1880 for political purposes, incorporated rituals much like those of the Patrons.[37]

Insurance societies. The first American fraternal insurance society, the Ancient Order of United Workmen, was founded in 1868 in Meadville, Pennsylvania, by John J. Upchurch, a Freemason. He wrote four initiatory degrees, culled from Masonry and Odd Fellowship, and envisioned a ritualistic order; providing insurance was then only a minor consideration.[38] By 1897 the AOUW had 315,000 members, most of whom experienced all four separate initiations of the order. Between 1869 and 1896 it accumulated revenues of nearly $100 million.[39] Hundreds of similar secret beneficiary societies offering fellowship, cheap insurance, and initiatory ritual came into existence from 1880 to 1900. Many did not bother to report to state insurance departments; those that did reported a total of more than 2.6 million members with annual revenues of nearly $50 million in 1898.[40] The leaders and historians of the successful beneficiary societies almost uniformly attributed the growth of their orders to ritual.[41]

Knights of Labor. The Holy and Noble Order of the Knights of Labor was the most prominent example of the use of fraternal ritual in labor unions.[42] The group was founded in 1869 by Uriah S. Stephens, a tailor who belonged to the Masons, Odd Fellows, and Knights of Pythias.[43] He created a long and complicated ritual with many Masonic motifs and phrases.[44] Stephens was not an effective leader, and the transformation of the Knights of Labor from a small secret society to an organization with nearly 730,000 members in 1886 was largely the work of Terence V. Powderly, who shifted the focus of the order to labor issues rather than ritual. Yet the rituals remained, and millions of workers knelt before a black-gowned, masked official and participated in and witnessed quasi-Masonic initiations. Recent historians have concluded that such rituals were "part of the very fabric" of the cultural life of late nineteenth-century skilled workers.[45]

The founders of fraternal groups emphasized ritual from the outset and added other activities almost by chance. Officials and members constantly debated the adequacy of their rituals and proposed revisions whenever membership flagged. In 1858, for example, a faction within the Good Templars complained that the order would collapse unless it adopted better initiations. Grand lodges in several states, angered by the national lodge's inactivity, offered prizes of fifty to one hundred dollars to the member who submitted "the best and most perfect Ritual." Others threatened to establish a rival order with rituals suitable to meet "the growing demands of the Order, and of the Age." The revisionists eventually took control of the national grand lodge and greatly expanded the rituals. At the time of the 1868 annual convention, the leaders, noting an increase in membership of 310,000 in four years, claimed that the new rituals were responsible for this growth.[46] In

1887 a historian of the Knights of Pythias attributed its success to a ritual that had "taken hold of the hearts of men [so] that, today, the growth of the order is without parallel in the history of secret organizations."[47]

In nearly every organization some leaders complained that the emphasis on ritual deflected money, time, and effort away from tangible political or economic objectives. Oliver M. Wilson, Commander of the Indiana Department of the Grand Army of the Republic, condemned "the bauble of ritualism" for sapping the organization of energies that should have been used to push for government pensions and health benefits.[48]

Much of Terence Powderly's career with the Knights of Labor was similarly occupied in struggles with the pro-ritualists. "If the object of the Order was to waste the time of each meeting in a long rigamarole of senseless phrases," Powderly told one master workman who balked at giving up the Stephens ritual, "then [keep] the old A.K. [Adelphon Kruptos] by all means." He urged local assemblies to concentrate instead on labor organizing. "For years I have been opposed to the old style of initiation," he wrote in 1881, explaining that "the best part of each meeting in the local assembly was taken up in initiating new members, in instructing them in the use of symbols, in hymns and formula that could not be put in practice in the interest of labor outside the meeting room."[49] But these were private thoughts. Although he sought to eliminate the ceremonial features of the Knights, Powderly himself was ultimately forced to prove his credentials as a ritualist.[50]

If labor leaders struggled with the mysterious attraction of ritual, outsiders found it even more difficult to explain. During the railroad strikes of 1877, Allan Pinkerton infiltrated the Brotherhood of Locomotive Engineers to prove that its secret initiations masked subversion. What his agents uncovered, however, were rituals similar to those of scores of orders. Pinkerton tried to work up an impassioned denunciation of the organization but finally acknowledged that the rituals were "simply a mess of the silliest bosh imaginable." The danger, he noted, was that many workers nevertheless were transfixed by these ceremonies: "Men are initiated with all the impressiveness which mystery and fear can give and are subsequently held and controlled by these communistic scoundrels."[51]

A French economist named Georges Tricoche visited the United States in 1897 to determine why so many American men put so much money into fraternal beneficiary societies. He discovered that the orders neglected actuarial principles, suffered from inept management and frequent defalcations, and lacked the financial resources of the private companies. Yet by 1898 they had over two and a half million members, nearly a half million more policyholders than the private companies.[52]

Tricoche was further puzzled that these were not the simple folk one might expect would be gulled by fast talkers or confidence men. Rather, the members were "mature men, serious well-informed men—great industrialists, professors, even Protestant ministers" who nevertheless chose to transform themselves into knights or Indians and to submit "to curious oaths and phrases." It was precisely this ersatz mysticism that accounted for the success of these orders, Tricoche concluded. Members made financial sacrifices in order to participate in rituals that possessed "the attraction of all that is mystical and secret."[53]

It is difficult for the modern reader not to sympathize with Tricoche—or, for that matter, with Powderly or Pinkerton. Temperance leaders, political schemers, veterans, farmers, insurance buyers, labor union members—all surely would have fared better had they paid less attention to ritual and more to bread-and-butter issues. It is hard to disagree with the historian Eric Hobsbawm, who described the intense ritualism of the labor orders as "misplaced ingenuity."[54] But present-minded assessments of this nature beg the real question: Why did so many men implicitly sacrifice economic, political, and social goals in order to perform these rituals?

This is not to argue that ritual was the sole or even primary reason why millions of men joined and remained active in these organizations. The growth of the Grangers was chiefly due to the rate practices of the railroads, and membership totals of the Knights of Labor were more sensitive to the outcome of labor actions than to modifications in ritual. What is at issue is why similar, elaborate rituals were found in so many organizations with such different purposes.

Nearly every nineteenth-century commentator acknowledged that this fascination was beyond reason. Members saw little point in attempting to explain the significance of rituals to the uninitiated, especially because this would have violated pledges of secrecy: Without referring to the secret symbols and arcana, how could one explain what they meant? Those who did publicly comment on the initiations often compared them to magnetism, an equally inexplicable and compelling force. This language suggested two important aspects of the phenomenon: There was something special about certain rituals that "attracted," "charmed," or "lured" members, and many men were somehow predisposed to "crave" or "desire" them. All rituals were not successful, nor did all men crave them.

Few Victorian men were given to self-analysis, and those who were rarely committed their introspections to paper, particularly on subjects they had promised to keep secret. With the exception of statements from apostate members, who attributed the ceremonies to Satan, there is little direct evidence about how the initiations affected members.

I therefore turned to the writings of nineteenth-century fraternal leaders and scholars. One cannot assume that members subscribed to the beliefs of their officials any more than one can attribute to the Puritans the views of the divines. I nevertheless followed the example of ethnographers, who often seek out priests or shamans. This seemed sensible enough, if only because fraternal scholars, like the religious leaders, had the most to say on the subject. And, unlike native priests, who were merely the custodians of a received tradition, the founders and scholars wrote and revised fraternal rituals. Surely no one was better suited to determine what they meant.

The ritualists themselves nonetheless could not predict which ceremonies would succeed, nor why. And they freely acknowledged an inability to understand the deeper meanings of their own rituals. In the closing lecture of the culminating thirty-second degree of Scottish Rite Freemasonry, the master of the lodge lectured at length on the symbols. He concluded by adding that, although the symbols had a still deeper meaning, "we have, as to this, ourselves succeeded in obtaining but a few hints, and we can therefore communicate no more to you." [55] If even the authors of the rite could not deduce its meaning, the historian's task is more difficult and necessarily speculative.

Psychoanalytical theory offers one way of bridging the gap between unconscious motivations and ceremonial practices. And the themes and symbols of fraternal rituals are often laden with the gender and interfamilial associations on which psychoanalytical models depend. Briefly consider the basic plot of the Master Mason degree: The master of the lodge "tortured" the initiate, who was naked from the waist up, by pressing the points of a compass against his left and right breasts. The initiate was then "killed" and buried. After various mystical incantations and processes, he was raised up to a new life as a Master Mason.

A Freudian explanation which focuses on the father's efforts to discourage Oedipal attachments in sons seems promising: Before the initiate (or son) is permitted to become a man (like his father), the master (his father) tortures him (threatens him with castration). Frightened by this display of paternal anger, the initiate ceases to identify with his mother and instead begins to identify with his father, which renders him fit to move in the company of men.[56] But an opposed psychoanalytic interpretation which argues that puberty rites are attempts by men to break a female monopoly on reproductive powers seems equally plausible. The Masonic initiate received his wound upon his "breasts," and, after dying, emerged from his grave (a new womb) and received a new life (rebirth through the agency of men).[57] Either psychoanalytical explanation is credible; because neither can be disproved or confirmed, however, they are of little use for this study.[58]

Many anthropologists have warned ethnographers, as they do not share the traditions and values of their subjects, against making assertions about unconscious (and uncommunicated) thoughts.[59] But others, most significantly Victor Turner, insist that this detachment gives the anthropologist an advantage over the participants, who may be too close to the rituals to perceive their more subtle meanings. Turner's work is relevant to this study partly because he confronted a similar methodological problem: Like the members of secret orders, his informants, the Ndembu, were not particularly communicative.

Turner proposed a middle ground between the psychoanalysts, who interpret ritual with relatively little attention to the people who practice it, and structural anthropologists, who consider ritual a reflection of social structure rather than an instrument of psychological mediation. He urged anthropologists to elicit from the participants the meanings of dominant ritual symbols in everyday life and then to compare how they are used in ritual contexts.[60]

Such an approach applied to the Master Mason ritual might entail asking a member who had just attended a funeral to explain the significance of the grave, the earth, and perhaps the act of burial; or, in the midst of activities unconnected with the lodge, the interviewer could ask the Mason what he associated with the compass or with the naked human breast. These responses could then be related to the structure of American society.

Historians of the nineteenth century obviously cannot proceed in this fashion. I have therefore reconstructed the public meaning of the predominant ritual symbols from more general sources. With respect to the Master Mason degree, for example, I have considered its funeral symbolism in light of nineteenth-century attitudes on corpses, burial, and death; the rebirth imagery in the context of the changing theology of conversion; the symbolism of the naked body and the breast in view of contemporary attitudes on sexuality and gender roles; and the juxtaposition of masters and novices in connection with relations between Victorian fathers and sons. The meanings of some symbols remained constant within the lodge and without, but many underwent a dramatic transformation. Much of the significance of fraternal ritual derives from this use of familiar symbols in unusual contexts.

At the outset of this study I endorsed the view of Emile Durkheim that ritual forms arise in response to transformations in the underlying structures of society. Because the orders were institutions of the emerging urban-industrial middle class, I initially looked at them through the lenses provided by theories of class, urbanization, and industrialization. But as I studied the phenomenon more closely and began to focus on the rituals themselves, it became apparent that I had neglected the obvious: Nearly all the orders were exclusively *masculine* institutions, and their rituals were closely linked to issues of gender. Farmers, industrial workers, and veterans practiced the rituals, not because they aspired to the way of life of the urban middle classes, but because they shared with them similar concerns about gender.

This book argues that fraternal ritual provided solace and psychological guidance during young men's troubled passage to manhood in Victorian America. Women's historians have shown that gender distinctions pervaded nearly all aspects of life; thus manhood entailed the acquisition of a wide range of roles and statuses. Fraternal rituals accordingly took on many different levels of gender meanings and significance. The expressed intention of the young man joining an order to make contacts and acquire status masked a desire to gain sufficient position to marry. When he intoned the sacred words of the rituals, he unknowingly ventured into a religious arena that had recently been transformed by evangelical women. When he left home for the lodge several evenings each week, keeping his wife in the dark about what transpired there, he imparted to her a painful message about the marital relation. When he performed the roles of Old Testament fathers or Indian chieftains, he reenacted paternal roles replete with gender significance. And when he ventured into the deepest recesses of fraternal secrets, he encountered ideas about gender expressed nowhere else in Victorian America.

Durkheim had no patience with those who sought to explain rituals through an examination of emotions, which are, he thought, "naturally refractory to analysis."[61] No science of society could be built upon so speculative an undertaking. But while the social scientist seeks empirical knowledge by discerning the common elements of human behavior in various periods and cultures, the historian's task is essentially reconstructive: to understand human behavior within a particular context. In the vignettes that precede all but the third chapter, I have taken this mandate beyond normal bounds. These episodes, though based on historical facts, have been presented in a way that suggests my sense of the operation of the fraternal mind. This is speculative, as is any attempt to penetrate the secret regions of the soul.

CHAPTER I

Masks

ENTERED ACCORDING TO ACT OF CONGRESS IN THE YEAR 1848 BY DR E WILLIS   BROWN & WORCESTER

He wondered what was taking so long. Surely they were not still debating his merits. Wilmot, who also clerked on Front Street, reported that the vote had been unanimous. "You're in," he had said, "assuming you make it through the initiation." They had laughed at this, but now, as he sat in what they called the preparation room, he was less confident. He certainly did not feel "prepared." He tried to recall the chapter on the initiation in Wilmot's book. "Fear nothing," it had said, "be appearances what they may." He couldn't make sense of the words. The phrase was intentionally mysterious, like the secret handshakes and passwords and symbols. Even Wilmot, who couldn't keep his mouth shut about anything, refused to discuss the ceremony.

He straightened the collar on his Improved French Yoke Shirt—it had cost two days' salary—and he felt moisture just below his chin. A drop of blood was smeared on his knuckles. He cursed. The notice for Glenn's Sulphur Soap said it would "cure blemishes of complexion, and prevent contagion," but it had only irritated his skin. Small wonder he had cut himself.

As he dabbed his chin, he stared at the straight-backed chairs along the opposite wall. Evidently men were sometimes initiated in groups, but tonight he would have to go through the oak door alone. On the wall were drawings and photographs of Past Noble Grands. Many had shopped at the Front Street store. He studied their faces and wondered if he, too, should grow a beard. These were men of substance, and the beards made their eyes appear more serious, their features more intense. He recognized the justice of the peace, James Penny. His pointed beard made him look like an Egyptian pharaoh. Jacob Dewitt, the town clerk, had a tangled beard that contrasted with his slick haircut. He wondered if Dewitt used Dr. Lyons Pomade. L. S. Rosencrantz, the town supervisor, and Charles St. John, who ran the National Bank of Port Jervis, had closely trimmed mustaches that grew downward, engulfing their chins. Floyd Goble's beard looked like General Meade's; Goble had been wounded at Gettysburg and no doubt wanted to remind people of his valor. Below Goble was Lemuel Elston, trustee of the Drew Methodist Episcopal Church and supervisor of the Sunday school, another veteran. Elston resembled Moses; his long white beard extended beyond the photograph. Solomon Van Etten, a surgeon in the war, now a principal in St. John's bank; and Francis Marvin, founder and director of the Port Jervis Gas Company, had shiny black beards that made their faces seem deathly pale. In the other photographs he saw the merchants of Pike and Front Streets, many of whose names he did not know. All stared at him through their whiskers implacably.

That he was about to join the ranks of such men was a signal honor, and one that would help his career. Membership in the order would place him among the substantial men of Port Jervis and bring him into contact with even more important men elsewhere, men such as Schuyler Colfax, whom Wilmot and he had heard in Poughkeepsie last month. The former vice-president had looked remarkably like his patron, President Grant. During Colfax's speech the clerk decided to join the order. Colfax had called it "a beautiful temple," its altars "consecrated to the purest morality, its walls profaned by no bacchanalian orgies." The clerk smiled at the thought of Colfax, or for that matter Dr. Van Etten or the venerable Floyd Goble rolling around drunk on the floor, their beards stained with the wine of Bacchus. Wilmot's book had said that while initiates in "olden times" were often treated with levity or rudeness, nowadays the ceremonies were "perfectly chaste, dignified, and serious." They were all damned fools, he thought, especially Wilmot, with that clown-faced grin.

Now muffled sounds came from beyond the far door. They were singing. It sounded like a hymn, but without female voices the song seemed ponderous. The music stopped and the lodge became silent. He heard a murmur, rising occasionally for emphasis and falling away again. Perhaps Elston was giving a prayer. The clerk became uneasy. He recalled Colfax's words about altars and temples. He wouldn't have minded being the butt of a joke; he had planned to laugh deeply and to glower at Wilmot in mock anger. But he didn't know how to act during the "serious and chaste" proceedings at the altars of this "temple."

Chairs scraped, doors opened and closed, and then a man in his fifties— a foreman in the gas factory—opened the far door. "Would you please come in here?" he asked. The door did not lead to the lodge room, as the clerk had thought, but to a room scarcely larger than the preparation room. Lockers lined the wall. A table and chair were in the middle of the room. The clerk walked briskly, trying to conceal his confusion.

The foreman sat down at the desk and began to ask questions and record his answers on a sheet of paper. The order had every right to know all about him, the clerk thought, but these questions were hardly necessary. A secret committee had been inquiring about him around town. Certainly they already knew his name, residence, occupation, and age. Dr. Van Etten could have told them—perhaps had told them—that he was in good health.

"Do you believe in the existence of a Supreme, Intelligent Being, the Creator and preserver of the Universe?"

The clerk hesitated. He believed in God, at least in some vague way, but he had never before been pressed on the point. He tried to remember the joke about the parson and the schoolmarm, but the foreman's eyes were stony. The clerk recalled the passage in Wilmot's book which told initiates to answer all questions "seriously and plainly" and to respond "promptly" to commands. He now hastened to say yes, he did believe in God. He tried to appear earnest.

"Are you willing to pledge on your sacred honor to keep secret all that may transpire during your initiation?" The clerk suppressed a smile and immediately said yes; he repeated an oath to that effect. The foreman stood, tied a black silk cloth over the clerk's eyes, and helped him to his feet. "Just follow my lead," he whispered. The clerk recalled the warning in Wilmot's book: "Give yourself passively to your guides, to lead you whithersoever they will." He felt dizzy. He had been sitting too long.

Three loud, wooden knocks resounded nearby. "Who comes there?" The voice from inside was self-consciously menacing.

"A brother" the foreman answered, "with a friend who desires to be initiated into the solemn rites and mysteries of this ancient institution."

The door opened and the foreman pushed the clerk forward. "You are now within a lodge of Odd Fellows—here the world is shut out—you are separated from its cares and distinctions, its dissensions and its vices." The clerk could not recognize the voice. The speaker continued to talk about friendship and charity, but the clerk was distracted. He sensed the presence of the members and recalled the somber, leonine portraits in the preparation room. Surely they were studying him now. He worried that the dull-witted foreman had mussed his hair while blindfolding him. He hoped he didn't appear ridiculous. The lecturer raised his voice: "Those who surround you have all assumed the obligations and endeavor to cherish the sentiments peculiar to Odd Fellowship; but before you can unite with them you must pass through an initiatory ceremony, which will lead you to primary truth." He paused. "Are you willing to proceed?"

"Yes." The clerk noticed that his voice was surprisingly thin. The room must be large. He feared he sounded as silly as he looked. "Be patient and firm," the lecturer advised. "Brothers, the stranger now awaits our mystic rites."

Suddenly the clerk was pushed to the floor. "Now, presumptuous mortal," someone declaimed, "where is your greatness? Low, level with the earth. This is the state of man. For thou art dust."

"Prepare the emblematic chains at once!" The clerk was jostled, and he felt chains being wound around his body, arms behind. Then there were shouts:

"Now! bind him to the stake!"

"Hold, brothers! Shall we proceed with these, our mystic rites, or shall we show mercy?"

"Mercy! Mercy!" The clerk couldn't recognize any of the voices.

"First, a solemn warning then. Lead on our friend."

The clerk was slowly pulled by the chains around the room. He stumbled against a chair and struggled to keep his balance. All the while a voice intoned, "Man in darkness and in chains! How mournful the spectacle. Yet it is the condition of millions of our race, who are void of wisdom, though they know it not. We have a lesson to impart to him—one of great moment and solemnity; a faithful exhibition of the vanity of worldly things—of the instability of wealth and power—of the certain decay of earthly greatness."

The clerk listened carefully. If they asked a question, he wanted to answer quickly and sensibly. Laughter was out of the question. He concentrated instead on his awkward, blind walk around the lodge. Continually he slowed, fearing that he would collide with a wall, but the room was far larger than he had imagined possible. His "conductors" kept pulling at the chains to make him keep pace. The lecturer mercifully drowned out the sound of his uneven footsteps.

After several painfully slow journeys around the room—the clerk lost count—he was brought to a stop. "Be serious, for our lesson is as melancholy as it is truthful," the lecturer warned. The room became silent. Suddenly someone tugged off the blindfold. He perceived a slate-grey skeleton in a coffin immediately in front of him. It was tinged with blood. The speaker, wearing a black robe and mask, stood above and behind. At both ends of the coffin were torchbearers in white robes and masks.

The speaker gestured toward the skeleton. "Behold a representation of the effect of death. That silent yet impressive lecturer is all that remains on earth of one who was born as you were born, who lived as you now live, who for many days enjoyed his possessions, his power and his pleasures. But now, alas! Nothing is left of him save that sad memorial of man's mortality." The clerk glanced back. The lodge members, standing, were wearing masks. Huge shadows, cast by the torchlight, loomed upon the back wall.

"Contemplate the scene!" The speaker again gestured to the coffin. "Should it not humble human pride? Should it not awake the soul to a just sense of responsibility to its God—of duty to itself?" The clerk wondered if the skeleton was real. Probably one of Van Etten's mistakes, he thought, and suppressed a snicker. "My friend, that gloomy monitor is but an emblem of what you are sure to be, and what you may soon become. Seriously meditate the solemn admonition it affords." The speaker paused. The lodge was silent.

When the speaker began again, his voice was gentler. He spoke of the need to purify the heart—"the fountain of all wrong"—otherwise hatred, crime, and war would continue to afflict mankind. As the speaker proceeded with a sermon—now he called for "Universal Brotherhood"—the clerk again became dizzy. The chains had made him top-heavy, and, with his arms bound tightly behind his back, he sensed that he was swaying. He prayed that the lodge members had not noticed.

When the sermon was finished, one of the white-robed torchbearers began to speak. He struggled to remember his part. His forehead glistened in the torchlight; his mask was stained with sweat. Now the words came. He described the rose, which, though beautiful in the morning, fades in the afternoon, "its loveliness vanished away." So it was with man, who rejoiced in his youthful beauty and power only to have breath soon depart. "Death is in the world and all that is born must die," he concluded.

The other torchbearer took up the theme. Leaves die and fall, their requiems sung by "wintry blasts." "And yet"—he paused for emphasis—"spring does come." "In the place of death there is life, beauty, and joy," he added, with an air of finality. The clerk, who had concluded that the skeleton was real, relaxed now that the ceremony had come to an end. Now he could sit down, smooth his hair, and blot his wounded chin. Now the heavy chains and silly masks would come off, and this shadow world of coffins and skeletons would be flooded with light. And now the mysteries of the order would be made clear. He had made it through the ordeal. He was an Odd Fellow.

But again the clerk was wrong. The ritual had just begun. In a few minutes he would again be blindfolded, dragged around the room, and subjected to more ordeals, oaths, prayers, and lectures. And after this evening was over, he would by no means be delivered from the ritualistic world of darkened rooms and somber incantations. Every week he would be expected to put on a mask and watch the initiation of others. If he proved adept at ritual, he might be chosen to "prepare" a candidate for initiation, to conduct him blindfolded around the lodge, or to offer a prayer or make a speech. And even then his initiatory experiences would have just begun, for by the 1860s there were eight different degrees of Odd Fellowship, each with its peculiar ritual. Members who wished to advance in the order were obliged to memorize new ceremonies, to don different costumes, and to spend much of their leisure time initiating and being initiated. Like the two million other men who were led blindfolded around a lodge of Odd Fellows and presented to a coffined skeleton during the nineteenth century, the clerk had merely crossed the threshold into the ritualistic world of the fraternal order.[1]

❖

The founders of the fraternal movement invariably insisted that their orders originated in the distant past. Initiates into Odd Fellowship were told that Adam was the first member, and that the order was "coeval with the advent of man."[2] Historians of the Knights of Pythias made a case that Pythagoras was the first Pythian, in spite of the awkward fact that the order had been founded in Washington, D.C., in 1864.[3] With little more justification, the Improved Order of Red Men at first claimed descent from the Sons of Liberty of the American Revolution, but this account of their origins failed to satisfy all of the members; a committee decided in 1864 to mark the commencement of the order with the discovery of America by Columbus.[4] In 1874 a historian of the Patrons of Husbandry claimed that his order, established seven years earlier, had been inspired by Vergil.[5] The Freemasons, supposed heirs of a tradition extending back to the founding of King Solomon's temple, computed time from the supposed date of creation (*Anno Lucis*), 4,000 years before Christ.[6] No idea was more commonplace, nor more palpably untrue, than the fraternalists' claims of ancient and venerable origins. Why leaders found it necessary to establish ancient pedigrees for their orders will be considered in more detail later, but certainly one purpose was to confer legitimacy upon institutions of recent origin.[7]

Contrary to the claims of some enthusiasts, Freemasonry originated in London in the early 1700s. Founded as a stonemasons' trade guild, the order became a club for tradesmen, merchants, and a few much-celebrated noblemen. In the 1730s and 1740s a handful of Masonic lodges were established in coastal towns in America; these were dominated by a mercantile elite, although genteel tradesmen were also admitted and even accepted as leaders.[8] During the early decades the order experienced little growth, met infrequently, and functioned chiefly as a drinking and eating club. A recent historian has concluded that the organization was at that time of little significance to its members or to anyone else.[9]

The colonists paid little attention to the ceremonies the English used to induct new members. The main purpose of these brief catechisms and lectures was to disclose secret passwords and recognition signals. Americans hurried over these ceremonies or did away with them entirely. Occasionally the three basic degrees—Entered Apprentice, Fellowcraft, and Master Mason—were conferred in a single evening. Many Entered Apprentices never bothered to take the higher degrees.[10]

During the late eighteenth century, however, large numbers of mechanics and military men, some of whom had been rejected by existing lodges, proposed a new variant of Freemasonry, which they termed "Ancient." (With complete consistency but little sense, they called the older lodges "Modern.") Preoccupied by issues of status in a rapidly changing society, these ambitious and politically active men did not intend to throw the doors of the lodges open to all comers, but rather conceived of the order as a means of validating their own attainments. Brushing aside the protests of the Moderns, the newcomers chartered lodges throughout the countryside and inducted tens of thousands of members.[11]

Meetings were generally held in taverns, where the "merry Masons" spent the evening proposing toasts and singing songs. The importance of drinking was reflected in eighteenth-century lodge constitutions that required members to pay liquor bills before leaving. Lest the tavernkeepers reap all of the profits, some lodges appointed "closet stewards" to purchase beer and prepare wine punches; often lodges acquired elaborate drinking paraphernalia, including silver punch bowls and sugar tongs. One nineteenth-century historian of Masonry gingerly conceded that in the early part of the century excessive drinking in the lodge was "not looked upon with the loathing which is now so generally bestowed upon it."[12] By the early 1800s the Masonic lodge, amply provisioned with liquor and refreshments, had become a place to celebrate the limitless possibilities of the secular world. In Masonic latitudinarianism these men discovered an outlook on life which resided comfortably with their growing economic ambitions.[13]

Although status and convivial entertainments were its chief attractions, some members became intrigued with the ritualistic possibilities of Freemasonry. As they began to compare notes with Masons in different lodges and with English visitors, they learned that the ceremonies were everywhere performed differently. At the time Freemasonry was transmitted to America, English practices were in a state of confusion; the situation in America was even more chaotic. Grand, or governing, lodges issued charters throughout the colonies. Responding to the absence of written degrees or a central organization to dispense them, the Grand Master of each lodge performed whatever rituals, if any, he thought suitable. In the post-Revolutionary era particularly apt alterations were picked up by visitors, itinerant lecturers, or lodge members who attended the annual meetings of each state's grand lodge. Officials at the state level combed Masonic documents to determine the validity of new and different versions.[14] In 1810 De Witt Clinton, Governor of New York and Grand Master of the New York City lodge, observed that nearly every lodge within his state performed its own version of the rituals. He formed a committee to instruct lodges in the correct forms, but when they failed to come to agreement the project was abandoned. If a venerable and ancient Masonic tradition existed, no one could determine what it was.[15]

Liberated from the constraints of immutable precedent, American ritualists invented their own Masonic rituals or variants. Taking what a nineteenth-century historian called "marked liberties" with the fragmentary English ceremonies, Americans changed the lectures, dramatized existing legends, and created entire successions of purely American degrees which proliferated rapidly during the early nineteenth century. American Freemasonry took many forms, the legitimacy of each determined by the persuasiveness of its innovator.[16]

The enthusiasts and supporters of the new rituals often found themselves at odds with members who wanted to spend the evening gathered around the punch bowl. It is not clear whether this schism was originally rooted in class differences, but by the early decades of the nineteenth century the order increasingly attracted an emerging middle class of lawyers, prosperous farmers, and independent tradesmen.[17] The infusion of this group coincided with new demands for sobriety and self-restraint and with the rise of emotionally intense rituals. Some new members chafed at the displays of drunkenness and debauchery; others complained of the order's lack of moral purpose. Typical of this new Mason was the member who in 1818 tabulated the expenditures of his lodge for the year. He was incensed to learn that it had spent $741 on liquor but only $64 to assist needy members.[18]

Because these factions worked at cross-purposes, the public perception of the order was confused. By the 1820s conservative ministers, who opposed the "extravagant mirth and bacchanalian revelry" as well as the quasireligious rituals, assumed that the former was a product of the latter.[19] They imagined that the rituals transported members into a drunken frenzy, in which state they finally surrendered to Satan. Having witnessed the disestablishment of their churches, moreover, the ministers resented that their influence in secular matters was waning just as Freemasonry was becoming popular and politically influential.[20]

Relations between conservative ministers and the Freemasons smoldered until 1826, when an event in western New York ignited a firestorm of Antimasonic activity. A disgruntled ex-Freemason, William Morgan, announced his intention of publishing the secret Masonic rituals. Shortly thereafter several Masons abducted Morgan on a charge of petty theft and imprisoned him in Canandaigua. The following night someone coaxed him into a carriage. It disappeared and Morgan was never seen again. Some evidence was later produced that Masons had drowned him in Lake Niagara, and twenty-six Masons were indicted on related charges. Only six came to trial; four were convicted of conspiracy and sentenced to terms ranging from several months to two years in jail. Many of the jurors and prosecutors were Masons, as was Governor Clinton—facts which persuaded some that justice had miscarried.[21]

Ministers thundered against the order, scores of Antimasonic newspapers denounced its activities and published exposés of the rituals, and politicians formed Antimasonic coalitions throughout the Northeast. That many Masons held public office suggested the possibility of widespread political subversion. Pointing to the trial of the alleged Morgan conspirators, critics asked how Masons could be expected to fairly discharge their duties as jurors when bound by secret obligations. Fueled by fears such as these, the Anti-Masonic Party became the first significant third party in American politics. In 1832 it nominated a candidate for President and carried Vermont; in New York it received 157,000 votes.

Though short-lived as a political movement, Antimasonry generated intense public pressure that forced thousands of members to renounce the order and hundreds of lodges to relinquish their charters. By best estimate membership declined from 100,000 in the mid-1820s to 40,000 a decade later. Those who remained did so circumspectly, rarely holding public events and refraining from publicizing meeting places and times.[22]

The middle-class stalwarts who kept the movement alive after the Morgan affair resolved to efface the popular image of the "merry Mason," whose drinking and debauchery had left the order vulnerable to public censure. By the 1840s few lodges allowed liquor on the premises and none permitted it during meetings.[23] The order also insisted upon a waiting period to determine whether new members were worthy of higher degrees. Masonic jurisprudence was codified and strengthened, culminating with the publication of Albert Mackey's *Masonic Landmarks* in 1856. Those accused of unmasonic conduct were put on trial during special juridical meetings of the lodge; those adjudged guilty were expelled.[24]

As liquor was banned from the lodge and a more rigorous standard of behavior imposed upon members, Masonic meetings lost their boisterous and festive atmosphere. Money previously spent on liquor and refreshments now went for expensive costumes and paraphernalia, and the portion of meetings allotted for socializing was crowded out by the increasingly complex and time-consuming rituals. The printed exposés and public performance of Masonic rituals by the Antimasons strengthened the proritualists, for new members came to the lodge expecting elaborate initiations.

Antimasonry contributed to the rise of fraternal ritualism in another way. The stigma attached to the order was so great that even when the public outcry had died down in the late 1830s, many ex-Freemasons were reluctant to return. They flocked instead into the Odd Fellows and the Red Men, which they proceeded to transform into middle-class organizations devoted to ritual.

Odd Fellowship originated in the late eighteenth century in Great Britain. Its working-class founders sought to mitigate the effects of the Industrial

Revolution and the English Poor Laws. Members in dire circumstances could freely appeal to "brothers" for aid; the order also guaranteed members a decent burial. The first American lodge of Odd Fellows was established in Baltimore in 1819 by immigrants who were affiliated with the English governing lodge, the Manchester Unity. James Ridgely, a nineteenth-century historian of the order, described the American founders as men of "limited education, and in a humble sphere of life."[25] They usually met at night in taverns "of not the most select character" to drink beer, sing ribald songs, and take part in revelries that sometimes attracted the attention of the constables. "Spirituous liquors soon began to supplant the beer and what was before comparatively an innocent indulgence became a serious and growing evil," Ridgely added.[26]

The early historians of the order lionized one Augustus Mathiot, the only founder who shared their middle-class sensibilities. Though he was a mechanic, he differed from others in "habits and education." Born into a religious and well-respected family, he was apprenticed to a chair painter when his father died. His schooling was limited, but Mathiot taught himself to read and became absorbed in history and romantic novels. In 1823 he applied to join the Freemasons but was rejected because he belonged to "that Bacchanalian Club of Odd Fellows." Mortified, Mathiot labored for the rest of his life to persuade the Odd Fellows to adopt middle-class reforms, especially temperance.[27]

His proposals were initially defeated. But during the 1830s an influx of lawyers, physicians, merchants, skilled mechanics and tradesmen, engineers, and well-to-do farmers, many of them ex-Masons, transformed the order completely. Ridgely, a lawyer, explained that this "new and refined element" shared a commitment to self-improvement, self-control, sobriety, and sound business practices. Critics complained that Odd Fellowship was becoming Freemasonry "revived," a charge the leaders disputed, but by the 1840s the order closely resembled the middle-class variant of Freemasonry.[28]

The new leaders no longer passed the hat to aid needy brethren; such degrading practices, they argued, discouraged thriftiness and initiative. They replaced the charity with a system of fixed weekly assessments, which instilled the habit of saving. (Over $20 million had been collected by 1862.[29]) They scorned the sloppy record keeping of their predecessors and taught lodge treasurers double-entry bookkeeping and money management. And they ensured the essentially middle-class character of the order by raising initiation fees and weekly dues, establishing committees to ascertain the moral and financial background of applicants, and convening trials to expel "dissolute" or disreputable members.[30] To prevent the rural lodges from resisting the measures of the mostly city-based middle-class reformers, the

Grand Lodge of the United States centralized its control and extended its jurisdictional powers. Finally, the officials embarked upon a major construction program to build Odd Fellows' temples, thus ridding the lodge of the influence of the tavern. By 1860 alcohol had been prohibited in all lodges.[31]

For the reformers the temples were also a means to a greater end: the performance of ritual. English Odd Fellowship lacked formal initiation ceremonies; applicants simply affirmed loyalty to their new brethren and promised to aid them whenever possible. In 1820 the American founders received a set of rituals from the Manchester Unity, but these were short and simple, consisting mostly of lectures. Perhaps in response to Mathiot's urgings, the grand lodge expanded these into a quasi-Masonic catechism drawn almost verbatim from the Bible.[32]

But the simple rites did not satisfy the new middle-class Odd Fellows. In the early 1840s a "general, earnest, irresistible" demand of the membership forced the grand lodge to revise its rituals. Some leaders urged adherence to the simple catechisms of the 1820s and 1830s, but the revisionists insisted on an entirely different type of ritual. They won by a decisive margin and undertook to provide "a moral more distinctive and didactic, a sentiment more elevated and inspiring, a principle of deeper significance, a purer and truer tone, and the embodiment of all these in a literature worthy of a cause so noble and a work so great."[33] A five-man committee, which included Ridgely, met throughout the year to revise the rituals. It decided to exclude "*all* of the English work" and to discard most of the lectures and catechisms of the previous decade. The committee presented its recommendations to a special session of the grand lodge which, after much discussion and some minor changes, approved the new ritual in 1845.[34]

English Odd Fellows who visited American lodges were amazed by the sober settings and religious ceremonies. Americans, on the other hand, were increasingly appalled by the boisterous, hard-drinking English immigrants who knocked on the doors of their temples. A delegation from the Grand Lodge of the United States journeyed to England and announced that the "convivial practices" that prevailed there lowered members below the moral standard in America. English Odd Fellows, accustomed to having a good time on lodge nights, were unsuited to the personal reformation that constituted the chief work of American Odd Fellowship.[35]

After the Americans returned home, they urged their English brethren to emphasize ritual rather than fellowship; the perception of the order as a "mere merrymaking concern" had inhibited its growth in America. After "discarding conviviality," they explained, the order had grown rapidly. "Our career affords an example not unworthy of your imitation," the American secretary noted pointedly.[36]

The Englishmen refused to accept the American ceremonies, and ultimately the Grand Lodge of the United States, claiming that the Manchester
Unity had neglected the ritual, severed all connection with its parent body; it
now called itself the Independent Order of Odd Fellows. The entire episode
left the English officials bewildered.[37]

The centralized structure of its governing system ensured that the rituals of American Odd Fellowship would remain subject to the authority of
the grand lodge. On the other hand, Freemasonry, which began to recover
from the Antimasonic crusade during the 1840s, found it nearly impossible
to control innovations. In 1843 Masonic lecturers and ritualists representing grand lodges from different states and jurisdictions met in Baltimore to
produce uniform degrees. Six months later those who attended could not
agree on what had been decided. (Whether they were aware of the parallel
deliberations in Baltimore of the Committee on Ritual of the Odd Fellows is
unknown). Masonic officials abandoned attempts to standardize the rituals
because "all have agreed it is an impossiblity." [38]

From 1853 through 1864 all twenty-nine existing degrees of the Scottish Rite were rewritten, and the ten higher degrees of the American Rite
were "arranged to suit the American mind." [39] From 1840 to 1860 American Masonry was entirely transformed; seasoned members observed that
after two decades of revision only the "mere shell" of the original rituals remained. Critics complained that the ancient traditions of Freemasonry had
been "annihilated, or murderously perverted." English officials urged the
Grand Lodge of New York to abolish all of the higher, York Rite, degrees.
American Freemasonry had become "too progressive," and the new rituals
were "too long, too complicated, and too theatrical." [40]

Americans defended the revisions as attempts to recreate the primitive
"Masonry" of the ancient Egyptians, Druids, Persians, Eleusinians, or Kab-
balists.[41] The English grand lodge, they argued, was the custodian of only
the latest and most corrupt variant of Freemasonry. One American official,
after an attempt, unpersuasive even to himself, to prove the antiquity of his
version of a higher degree, concluded that the true standard for Masonic
ritual was whether it conveyed "great and solemn truths." Any ritual which
failed this test, "no matter what its age," was not true Masonry.[42] The argument was tautological: Ancient Masonry, if it lacked powerful rituals, was
not real Masonry; modern revisions, if compelling, necessarily contained the
germ of ancient Masonic genius.

By the late 1870s and early 1880s Masonic forms had stabilized, and officials demanded that the "mania for tinkering with degrees" cease.[43] After
the period of revision ended, some writers insisted it had never really occurred. In 1876 William Rounseville, editor of the *Voice of Masonry*, derided

those who claimed that Masonry had undergone a radical overhauling during the decades after the Morgan affair. He commented that although most
secret societies had changed their rituals almost entirely, Freemasonry was
"sublimely quiet and unmoved" throughout the memory of man. Another
editor of a fraternal journal noted that although the wording of the rituals
had undergone "astonishing" changes, Masonry remained the same in form
and feature. He offered no explanation of this contradiction.[44]

Nineteenth-century historians of Odd Fellowship and Freemasonry underscored the importance of the revised rituals to the orders' subsequent
success. Ridgely subtitled his history of Odd Fellowship of the 1840s "The
First Decade"—as if the previous two decades, when the order was run by
laborers, were not Odd Fellowship at all. The ascendancy of the middle
classes had resulted in a "memorable period when our arcana took new form
and significance."[45] Despite higher fees, stricter admission standards, and
effective rules against keeping inactive members on the books, membership
in the Odd Fellows climbed from 30,000 in 1843 to 200,000 in 1860 and
nearly a million by 1900.[46]

So, too, with Freemasonry. The revisions of ritual in the 1840s and 1850s
were the culmination of a "glorious reformation" that had transformed the
lodges into temples and had conferred upon lodge masters the title "Most
Worshipful."[47] The lodge historians commonly attributed the success of
their orders to the new ritualism of the mid-nineteenth century. They did
not explain why this should be so, for they assumed that their readers understood the relationship, having themselves been blindfolded, bound, and
brought before the emblem of mortality.

❖

From the moment the lodge opened, a member's sense of time was blurred.
Although meetings were always held in the evening, the ceremonies charac-
teristically began at "daybreak," further distancing members from the outside world. While initiates were being prepared, the actors for the evening
took off their clothes and put on robes, loincloths, or aprons. Others placed
the scenery, lit the candles and turned off the lights. Gradually the present
dissolved, and a conjured scene of the past appeared before their eyes. After
the initiations, the process was reversed. The lodge was closed with a prayer
or perhaps a song and an announcement that, because the sun had set, one's
labors as a Mason, Odd Fellow, or Pythian had come to an end. Time within
the lodge now corresponded to that outside.

In all the rituals time expanded or contracted according to the exigencies
of the plot. Pythians moved from ancient Syracuse to the Middle Ages in an

instant. Royal Arch initiates experienced the entire Babylonian captivity in a few minutes. But the preoccupation with the past did not lead to historical accuracy, and many of the depictions were patently ludicrous.[48] The Pythians superimposed the imagery of medieval knights upon the Greek legend of Damon and Pythias. In the ritual of the Knightly Rank Pythagoras himself appeared before the armor-clad initiate. The candidate for the Council degree of the Good Templars, a temperance order, was advised to peruse the "history of the middle ages," a period not known for sobriety.[49] Old Testament patriarchs went on processions through the desert while organists played fraternal versions of stolid Protestant hymns. And Red Men gathered around a council fire that was regulated by gas burners.

Some ritualists frankly admitted that they cared little about historical authenticity. Mackey conceded that there was no evidence for the existence of the Secret Vault of Enoch, described in an important Masonic legend as a temple antedating Solomon's by several millennia. He wrote, "Like every other myth and allegory of Masonry, the historical relation may be true or it may be false; it may be founded on fact or be the invention of imagination; the lesson is still there, and the symbolism teaches it exclusive of the history."[50] The members' need to commune with an alternative past was so great that they made little effort to verify its authenticity.

Mircea Eliade has suggested that there is a difference between the way traditional and modern societies conceive of the past. The former hold that the crucial transformations of the world occurred at the dawn of time. By ritualistically recreating these seminal events, traditional societies preserve and transmit the ancient truths necessary to retain the favor of the gods. But modern man, Eliade believed, builds upon the past, and thereby rises above it. Ancient truths become outmoded; to celebrate them would be pointless.[51]

There is little apparent reason why Victorian American men would go to such extremes to celebrate the past, much less choose to invent one. Their fortunes were not tied to land or traditional privileges; they did not toil long hours in factories nor lament the passing of farm life. Rather, they were the architects and builders of a new and vital urban-industrial order. Their energy, ambition, and enshrinement of progress were the hallmarks of the age. "We may well be called fast men," one Masonic editor observed.[52] Yet on lodge nights they retreated into an imaginary world of the past.

A clue to this paradox can be found in the explanations given by the orders' officials of the groups' mid-century transformation. In 1860 A. B. Grosh explained that the "noble rituals" of Odd Fellowship now provided the "substratem of our Moral Temple." Ridgely maintained that the revisions had exalted the order "almost to the dignity of a religion."[53] In 1869 Albert Mackey, an official of Scottish Rite Freemasonry, noted that the order, long viewed as merely a social institution, had become a speculative science. Sociability continued to bind Masons, but it was no longer sufficient, for

> the Masonic mind is everywhere beginning to look and ask for something, which, like the manna in the desert, shall feed us, in our pilgrimage, with intellectual food. The Universal cry, throughout the Masonic world, is for light . . . [T]he types and symbols, the myths and allegories, of the institution are beginning to be investigated with reference to their ultimate meaning; our history is now traced by zealous inquiries as to its connection with antiquity; and Freemasons now thoroughly understand that often quoted definition, that "Masonry is a science of morality veiled in allegory and illustrated by symbols."[54]

Members looked to a past in which they embarked on a pilgrimage for manna because in some sense the present had proven barren, devoid of emotional and intellectual sustenance. Precisely what the Masonic mind expected to find at the end of the journey was unclear, even to the ritualists. But they were convinced that the yearning to search was widespread and profound, and that whatever one meant by "light," "manna," or "intellectual food," it was to be conveyed through successions of religious ceremonies and mystical symbols.

❖

"Consensus" historians believe that during the nineteenth century middle-class values were diffused throughout American society almost effortlessly. This untroubled coalescence of a national culture of liberalism was in marked contrast to the situation in Europe, where middle-class values became ascendant only after an embattled bourgeoisie prevailed over the working class and the aristocracy.[55]

Scholars such as Paul E. Johnson, Mary P. Ryan, and Anthony F. C. Wallace have challenged consensus assumptions. America did not almost inevitably become a middle-class nation, they argue; this outcome resulted instead from the efforts of a self-conscious middle class which promoted its own interests and values.[56] Evangelical Protestantism was central to this new middle-class agenda. In Johnson's view, the revivals of the 1820s and 1830s provided the "moral imperative around which the northern middle class became a class."[57]

The rise of fraternal orders at mid-century provides evidence of the emergence of a middle-class institution parallel to evangelical Protestantism. Fraternal leaders were proud of their middle-class orientation, and their frequent preachments on sobriety, self-restraint, and personal reform accorded with the needs of capitalism. One scholar has regarded the lodge as a "moral policing institution" whose symbols and regulations reflected capitalism's needs for free labor; another concluded that the "entire ethos and spirit" of the orders was dominated by capitalism.[58]

The relationship of the growth of the orders to the rise of capitalism was more complex than these writers suggest. The evangelicals who spearheaded the "Christian capitalist" millennium also led the Antimasonic movement.[59] And fraternal leaders, despite their unequivocal endorsement of middle-class values and capitalist institutions, indicted evangelical Protestantism with equal venom.[60] If the underlying social function of evangelical religion and Freemasonry was to promote the same middle-class goals, why did they remain irreconcilably opposed to each other?

The revisionists have adopted Emile Durkheim's view that culture is generated by social structure. Johnson, who states from the outset that he was guided by Durkheim, argues that the revivals arose to fulfill entrepreneurial capitalism's need to discipline workers and sever their ties to a larger network of social responsibilities and affiliations.[61]

Although the orders unquestionably adopted the institutional and promotional mechanisms of capitalism and articulated the values of the emerging middle class, it does not follow that members joined and continued to attend because of this structural congruence. Middle-class men, or workers who aspired to that status, did not have to go to the lodge to learn the merits of hard work and self-discipline. Moreover, the rituals repeatedly contravened basic tenets of capitalism. The Improved Order of Red Men, for example, advised initiates to emulate the children of the forest, who held all wealth and property in common.[62] Rather than reinforcing the forms and ideologies of capitalist social organization, the rituals often subverted them.

The fascination for fraternal ritual suggests that even as the emerging middle classes were embracing capitalism and bourgeois sensibilities, they were simultaneously creating rituals whose message was largely antithetical to those structural relationships and values. This concurs with anthropologist Victor Turner's belief that social life is a dialectical process whereby society fits individuals into structures and defines their appropriate roles, yet these individuals, longing for a deeper and less restrictive range of experience and meaning, unconsciously react against the structures by participating in what he calls "liminal rituals," the symbols of which are in opposition to existing hierarchies and rules. The rigidity of feudal social relations thus gave rise to the alternative *communitas* of the monasteries and Christian faith. In simpler societies "anti-structure," as Turner termed these liminal ritual states, was often expressed through ceremonies such as initiation rites, in which the ordinary regularities of kinship, law, and custom were replaced by a "weird domain" of strange symbols and secrecy.[63] "No society can function without this dialectic," Turner added.[64] Whereas Durkheim focused on social structure, from which he imagined the requisite function of culture could be inferred, Turner insisted on a close examination of the rituals and their symbols, which mediate between unconscious psychological concerns and social structures. Turner found that rites of this nature most commonly appeared in societies experiencing cultural change, wherein the imposition of new structures and roles is intensely perceived. This would have been especially true of young middle-class men during the early and mid nineteenth century.

Much that seems silly, foolish, or downright preposterous about fraternal ritual gains meaning when viewed from a Turnerian perspective. Odd Fellows acknowledged that once they had wrapped themselves in biblical robes and fixed masks upon their faces they were indeed odd; and lawyers, shopkeepers, and industrialists understood that it was bizarre to pretend to be Old Testament patriarchs, Roman senators, or medieval knights. But this incongruousness provided much of the meaning of the ritual by conjuring a world that offered solace from real life.

The historian Dorothy Lipson identified Masonry during the Federalist period as part of a "play element" in American culture.[65] It is tempting to infer that as a nascent capitalism imposed work discipline and circumscribed social relations, members sought refuge in the lodge. After adding figures all day in a counting room or superintending workers in a shop, a clerk or foreman could spend the evening drinking, making toasts, and singing. Recharged by an immersion in this undisciplined, unstructured, and emotionally expressive domain, he could return the next day prepared to make the sacrifices and sober judgments demanded by work.

This may explain the significance of Freemasonry during the Federalist period, when the "merry Masons" commonly disported in grogshops and taverns, but it makes less sense after the 1830s and 1840s, when middle-class members banned alcohol, replaced the drinking songs with fraternal hymns, recited long lectures from memory, and bound initiates in chains. Officials did not oppose humor and pleasantry but allowed them only if time remained after the serious work of initiation.[66] Determining why members should "crave" these new forms of discipline and structure requires a close consideration of the rituals and their symbols.

❖ REVELATION AND CONCEALMENT ❖

Many of the rituals written during the 1830s and 1840s made use of masks. Some were comical, some frightening; others simply obscured the face. The masks, worn by the entire membership, were not necessary to conceal members' faces from a blindfolded initiate, nor even from each other in a darkened lodge. Instead, by covering their faces with masks, members in effect effaced the most visible expression of self. This underscored an important premise of fraternal initiation: Within the lodge everyone acquired new and mysterious identities. The masks concealed one identity and conferred another.

The visible imposition of new forms of identity is always perilous drama, for the confusion and inversion of social relationships is at the heart of humor.[67] We laugh at the idea of dogs writing novels, at children tyrannizing parents, or at bosses who trip as employees look on. It was potentially funny, therefore, when the neighborhood tobacconist, wearing the mitre of a Jewish high priest, dragged the blindfolded local industrialist around the room. Lodge members pressed by friends to describe initiations commonly chose humorous prevarications, and new initiates often expected the ceremony to be funny. The most common jokes had it that candidates were forced to ride a goat or were stretched upon a gridiron and tortured. At least in the case of the lowest degrees, the emotional tenor of the proceedings was always perched precariously at the edge of humor.

During the 1850s and 1860s leaders struggled to eliminate features that might undo the serious work of initiation. Officials insisted that anything resembling levity or jesting be "promptly repressed" and, if necessary, rebuked or punished. Odd Fellows were instructed to wear masks "not of a ludicrous character."[68] The success of these efforts was apparent by the 1860s and 1870s. Members now reported that candidates generally presented themselves in a serious frame of mind; some approached the lodge with "a feeling of solemnity beyond seriousness." The proceedings commenced in so grave a manner that even sceptical and inattentive initiates became quiet; never did they attempt humor. Some, especially the better-educated, were "so wrought upon and their feelings so excited that they shed tears."[69]

Without explanation, the use of masks soon disappeared. This suggests that the purpose of the ritual was not to efface personal identity utterly and replace it with a socially induced alternative but to bring issues of personal identity to the fore, where they could be challenged and examined within differing contexts and environments. When the local tobacconist wore biblical robes and repeated lines attributed to Abraham, he did not cease being Mr. Smith. Liberated from the impersonality of the mask, he was encouraged to internalize what it was like to rule a tribe, to transmit God's ineffable word to the people, or to offer his son for sacrifice.

Scholars insisted that the emotional meanings of the rituals were bound up with its symbols. A skeleton was not just an abstract emblem of mortality; it also elicited revulsion or fear. Albert Pike, the foremost nineteenth-century Masonic ritualist, observed that even if members failed to comprehend the intellectual nuances of the rituals, the symbols evoked an "appropriate *feeling* [his emphasis]."[70] Joseph Weeks, a ritualist for the Knights of Pythias, noted that men relied upon symbolic communication because words failed to express "the soul's deepest and truest thoughts" and imprisoned their "holiest emotions."[71] Fraternal ritual, another scholar explained, was an emotional pilgrimage through a "forest of symbols."[72]

It is no easy matter to determine the emotional significance of these symbols, partly because there were so many. One scholar for the Knights of Pythias stopped counting when he reached twenty thousand.[73] Most of the symbols appear banal, and the presiding official's long-winded explanations at the conclusion of a ritual gave them seemingly trivial significance. For example, in the Fellowcraft degree (the second degree in Masonry), the initiate was told that the two columns at the entrance to the lodge were named Jachin, denoting *establishment* or *house,* and Boaz, denoting *strength;* together, they referred to a passage in Scripture: "In strength shall this house be established." On the top of each column were two large globes or balls, representing maps and charts of the celestial and terrestrial bodies; these were symbolic of the order's universality.[74] How information of this character could have been replete with emotional significance is hardly apparent.

The rituals themselves informed initiates that the facile meanings were wrong, or at least incomplete. Every symbol contained deeper meanings than even the rituals' own authors could fully comprehend. Pike explained that fraternal truth was "hidden under symbols and often under a succession of allegories." Lower-degree initiates, such as those who were told the trivial meanings of Jachin and Boaz, had been "intentionally misled by false interpretations." Only the adepts—the thirty-second-degree Masons—could understand the deeper meanings of the order.[75] Yet in the closing lecture of that degree, after the master of the lodge had provided a long explication, he confessed that he had obtained only a few hints of the deeper significance of the symbols. The adept was now to discover those meanings for himself, through reflection and introspection. The final unmasking of the ritual laid bare the self.[76]

As the ritualists repeatedly insisted, the symbols simultaneously offered concealment and revelation, as some mysteries were explained while others were newly propounded.[77] This paradox is closely related to the rituals' mediation between the visible, concrete aspects of members' lives, and the hidden fantasy world of solace. Successful ritualists intuitively summoned up the symbols that addressed members' anxieties without raising them explicitly. The masks and disguises, the pervasive secrecy, and especially the mystical symbols were part of a process of concealment and revelation in which middle-class men, and many workers as well, became accommodated to a social order largely of their own making.

To determine what was subconsciously "revealed" requires a closer consideration of the symbols within the context of the rituals and of American society more generally. One clue is suggested by the fact that the elements of secrecy impeded vision: Lodges were cast into darkness and initiates were blindfolded. This enhanced the impression of secrecy, but it also caused a reorientation in sensory perceptions. For many candidates the peculiar sound of the first initiation was its most memorable aspect, particularly the flat, low tones of male voices chanting, singing hymns, or reciting lines in the echoing expanses of the lodge. When I asked Masons to explain their response to modern fraternal rituals, they described a darkness that seemed to seep through the blindfolds. Within it they became acutely aware of the sound of the ritual—and particularly of its words.

CHAPTER II

Words

From [Benjamin Henry Day], *Richardson's Monitor of Freemasonry*
(Philadelphia: David McKay, 1861?)

"**G**rand Architect of the Universe—to whose holy sight the centuries are as days and to whose Omniscience the past and the future are as one eternal present—look down upon us, Thy children who still wander amid the delusions of time; look down, O Grand Architect . . ."

Charles Estabrook again winced at the Grand Chaplain's upstate accent; the first syllable—"Ark"—pierced the solemn stillness and reverberated against the stained-glass window: David and Jonathan, in their loose biblical robes, seemed to huddle closer, the grey glass shards of their flesh unwarmed by daylight. Estabrook looked at the empty Chaplain's chair, now draped in black cloth. He thought of Dr. Brown's genteel British accent, which, coming from an Anglican minister, had no doubt offended many during the War of 1812. But that was, incredibly, more than seventy years ago, and Brown's exhortations to the troops of Lincoln had subsequently proven his patriotism.

"Look down, we beseech Thee, from Thy glorious and eternal day into the dark night of our errors and presumption, and send a ray of divine light into our hearts, that in them may awaken and bloom the certainty of life, reliance upon Thy promises and assurance of a place at Thy right hand."

Estabrook's gaze moved slowly from the place called the East to that called West. The Bible was open upon the altar. Three white candles, carefully arranged in the shape of a right triangle, were unlit. Estabrook knew that they symbolized the Masonic motto—"Wisdom, Strength, and Beauty"—but on Tuesday evening Halstead had said something about the triangle also representing Isis, Horus, and another Egyptian god whose name Estabrook had forgotten. A decoding of hieroglyphics, Halstead had asserted, would confirm Freemasonry's Egyptian origins. Until that occurred, Masons would have to figure out the mysteries on their own. Estabrook resolved to look up the name of the forgotten Egyptian deity tomorrow.

Forty years before—in 1844, when Estabrook was only twenty—Brown, then President of the Newburgh Library Association, had given him the job as city librarian. Brown had taught him in Sunday School at St. George's and had become his patron and adviser. Often Brown would stop by the library to check biblical references and to peruse the acquisition list. As Chaplain, he officiated and played the organ when Estabrook was initiated into Masonry.

"Be with us now that we may serve Thee in spirit and understanding. And to Thy glorious name shall we ascribe the praise forever." With the others Estabrook said "Amen." He was pleased, despite the desecration of the language, that the Grand Chaplain of New York had come after all.

Worshipful Master Sterrit rose and began reading from a sheaf of yellow papers. Estabrook knew the chronology almost by heart: "Born, 1791"; "valedictorian at Columbia College, 1811"; "studied theology under the Right Reverend John H. Hobart . . ." Brown had often spoken of Hobart, a stiff man who ridiculed the "unlettered, unauthorized, and uncouth" itinerants who preyed upon the ignorance of the common people. Christian worship, Hobart insisted, must rest squarely upon the rites of the Church and upon the literal meaning of Scripture. Estabrook recalled how Dr. Brown began his sermons by putting on wire-frame glasses; pulling out a single piece of paper, folded over; and then announcing the scriptural passage he intended to discuss. The Word of God, he would say, must take precedence over all else.

"He delivered his inaugural sermon on the day before the Festival of the Nativity—December 24, 1815. The text was taken from 1st Timothy 4:16 and was an excellent discourse. But there was much to discourage the young clergyman. St. George's was then the most feeble of all the congregations which had a name to live. And infidelity having flourished in Newburgh at the beginning of the century, the minds of a large portion of the inhabitants were poisoned with infidel doctrines."

Estabrook, while rummaging through a locked cabinet in the library basement, had come across some issues of the newspaper published by the Society of Druids. The rise of this organization was one of the stranger episodes in the history of the town, but the subject was rarely discussed. Many of the more prosperous local farmers and tradesmen who had provisioned General Washington's forces became infected with the enthusiasms of infidel France. In addition to establishing a newspaper, the society hired a lapsed clergyman to lecture on Rousseau, Paine, and Voltaire. What is more, at midnight sessions they performed unspeakable acts which local gossips blushed to tell. Estabrook thought it best to seal the newspapers in the dusty basement tomb.

"They encouraged each other in their unbelief, offered the Bible as a burnt sacrifice upon their sacrilegious altars, and ridiculed the sacraments of the church in their nocturnal revels. But Dr. Brown determined to do what he could, and unbelief began to hide its head. In course of time the children and descendants of these people became attached to the principles and sacred ritual of the church."

As Estabrook fingered the triangular pendant suspended from his neck, Sterrit described General Lafayette's return to Newburgh in 1824, especially his visit with members of the Hiram Masonic Lodge. Brown, then its

Junior Warden and Orator, had delivered the welcoming address. Shortly thereafter, Sterrit noted, all of the local Masonic chapters had been forced to close due to the "anti-Masonic excitement." Brown had proven indispensable in their subsequent resurrection.

Estabrook recalled his nervousness that Sunday in 1855, two days after Christmas, when Doctor Brown had asked him to assist in a service celebrating the anniversary of the birth of St. John the Evangelist, the patron saint of Freemasonry. It had been nearly thirty years since William Morgan had disappeared, yet many people still spoke of Freemasons as the "murderers of Morgan" and the "legions of Satan." Estabrook had worried that even the venerable Dr. Brown—the only local clergyman with a national reputation—might stir up opposition by holding a Masonic service in the church.

"On that date, December 27, 1855, when the Masons had proceeded to his church in a body, and took seats reserved for them in the center aisles, the Reverend Dr. Brown said, 'We have met not to excite public curiosity but for the more noble purpose of illustrating the benevolent principles of our association and of paying respect to that ancient saint, the most distinguished of the apostles, who, besides being a Christian of the highest order, was also one of the highest ornaments of the moral and spiritual temple of Masonry.' "

Estabrook recalled how Brown had motioned the chapter forward and instructed the organist to play "Hail, Masonry Divine." The members passed silently in two lines around the congregation and up the center aisle. They wore white lambskin aprons over their dark suits; the square and the compass were, like Brown's vestments, trimmed in red.

"Dr. Brown died at his home in this city August 15, 1884, aged ninety-three years, two months and twenty-six days. And how cheerfully did he detach himself from all earthly ties! With what gracefulness and expectation as if returning to his native element did he ascend from the bed of death to immortality! 'He knew in whom he had believed.' "

Jeremiah Searle, a Presbyterian minister and Brown's successor as Senior Chaplain, now arose in the East: "I am glad to introduce just here the prayer which Dr. Brown had prepared for use in the lodge, the manuscript of which in Dr. Brown's handwriting has been placed in my hands. This is the prayer which he was wont to use in closing the lodge:

Supreme Architect of Universal nature, who by Thine almighty word didst speak into being the stupendous arch of heaven, we humbly adore and worship Thine unspeakable perfections. We thank Thee that amidst the pains and calamities of our present state, so many means of refreshments and satisfactions are reserved unto us while traveling the rugged path of life. We thank Thee for the light we enjoy and that Thou hast been pleased to show us strong inducements to virtue and holiness. May these inducements sink deep into our hearts and bring forth in us good fruit. Pardon the imperfections of our present meeting, and enable us more faithfully to perform the obligations here enjoined on us, and invariably to practice all those duties out of the Lodge which are inculcated in it. Dismiss us with Thy blessing, and may the approbation of heaven and the testimony of a good conscience be our support, and may we be endowed with every good and perfect gift, while traveling the thorny path of life, and finally be admitted within the temple of eternal light and life.

Gilbert E. Jacobs, seated in the North, just to the left of the organ, stood and read slowly: "Doctor Brown's funeral, by request of his relatives, will not be attended with the ceremonies of Masonry, which, doubtless from the circumstance of the case and his warm church relations, is perfectly proper." Estabrook shifted his legs, which had crushed the red velour of his pew cushion, and he looked down at the black and white tile of the Masonic temple.[1]

❖

At first glance the prayer with which the Reverend Brown closed lodge meetings seems hardly worthy of note; with small alteration, he could have substituted it for the Episcopal doxology. However, this prayer, though it was in his own handwriting, had been taken almost verbatim from the High Priest's second prayer in the Royal Arch initiation. Brown no doubt came across the ritual when he joined the Royal Arch Masons in January 1818, three years after his ordination. In the following December he was elected High Priest of the local Jerusalem chapter, or lodge. Apart from the two decades after 1826, when all of the Masonic lodges in Newburgh had closed, he remained intimately involved in Royal Arch Freemasonry.[2] As High Priest he performed the central role in the Royal Arch initiation; he surely memorized the requisite prayers. Late in life, perhaps as his memory began to falter, he committed the secret prayer to paper.

Why Brown used this prayer to an audience incapable of understanding its allusions is puzzling. Perhaps he and the other attending Royal Arch Masons enjoyed this private deception of Blue Lodge members; more probably, Brown, who was little given to humor, believed that the prayer contained a message central to all Freemasonry. Once the Blue Lodge Masons took the

Royal Arch degrees, they would begin to perceive that in its essence Masonry was a system of occluded yet cohesive meanings. Deeply hidden in the rituals and the prayers were successive layers of revelations.

As a disciple of Bishop John Hobart, who nearly endorsed the Catholic position on ritual efficacy, Brown may have believed that Blue Lodge Masons, though unaware of the deeper meanings of this prayer, would still benefit from it. And the High Priest's second prayer, as Brown no doubt recognized, was one of the most powerful condensations of Masonic symbolism, an allegorical summation of the Royal Arch initiation, and thus of Masonic theology.

The first sentence of the prayer included several allusions to its ritualistic referent: "Supreme Architect of Universal nature, who by Thine almighty word didst speak into being the stupendous arch of heaven, we humbly adore and worship Thine unspeakable perfections."[3] The "stupendous arch of heaven" hinted at the prayer's provenance—the Royal Arch degree—and the other phrases referred to its opening ceremonies. Members gathered around the altar, prayed, divided into groups of three, took hold of each other's wrists and lifted them three times. The procedure was called "raising a living arch." While doing this, they whispered the "Grand Omnific Royal Arch Word," the ineffable name of God.

The symbolic richness of Masonry defies any single interpretation, and this is particularly true of the exceedingly complex Royal Arch degree.[4] Yet for American Masons the basic meaning was fairly explicit. The number three, the most sacred of all numbers, was closely associated with divinity. Among Royal Arch Masons it also signified the triangle, which symbolized the "Grand Architect of the Universe." The equilateral triangle was regarded as "the most perfect" of Masonic figures. Similarly, when the members took hold of one another's wrists, they formed a geometric figure known as the Triple Tau (which can be visualized as a broad H with a T placed upon its crossbar). Among American Masons the Triple Tau signified, after Ezekiel, those who were to be saved from the wrath of God "on account of their sorrow for their sins."[5]

The first sentence of the High Priest's prayer thus presented a symbolic code for the opening ceremony of the Royal Arch. The prayer can be roughly "translated" as follows: "Supreme Architect of Universal nature" (that is, God), "who by Thine almighty word" (the Grand Omnific Royal Arch Word, the secret name of God), "didst speak into being" (by mystically whispering) "the stupendous arch of heaven" (the living arch), "we humbly adore and worship Thine unspeakable perfections" (the mystical attributes of deity, as denoted by the triangle and the number three).

The opening ceremony of the Royal Arch established that members possessed the lost Word of God. Initiates, who lacked that crucial knowledge, were meant to embark upon a journey to discover it for themselves. The second section reenacted the destruction of the temple of Jerusalem and the Babylonian captivity. After the blindfolded candidates had been thrown to the floor, bound, and carried into the preparation room (symbolic of confinement in Babylon), a lodge official representing King Cyrus of Persia would announce that God had charged them to rebuild the temple at Jerusalem. Blindfolded again, the initiates slowly made their way towards Jerusalem, crossing raging rivers and journeying through the inhospitable forest of Lebanon. Upon reaching Jerusalem, the sojourners, described as "strangers" and "enemies," were denied entrance to the construction site of the second temple until they spoke the secret phrase: "I am [God] hath sent me." They then passed through the seven veils of the Temple, each time being obliged to repeat this allusion to the God of the Old Testament.

This part of the ritual, which required at least half an hour to perform, was encapsulated in the second sentence of Brown's High Priest's prayer, which thanked God for providing assistance "amidst the pains and calamities of our present state" (the Babylonian captivity) while members traveled "the rugged path of life" (the return to Jerusalem, with its attendant obstacles).

In the third section of the ceremony the repatriated captives were allowed to help rebuild the Temple. Often they were taken to a corner of the lodge and told to dig among boards and stones representing the ruins of the first Temple. They would eventually discover a trapdoor, attached to the keystone of an arch, that concealed a darkened chamber below. (See the illustration at the beginning of this chapter.) A rope was placed seven times around the body of one initiate; the other two lowered him into the "vault." On the first descent he usually found three squares, which the High Priest said were the jewels of "our ancient Grand Masters—King Solomon; Hiram, King of Tyre; and Hiram Abiff." On the second descent he discovered a chest "having on its top several mysterious characters." Inside were a pot of manna, Aaron's rod, and the "long lost book of the law." The High Priest also uncovered several pieces of paper that together provided a key to the letters on the outside of the ark of the temple. Lodge members sang the Royal Arch ode:

> Joy, the sacred law is found
> Now the temple stands complete
> Gladly let us gather round
> Where the pontiff holds his seat.
>
> Joy, the secret vault is found,
> Full the sunbeam falls within,

Pointing darkly underground,
To the treasure we would win.

They have brought it forth to light,
And again it cheers the earth;
All its leaves are shining bright,
Shining in their newest worth.[6]

The High Priest informed initiates that the characters on the outside of the ark formed the Grand Omnific Royal Arch Word—the "great, mysterious, and sacred name of Deity, which was communicated by the Lord unto Moses at the burning bush, and was in use until just before the completion of King Solomon's temple, when it was lost by the death of our Grand Master, Hiram Abiff."

The third sentence of the High Priest's prayer offered thanks to God for the "light we enjoy" (the "sunbeams" and "shining light" of God's word) and for other "strong inducements to virtue and holiness" (the various "treasures" inside the ark). He also asked that God's treasures "sink deep into our hearts" (the descent into the vault) "and bring forth in us good fruit" (manna, the "spiritual food" of God; and Aaron's rod, which, according to Scripture, "brought forth buds, and bloomed blossoms, and yielded almonds"). The prayer concluded with a request that "we be endowed with every good and perfect gift" (again, God's treasures) while "traveling the thorny path of life" (the Babylonian captivity), and "finally be admitted within the temple" (the Second Temple of Jerusalem) of "eternal light and life" (the heaven illumined by the newly discovered word of God).

The allegorical possibilities of the High Priest's prayer, and of the ritual itself, were boundless. On the simplest level, the initiate reenacted a historical pageant which in some ways was congruent with contemporary concerns: Many lodge members probably assumed that the "pains and calamities of our present state" and the "thorny path of life" referred to the trials of everyday existence. Even on its simplest level the ritual was a quest for an understanding of God, but the mysterious language and symbols called out for theological exegesis, as Masons like Brown well understood.

The essential premise was man's innate deficiencies: His "calamities" were due to his own "imperfections," which had caused his separation from God. Initiates who dug in the ruins of the temple were told that the rubble symbolized the "long habits of sin and folly" that had prevented them from "beholding that eternal foundation of truth and wisdom upon which they were to erect the spiritual and moral temple of their second life." When they sought God's deliverance on the return to Jerusalem, their conductor depicted them as "frail, dependent and needy creatures," who were afflicted with the "leprosy of sin." The initiate could not begin to comprehend God, nor to acquire His Word, until he had first been delivered from Adam's stain.[7]

The second section of the ritual sought to resolve this troublesome question: How could man, burdened with original sin and myriad imperfections, hope to gain admittance to God's temple, find the key to His Word, and be saved from the horrible consequences of sin? The High Priest's prayer, as read by Brown, addressed the issue indirectly. After acknowledging man's sinfulness, it thanked God that "amidst the pains and calamities of our present state, so many means of refreshment and satisfactions are reserved unto us." The passive structure is confusing; it is not clear what "refreshments and satisfactions" are reserved, or by whom. These ambiguities were resolved in the next sentence of the standard version of the High Priest's prayer: "We bless Thee, that, when man had fallen from his innocence and happiness, Thou didst leave him the power of reasoning, and capacity of improvement and pleasure."[8] With this the Royal Arch boldly ventured upon some of the most troublesome currents of Protestant theology: Adam's fall, it suggested, was not so tragic, nor his moral burden so onerous, for, through reason, man could enjoy life and elevate himself to grace. Brown, for good reason, chose to exclude this sentence from his otherwise verbatim version of the High Priest's prayer. A minister of God could not deny that Christ was the only instrument of man's salvation.[9] By suggesting that redemption could be accomplished through human reason, the Royal Arch contravened the most fundamental tenet of Christianity.

The Royal Arch rite was largely based on Ezekiel, a prophet who endured the Babylonian Captivity and had a vision of God's destruction of Jerusalem (Ezekiel 9–10). He saw that God placed the tau symbol upon the foreheads of the righteous; everyone else He slaughtered for persisting in sin. The ritual borrowed Ezekiel's narrative and many of his symbols. It specified that the chains, the hoodwinks, and the confinement of the simulated Babylonian captivity symbolized man's bondage to sin, which had "destroyed within us the first temple of purity and innocence."

By using the Babylonian captivity as a metaphor for the initiate's own sinfulness, the degree also resurrected typology, a metaphorical analysis of Scripture popularized by John Bunyan.[10] In one of his most popular works, *Solomon's Temple*, Bunyan described Solomon as a "type of Christ" and Solomon's Temple as an allegory for the house of God.[11] Bunyan believed that a literal interpretation of the Bible engendered passivity among Christians, who often approached its lessons with the detachment of a scholar. A typological interpretation, on the other hand, invested the present with limitless religious significance. If Solomon could be a type of Christ and his temple a prefiguration of Christ's church, then everyday events in the lives of the Puritan Saints could take on meaning as allegories for the events of the Bible.

Masons were incessantly urged to apply, in effect, a typological approach to Masonic rituals. So conceived, the powerful symbolism of the Royal Arch could confer upon the lives of Masons the spiritual significance of events in the Old Testament: An arch in a railway station might bring to mind the temple of Solomon, an onerous business contract might gain meaning as a form of Babylonian captivity, and a business reverse could be seen as the "rough and rugged road" on the return to Jerusalem. But the typology of the Royal Arch differed in one crucial respect from that of the Puritans: Where Puritan typologists fused Old and New Testaments and insisted upon the applicability of both to contemporary situations, the Royal Arch omitted or disguised references to the New Testament, and it entirely excluded Christ.

In certain instances the omission was unsubtle. The High Priest, in his first prayer, commanded members to withdraw "from every brother that walketh disorderly" and to "have no company" with any man who "obey not our word."[12] This prayer was taken directly from the New Testament (2 Thess. 3). Royal Arch Masons, however, were not told of its provenance. All but the most astute Biblical scholars would assume that they were being enjoined to obey the word of the lodge rather than that of the Lord. Worse, the Royal Arch prayer excised one telling phrase from Scripture: "in the name of our Lord Jesus Christ."

Without Christ, how could the Royal Arch lead sinful men to salvation? The Reverend Dr. Brown apparently agonized over this problem and deleted the sentence suggesting the sufficiency of reason. Having warred with the deists in the local Society of Druids, he was perhaps more sensitive to the issue than most, but the Royal Arch did not elevate man so much as it evoked a towering and imposing God. Man's dependence on God was, as Ezekiel warned, absolute. Without access to His long-lost Word, man's depravity was infinite, his prospects for salvation nonexistent. Man must struggle mightily to discover His ineffable secrets, to endure the privations of captivity, to persist through adversity, and to dig deep into the mysteries of the past.

The deity of the Royal Arch was "great, mighty, and terrible."[13] He hid His secrets from most men—and from all women. Royal Arch Masons, and perhaps some others, might benefit from His assistance if they could surmount obstacles such as those experienced by the patriarchs of the Old Testament. Having descended into the vault and discovered His Word, they could finally set about the work of rebuilding His Temple.

The Royal Arch was susceptible to contradictory interpretations. For deists the descent into the vault symbolized man's appropriation of divine powers. Through reason, and particularly through the scientific study of Nature, man could begin to unravel the world's mysteries. Brown, on the other hand, was part of a movement in Masonry which sought to channel man's efforts into a heroic search for the true meaning of an unfathomable God.

❖

Brown's alteration of the High Priest's prayer was by no means exceptional. Candidates for the Royal Arch degree were told that its rites and mysteries had been unchanged by time and had been handed down "through a chosen few." [14] This was a necessary claim, for it linked the ritual's "lost" truths to the Old Testament. It was also untrue. Like most fraternal rituals, the Royal Arch underwent continuous revision.

Ceremonies bearing the Royal Arch name first appeared in England during the mid-1700s and in the American colonies shortly thereafter. English Masonry was then in a formative stage and many of its rituals were still in embryonic form. The most important thinker in eighteenth-century English Freemasonry was William Preston, who considered the order an avenue through which to provide instruction in geometry, ethics, and science to men who lacked formal education.[15] Inspired by Newtonian rationalism, Preston had little use for the mystical or religious interpretation of Masonry which had flourished in parts of France and Germany. Masonic symbols and rituals, he thought, were "visionary delusions," useful only if they illustrated some rational principle.[16]

It is impossible to determine what forms of Masonic ritual prevailed in eighteenth-century America; variants proliferated until 1797 when a so-called Grand Lodge was established to unify American Royal Arch Masonry. Its first task was to "systematize" the rituals of the order.[17] A Royal Arch committee—apparently chosen by the Grand Lodge—"then made improvements in the rituals," many of which were codified in Thomas Smith Webb's *Freemason's Monitor*.[18] Webb's Freemasonry was derived from Preston, and his rituals took the form of Prestonian lectures and catechisms on subjects ranging from architecture to the natural sciences. "Useful knowledge is the great object of our desire," Webb wrote.[19]

Superimposed upon Webb's rationalism was an indulgent God whose "good pleasure" had "spared us with great and exceeding patience." Webb insisted that man could, through the exercise of reason, make sense of the mysteries of the earth, which God had created for man's enjoyment. "The ways of wisdom are beautiful, and lead to pleasure," he wrote. Webb consequently approved of "innocent mirth" after the formal part of lodge meetings had been completed.[20]

After his death in 1818, Webb's amalgam of Enlightenment rationality and religious liberalism was gradually subverted. Itinerant Masonic lecturers organized new lodges, conferred their own variants of the rituals and lectures, and pocketed the charter fees. In the absence of written degrees, Masonic officials at the state level confronted with a variety of rituals combed earlier Masonic documents to determine the validity of the different versions. Because verbatim accounts were not available, attempts to "prove" a pedigree for any ritual fell short.

The Reverend Salem Town, a minister from Aurora, New York, who was the author of the widely cited *A System of Speculative Masonry*, rejected Webb's rationalism and imposed upon the most common American Rite sequence a more ominous conception of God. In the Entered Apprentice degree the candidate (who was prompted to request light prior to the removal of his hoodwink) represented Adam, a victim of moral blindness. The Fellowcraft degree, which consisted of a sequence of Prestonian catechisms on geometry and natural history, indicated Adam's "sincere desire to make advances in knowledge and virtue." The death and resurrection pageant of the Master Mason degree denoted Adam's wanderings "into devious and forbidden paths." The fourth through sixth degrees further prepared the candidate for "those mansions above, where a higher and most exalted heaven has been prepared for the faithful." In the seventh, or Royal Arch, degree the initiate received "redemption from the Egypt and Babylon of the world." [21]

No initiate, subsequent Royal Arch theorists added, could fail to perceive that the Royal Arch was in fact a pilgrimage, a search for Divine Truth, symbolically represented as "Logos, the Word, the Name." Entered Apprentices (first-degree Masons) were required to affirm a belief in God; otherwise there was no point in commencing the ritualistic journey. The veil of secrecy surrounding the order imparted to its ceremonies the mystery which one should associate with so exalted and difficult an endeavor. And the profusion of symbols expressed the sublime mystery of God. "It only remains for the [initiate] to study their deep and hidden meaning," one manual on the degree asserted.[22] By mid-century, particularly after Albert Pike and Albert Mackey had become members of the Grand Lodge,[23] the Royal Arch constituted a dramatic expression of religious conversion.

While innumerable variants of Masonic rituals had become diffused throughout America during the eighteenth century, the rituals of American Odd Fellowship, established in 1819, are less difficult to trace. From the outset the Odd Fellows established a Grand Lodge and kept a close

rein on itinerant ritualists. Nevertheless, its rituals, like the American Royal
Arch degrees, underwent a transformation from a liberal and latitudinarian
system to a harsher and more foreboding theology.

The Odd Fellow's White degree, written during the 1820s, identified
Adam as the first Odd Fellow, and examined his relationship to God.
"White" referred to Adam's purity. Adam was said to have received from
God "mental faculties superior to all earthly creatures." These he was to use
to do good works, for "God rewards and blesses" those who practice charity.
When asked, "What were the commands of God to Adam?" the initiate was
told to reply: "That he should act with humanity and kindness" and "live in
brotherly love with all his fellow creatures." The Odd Fellow who cultivated
the seeds of friendship and brotherly love could expect eternal bliss and
happiness beyond the grave, when his spirit would "ascend to the heavenly
Mansions."[24]

Many of the passages of the White degree were taken directly from the
Bible; others were paraphrases of biblical incidents. Yet the early ritualists
did not hesitate to modify Scripture to suit their purposes. The degree replaced the language of Genesis with an affirmation of man's innate capacity
and his essential goodness. There was no reference to the garden of Eden
or to Adam's fall. This new Adam, unburdened with original sin, did not
require a wrenching conversion experience, and the catechisms of the ritual
provided no room for dramatic displays. The "great and universal law" of
the degree was Christ's message: "Do unto others as you would have them
do unto you." The God of this ritual was loving, even solicitous, and His
glory was magnified by the accomplishments of His creations.

The immigrant tradesmen who established American Odd Fellowship
first met in Baltimore in March 1819. On April 26 they organized the first
lodge and soon thereafter, in May, they drafted the White degree.[25] On
May 5, also in Baltimore, William Ellery Channing delivered a sermon,
later to become famous as the "Pentecost of American Unitarianism," at the
ordination of Jared Sparks.[26] His text was a response to Jedidiah Morse's
stinging attacks upon the ascendancy of liberal theology at Harvard.[27]

Channing asserted that man was to use reason to interpret God's will, for
God was not an incomprehensible and terrible despot, but an expression of
"moral perfection" who exhibited "a father's concern for his creatures." He
called predestination a "dreadful system," for, he argued, a just God would
not stamp depravity upon mankind. Channing abhorred the notion that it
was a wrathful God who inflicted upon Christ the agony of the cross. Christ,
Channing preached, had come not to rescue man from divine punishment,
but to deliver him from sinful ways. Channing also distinguished between
God the Father and a Christ with essentially human attributes whom man

might hope to emulate. At the heart of the Unitarian faith was a belief that man must reflect God's love by following the loving example of Christ.[28]

Channing's views on the attributes of man and God and the mission of Christ were echoed in the White degree. Although the ideas of Channing were in the air, the Odd Fellows' liberal theology may have been unrelated to the theological disputes of the day. The order was initially a social club, a place to join, in the words of a favorite song, "With friends so blithe and jolly, / Who all delight for to dispel / The gloom of melancholy." For men who found the pleasures of this world more compelling than the terrors of the next, the biblical references in the ritual probably helped quiet any lingering pangs of conscience.

The middle-class men who swarmed into the Odd Fellows during the 1840s complained that these rituals were "formal" and "unmeaning." Their criticisms led to the radical revision of 1845 described in the preceding chapter.[29] The Initiatory degree they adopted totally rejected the theology of the White degree. It continued to identify the initiate as Adam, but now it elaborated on the consequences of his fall.[30] Like Adam, the candidate was "naked" (his shirt had been removed) and he was repeatedly told "Thou art dust" and placed on the floor to the exclamation "Low! level with the earth! This is the state of man" (and, in Genesis, the fate of snakes).[31] The chains around the initiate's body were said to represent his "guilty soul." The blindfolded initiate was asked: "If you had light, should you know the person that recommended you?" After he had responded "Yes," his blind-folds were removed, and a skeleton was thrust into his face. "Contemplate that dismal, ghastly emblem of what thou art sure to be, and what thou mayst soon become."[32] One nineteenth-century commentator on the ritual observed that the "depravity of man" required special measures to effect his salvation. The "emblem of mortality," another wrote, would fill the initiate's heart "with a salutary horror of that monster, SIN [emphasis in original]."[33]

The initiate, "bound by ignorance and fear," required the sudden reve-lation of light, and of God. No longer a mute spectator, he had become the central figure in an ancient drama, "coeval with the first inhabitants of the earth." His development in Odd Fellowship, and in life, would not be easy: Obstacles were inevitable, pain and death man's destiny. The skeleton served as a reminder that no comfort could be expected even after death. The easygoing God of the White degree had been replaced by a "Supreme, Intelligent Being" whose "holy name" was to be mentioned only with "that reverential awe which is due from the creature to the Creator."[34]

During the 1850s and 1860s an almost identical transformation per-vaded the upper levels of Scotch Rite Freemasonry. This is most evident in the "modern ritual" of the twenty-eighth degree ("Knight of the Sun") of the Scottish Rite. In this—"by far the most learned and philosophical of the Scottish degrees," according to Mackey[35]—the Worshipful Master represented Father Adam; the initiate was his child, one whose eyes were bandaged and arms bound with chains. A mask was fastened to his face and a crown placed upon his head. He wore a ragged and bloody robe. In his left hand he held a purse; in his right, a sword.

When asked what he most desired, the conductor (speaking for the initiate) answered: "To divest myself of original sin." The "child" of Adam was conducted around the temple while another official spoke of God as "the living and awful being, from whom nothing in the universe is hidden." Man had "wandered far into darkness"; around him hovered "sin and shame." The candidate for the Knight of the Eagle and Pelican of the Scottish Rite similarly commenced his initiation wearing an elaborate uniform, including white gloves and a sword. Each element of his fine costume was replaced during the rite with more common clothing. Finally, the Master of Ceremonies noted that "these marks of indignity are not sufficiently humiliating" and covered the initiate with a black cloth sprinkled with ashes and dust.[36]

By mid-century the rituals of American Freemasonry and Odd Fellowship had been completely transformed: References to man's goodness had been replaced with an assumption of his innate sinfulness; approval of his innocent enjoyment of life's pleasures with a "dreadful track" of trials and tortures; a solicitous God with an "awful being" who was prepared to "thrust a red hot iron through the initiate's tongue, pluck out his eyes, cut off his hands, and leave him to be devoured by voracious animals" should he reveal the secrets of the order.[37]

The ritualists of the 1840s and 1850s established the theological foundation for the rituals that proliferated during the last third of the nineteenth century. And despite the public endorsement by all fraternal orders of good works and tolerance, the rituals of all major and most minor orders offered a form of religious expression far removed from the liberal beliefs which had come to prevail in the churches of the middle classes.

The highest degree of the Knights of Pythias opened when the Master of Arms asked the initiate "by what right" he sought admission to the degree.[38] The initiate, having been rehearsed in the preparation room, responded, "By that of being a brave man." After considerable debate the participants would move to test the courage of the initiate through an ordeal to be administered by Pluto, the god of the underworld.

The lodge room was darkened to represent hell. A pile of skeletons was placed near a cauldron. Pluto, wearing silver mail, a cloak of black, and a helmet, led the initiate by the arm past swarms of "deadly adders" and the "calcined" remains of "coward souls." He picked up a piece of oak pierced with long iron nails and invited the initiate to examine it. He then turned the candidate away from the torture device and stared into his eyes, intoning: "When Adam fell from his primeval bliss he had been tempted by me through unsuspecting Eve." By this means, he continued, he had peopled this "wild waste." While Pluto thus diverted the candidate, lodge members replaced the oak board with another, fitted with rubber nails. As Pluto finished his disquisition a curtain was drawn open, revealing the Chancellor Commander in a scarlet robe with a white cross upon his breast. Pluto fled. The Commander stepped forward and told the "pilgrim" to remove his sandals and mount a small ladder placed over the oak board. He also asked that the fellow Knights crowd close to "bear witness in the act." Finally, he instructed the initiate: "Now, if you are a brave and steel-souled man, Leap down!"[39]

Very few heeded the command. Many became confused and agitated. The command was twice repeated. Then the Chancellor Commander pushed his foot down on the rubber nails and instructed the "pilgrim" to do likewise. Afterwards the Commander explained the symbolism: The wilderness of hell was to remind the initiate of life's difficult journey; the snakes, of the "trials and temptations of life;" and the skeletons, of the "penalty of Cowardice." The Vice Chancellor announced, "As a brave and obedient man I cannot give you cordial greeting, yet will, in consideration of the many trials you have undergone, proceed to give you knowledge of our secret work, that you may know that he who wears the spurs should fairly win them." Then he dubbed the initiate a Knight, saying, "You have been severely tested, and passed the ordeal unscathed."

But of course the initiate commonly had done no such thing, for he had failed repeatedly to jump upon the nails. The ritual had not delivered him from the stain of Adam; it had confirmed it before all of the Knights of the lodge. Logically his behavior warranted not knighthood, but torture and damnation.

Fraternal societies competed to attract the "better" members of the community, and potential initiates were always obliged to attest to their physical and mental fitness. Yet this Knights degree and many other rituals were predicated on the assumption that the candidate would fail his trials. Often he was depicted as an assassin (Scottish Rite rituals), intruder (Red Men, Ancient Order of Foresters), spy (Grand Army of the Republic), or coward. Occasionally he was ordered to perform impossible tasks or was tricked into violating his oath.[40] The darkness brought on by the blindfolds symbolized his benighted soul and evil nature. He was obliged to prostrate himself to express his humiliation and debasement.[41] He was not merely inexperienced, but fundamentally flawed. It was not enough that he learn new ideas; he would first have to be purged of the old.

Members expected the rituals to be charged with emotion. Having been led to believe that his initiation would be momentous, the candidate undoubtedly felt nervous, certainly curious, as he waited in the anteroom. Within the temple, meanwhile, the sense of expectation became still more acute. Scenery was prepared, costumes were donned, lights extinguished. As the candidate was escorted past the guards and led to the altar, members were often reminded of their own initiations. And as the candidate repeated the oath of secrecy and embarked upon the ritualistic circumambulations, tension mounted. Members knew, and the candidate half suspected, that the ritual would reach a climax.

As if skeletons, skulls, bloody daggers, executioners' devices, and assorted funereal accoutrements were not enough, ritualists frequently employed other mechanisms to unnerve the initiate at the moment of climax. The tension usually culminated in a sudden revelation of frightening objects or in an explosion of light and sound. Disoriented and embarrassed, the initiate would now rearrange conventional images into different patterns —and new meanings. "The Shock of Entrance," Mackey observed, "is the symbol of the disruption of the candidate from the ties of the world, and his introduction into the life of Masonry. It is the symbol of the agonies of the first death and of the throes of the new birth." His new life as a member would entail a quest for the true meaning of God.

❖ A FARTHER DEGREE ❖

Death was the central theme of most rituals. The candidate commonly was "killed" during the initiation; one instance is Hiram Abiff's assassination in the Master Mason ritual. Often the initiate's metaphorical voyage stopped just short of death. The candidate for the Grand Army of the Republic, for example, was pronounced a "traitor" and led before a firing squad; his execution was interrupted at the last moment. In other rituals initiates were nearly slain by Indians, Old Testament patriarchs, or by God himself.

Often they examined the physical consequences of death: the ubiquitous skulls, skeletons, and funeral paraphernalia—particularly coffins. In several Masonic degrees candidates were consigned to a Chamber of Reflection occupied by a coffin and a corpse. Candidates for the Odd Fellows, Grand

Army of the Republic, and the Knights of Pythias took their oaths before a coffin. Icons of death figured prominently in more than thirty of the forty-five degrees of American Freemasonry. Occasionally, as in the Pythian journey through Hades, the fraternal pilgrimage ventured beyond the margins of life and death.

Ritualistic representations of death reminded initiates to pay their dues. This was particularly evident in the Ceremony of Adoption of the Modern Woodmen of America, an insurance order. The candidate, led in search of the Woodmen's Camp, would encounter a "Youth" who urged him to enjoy himself rather than worry about death. No sooner had the candidate resisted this temptation than "Death" appeared, saying "I have remained here that I might turn you into lifeless clay." The conductor then pleaded for clemency: "If you demand his life now his loved ones will be objects of charity." Death, noting the purpose of their journey, allowed them to pass—"this time." The conductor and the candidate eventually arrived at the camp just in time to join a funeral procession. During the eulogy they learned that the deceased member's widow and orphans would "receive the care and protection of this Society." The moral was obvious.

But representations of death also were found in orders, such as the Masons, which did not offer insurance provisions. And there was no reason why those who sought to sell insurance should be led to depict death in such graphic detail. Insurance benefited the deceased's family; it did nothing to retard the decomposition of the flesh.

Ghastly depictions of death supposedly reminded members of what would happen if they violated their oath of secrecy. The initiate for the "Knight of the Sun" degree asked the brethren, should he fail them, to "seize me and thrust my tongue through with a red hot iron, to pluck out my eyes and deprive me of smelling and seeing, to cut off my hands and expose me in that condition in the field to be devoured by voracious animals."[42] But the hyperbole of such oaths diminished their efficacy.

More probably, repulsive images of death were initially included to generate an emotional response, not unlike the visceral excitement teenagers find so compelling in horror movies. The Master Mason degree depicted in lurid terms the decomposition of Abiff's body, represented by the prostrate candidate. Because, they said, he began "to smell a little already," the assassins buried him, covering his body with sticks and papers. Master Masons fought off the stench and attempted to raise him, but, according to their spoken narrative, his flesh separated from the bone.

These scenes, which bordered on the burlesque, were salvaged from it by their pervasive religious imagery. In the Knight Kadosh ritual (thirtieth degree of the Scottish Rite) the initiate was instructed to thrust a dagger into a skull. An inscription on the back wall of the lodge was then read aloud: "Whoever shall overcome the dread of death, shall emerge from the bosom of the earth, and have a right to be initiated into the greater mysteries."

All rituals promised to reveal "great mysteries," "impenetrable secrets," or equally arcane forms of religious knowledge. Novices often assumed that the "secrets" of the order referred to the passwords, handshakes, recognition signs, and signals of distress, but a preoccupation with death forced members to ponder the nature of God and the afterlife. This is hardly remarkable: Protestant ministers inevitably used the occasion of a funeral sermon to remark on the brevity of life and the meaning of death. The grisly scenes and gruesome iconography of the fraternal rituals, however, bore little resemblance to the domesticated imagery that increasingly characterized American attitudes toward death.

In the Protestant churches the emergence of a gentler, more hopeful attitude was the work of liberal theologians who believed that a God who sacrificed His son to deliver mankind from sin had no desire to torment His creatures in the hereafter. Death thus delivered men from the woes of life. "Death," John Pierpont, minister of the Hollis Street Unitarian Church in Boston, wrote, "lays his hand upon the burning brow, and it is cool. He touches the aching heart, and its pain is gone." Its inducements were so powerful that God had to implant in man a fear of death to "keep his children from rushing uncalled into his [God's] presence.[43] "That we are so near death is too good to be believed," Henry Ward Beecher insisted.[44]

During the nineteenth century this view became a commonplace of American culture. The death's heads and foreboding epitaphs on tombstones that for eighteenth-century Calvinists had expressed God's hatred of sin gradually gave way to somnolent and peaceful images with inscriptions describing death as a gentle, even pleasant release from life. In 1831 Unitarian clergymen and literary figures established Mt. Auburn Cemetery in Cambridge; soon afterwards similar invitingly landscaped garden cemeteries appeared in New York, Philadelphia, Baltimore, and other American cities. Corpses, too, were doctored in response to the demands of a public which no longer cared to contemplate the grim physical realities of death.

Death grew more appealing partly because hell began to lose its terrors. The young Henry Ward Beecher had imagined that the tolling funeral bell signaled "Death! hell! damnation!" but by the mid-nineteenth century he learned to think of it as God's reassuring call to "Come home."[45] In 1878 E. L. Youmans, editor of the *Popular Science Monthly*, announced that due to the advance of science and human progress, the hell of Jonathan Edwards had been abolished.[46]

But the vanquished hell of the Puritans reappeared each week in the temples of the orders. The skeletons, coffins, grisly oaths, and voyages through Hades were striking refutation of the new Protestant interpretation of death. Whereas for the liberals death confirmed the goodness of God, the perfectability of man, and the moral values of Christian nurture, fraternal rituals taught that God was imposing and distant, that man was fundamentally flawed, and that human understanding of religious and moral issues was imperfect. Only by experiencing the greatest of transformations—death —could man begin to comprehend the truths of human existence.

The fraternal conception of death acquired practical significance from the fact that, apart from regularly scheduled meetings, the most common occasion upon which the lodge was convened was the death of a member. Every major order made use of special burial rituals.[47] When they learned of the death of a lodge brother, officers sought permission from his family to have their own private moments with the corpse. If the member had requested a fraternal interment, the lodge made all the arrangements. As it was so common to belong to several orders, disputes often arose over which order was entitled to lead the funeral procession and to conduct the burial service.[48]

Lodges had good reason to quarrel over these questions, for they held that the funeral service marked the culmination of the initiatory sequence. Masonic handbooks explained that the burial service was "in strictness a part of our ritual." The death and resurrection of Hiram Abiff in the Master Mason degree was merely a "rehearsal" for the burial service. (Members who had not attained that degree were denied Masonic interment.) The procession to the graveyard was analogous to the circumambulations of the lodge by the initiate. The grave itself, through various mystical processes during the Masonic service, became an extension of the lodge temple. "No brother," the handbook noted, "has completed his course of Blue-Lodge Masonry until he has been *actually* dealt with by the hands of kind bearers and depositors." At the grave the Worshipful Master was to announce that the deceased had experienced the greatest initiation of all: "He has advanced one degree farther than any of us! He has received light that is ineffable to mortal eyes. All that to us, is enwrapped in cloud, in mystery, in emblems, is clear and plain to him."[49]

But what would the deceased brother find at the end of his final journey? Masonic scholars could only speculate, and these speculations were the subject of countless speeches and monographs. They were especially struck by the similarity of the ritualistic voyages into subterranean chambers to the interment of the dead. Mackey observed that the human body was a temple of life which ultimately decayed, collapsed, and was buried. Yet deep beneath its ruins—in "the profound abyss of the grave"—was to be found divine truth.[50] "We must descend," he wrote elsewhere, "into the secret vault of death before we can find that sacred deposit of truth which is to adorn our second temple of eternal life."[51] During the Royal Arch degree, initiates emerged from this vault of death bearing the glorious light of the Grand Omnific Word that signified God. "The search for the Word—to find divine Truth—this, and this only, is a mason's work, and the WORD is his reward," Mackey explained.[52]

The opening ceremony of the Royal Arch ritual offered the most complete exposition of the nature of God. Three officers placed their arms and legs in positions that formed several triangles. They then uttered three words, each made up of three sounds—Jah-bel-on, Je-ho-vah, and G-O-D—but, as each man began with a different word in the sequence, what they said was incomprehensible. During the initiation itself the candidates unearthed the Grand Omnific Word: the Hebrew tetragrammaton. They then repeated the mysterious phrases that had been intoned earlier.

Ritualists inscribed many meanings upon the facets of this complex ceremony, but there was no disagreement about its basic import. The recurrent references to *three*, as well as the symbolism of the triangle, denoted Deity. Jah was the sun god of the Syrians; Bel, or Baal, the fire god of the Chaldeans; and On, the sun god of the Egyptians.[53] Je-ho-vah indicated the ineffable God of the Hebrew tetragrammaton. And G-O-D, which in English "coincidentally" spelled God, actually alluded to the first letters of the Hebrew words gomer, oz, and dabar, so that the phrase meant wisdom, strength, and beauty, the Masonic motto.[54]

The blinding "light without form" that accompanied initiations ultimately denoted "Divine Splendor."[55] For this reason the Masonic lodge was always sited upon an east-west axis and the Worshipful Master stationed nearest the position of the rising sun. The candidate's journey toward Truth brought him to the easternmost part of the lodge, where, it was thought, he could better apprehend its meaning. The Knights of the Golden Circle opened ceremonies with a prayer to the "Divine Essence! God of our Fathers." The order's first principle outlined the attributes of this deity: "Essence, Ethereal, Eternal, Supreme—by us called God! hath created, pervades and controls the Universe!"[56] The 1845 Initiatory degree of Odd Fellowship informed candidates that "we pursue the universal religion of nature." The Red Men prayed to a "Great Spirit" whose image "appeared in the sun" and whose presence suffused the forest with His light.

Rarely was the implicit theology of the rituals articulated in public. An exception was a novelette entitled "The Mysterious Record: Manuscript of a Deceased Odd-Fellow," which appeared in the Odd Fellows' magazine, *The Rainbow*, in April and May 1843. A young man, meditating at the edge of a forest, is overwhelmed by the beauty of a sunset. He prays that he might commune with the God who created such beauty. He then has a terrible vision of God, whose "stern and piercing eyes" are full of wrath. The remainder of the story is a thinly veiled allegory for the Master Mason degree: God asks if he wishes to learn the secrets of Nature. The young man demands to receive Light, but what he learns drives him mad. God, he concludes, mercifully veils His "dim terrors" from mankind. Non-Masonic readers might think the story a cautionary tale composed by a conservative theologian. But Masons knew that it referred to the foreboding God who could be encountered only through the ritual.

The secret deity of the orders was distant and impersonal, a God to whom access, save at death, was impossible. This picture more closely resembled the God of the Puritans than the benevolent and human Christ of liberal Protestantism. Fraternal rituals sought to redress "the Divine displeasure,"[57] or to propitiate an "offended Great Spirit."[58] The fire triangle, its base upon the ground, which appeared in many Masonic rituals, delineated an "angry God."[59] A funeral hymn of the Odd Fellows implored the "Great God" to

> . . . afflict not in Thy wrath,
> The short alloted span,
> That bounds the few and weary days
> Of pilgrimage to man.[60]

The lurid descriptions of corpses and the insistence upon confronting one's mortality were also suggestive of Puritan mores and theology.[61]

A Masonic editor who happened upon John Bunyan's *Pilgrim's Progress* was struck by the ritualistic possibilities of Christian's humiliation, his struggle to cross the black river Death, and his ascent to the Celestial City. "How analogous is all this to the Masonic system!" he wrote. He thought it odd that, in spite of the "wholesale demand" for rituals, the degree makers of the preceding hundred years had neglected Bunyan's classic.[62]

In fact, American fraternal leaders had little use for an explicitly Christian ritualism. Prior to 1845 initiates in the Odd Fellow's Priestly Order, or Scarlet degree, were told that the scarlet ribbon with which they were invested symbolized "the Royal Dignity of Jesus Christ, and the bloody suffering of him and his church." But the revisions of 1845 eliminated the Scarlet degree; Christ ceased to have a place in the rituals of the order. By the 1850s Christ's name had also been excised from most Masonic rituals. The script written by Pike for the twenty-eighth degree of the Scottish Rite, for example, called for a return to the primitive truths which "faded out from men's souls before the world grew old."[63] In this rite Michael, the chief of the seven archangels ("Who is like unto God"), told initiates that the "truth of primitive revelation" was always "covered from the common people." Even in "the present day", he lamented, the Creator was degraded to the "rank of humanity."[64] After the Civil War only a handful of rituals offered prayers to Christ.[65]

The American rejection of Christ contrasted with the simultaneous ascendancy of a Christian interpretation of Masonry in England. George Oliver (1782–1865), the most prominent English Freemason, had become dissatisfied with Prestonian rationalism. Throughout Masonic rituals he perceived Christ's hand: The darkened lodge represented the state of the world before the birth of the Redeemer; the three assassins of Hiram Abiff stood for Pontius Pilate; Caiphas, the Jewish High Priest; and Judas Iscariot; the twelve Masons who searched for Abiff's body were the disciples of Christ; and the raising of Abiff symbolized the resurrection of Christ.[66]

Scholars within the American fraternal groups justified the omission of Christ by emphasizing the universal character of their orders; all men, whether Christian, Mohammedan, or Jewish, were theoretically welcome to share in the fellowship of the lodge. But the theorists also discussed a theological difficulty with a Christian interpretation of Masonry. The initiation, Mackey observed, came to a climax when the subject was confronted with a flash of light, a skeleton, the mysteries of the ark, or some other revelation. "There is to be," he noted, "not simply a change for the future, but also an extinction of the past; for initiation is, as it were, a death to the world and a resurrection to a new life."[67] The allusion to Christ was surely intentional, and its implication significant: Christ's own "initiation," by ensuring man's salvation, could be thought to render all other initiatory experiences superfluous. If Masonry were merely an allegorical rendering of Christ's message, as Oliver held, then members might just as well attend church. By insisting upon a disruption of the initiate's "ties to the world" and an "extinction" of his past, Mackey had implied the insufficiency of Christian worship.

The orders' exclusion of Christ was particularly significant because it occurred just as Protestant worship increasingly centered on Christ.[68] The Calvinists' anguished doubts about the workings of an unknowable God ceased to concern liberal theologians, who advised churchgoers to think less about sin and depravity and "more of Christ, his character, his love, his suffering."[69]

Lynn Dumenil observed that Freemasonry was a "malleable" system that succeeded in accommodating a wide spectrum of religious positions. She rightly noted that Freemasonry gained acceptance during the late nineteenth century because its dedication to universality, toleration, and morality was "in keeping with the tendencies of liberal Protestantism."[70] And though the rituals excluded Christ, fraternal leaders continually affirmed that their order was a "handmaiden to Christianity." Worshipful Masters, Noble Grands, and Grand Sachems consistently endorsed religious toleration and repeatedly articulated the quasi-Arminian doctrine that the measure of a man was to be found in his good works rather than his piety.[71]

But even as officials voiced the customary pieties, their rituals suppressed mention of Christ, delineated in grotesque detail the consequences of death, and evoked an awesome and mysterious Deity. Most important, they served as a means of personal transformation in which the rites of the lodge supplanted the mediation of Christ.

The theological tension between liberal Protestantism and fraternal rituals is all the more remarkable since the latter were often written by liberal ministers. The five-member committee that in 1845 revised the rituals of the Odd Fellows included Edwin Hubbell Chapin, a prominent Universalist minister; and John McCabe, a banker who three years later was ordained as an Episcopalian minister.[72] Chapin's background was particularly incongruous with his role in the order. Raised in a stalwart Puritan family, he rebelled against his family's orthodoxy. "I reject the doctrine of the trinity, of a vicarious sacrifice to appease the wrath of God, of total depravity, original sin," he said in 1840. His was a "religion of love, and not of fear."[73] Yet four years after making this statement, he helped, as chairman of the Odd Fellows Committee on Ritual Revision, to create a ceremony that asserted man's innate depravity and that culminated in the frightening encounter with a skeleton.[74] Justus Rathbone, who wrote most of the rituals for the Pythians, attended Carlisle Seminary in Pennsylvania.[75] Uriah S. Stephens, author of the Adelphon Kruptos—the secret work—of the Knights of Labor, had studied for the Baptist ministry.[76]

Many ministers also served as High Priests, Prophets, and Chaplains. In New York State in 1891 a large proportion of the ordained clergy belonged to the Freemasons, including approximately 26 percent of the Universalist, 22 percent of the Episcopalian, and 18 percent of the Methodist clergy. The percentage was much lower among Congregational (6 percent), Presbyterian (7 percent), Lutheran (13 percent), and Baptist (15 percent) clergymen.[77] Fraternal members were themselves drawn largely from the urban middle classes, where religious liberalism found its greatest support.[78]

Members were perhaps unaware of the theological implications of their rituals; surely, few recognized that the theology they received in the lodge was antithetical to that which they witnessed in church. That liberal ministers were equally unmindful seems doubtful. How, for example, did the Reverend John Brown reconcile his offices on Sunday mornings, when he donned the vestments of an Episcopalian minister and preached a Gospel of

Christian love, with his position on Wednesday evenings, when he wore the mitre of a Jewish High Priest and officiated as initiates struggled along the "rough and rugged road" in search of the mysteries of an unapproachable deity?

Pike insisted that the "profoundest thoughts" of the human mind were to be found not in its philosophies, but in its symbols. "There are thoughts and ideas which no language ever spoken by man has words to express," he added.[79] He urged members to go beyond the platitudes of officials and to ponder the meanings of the symbols. Pike's distinction between philosophical and symbolic meanings is suggestive. Members and ministers may have adhered to a liberal theology and a latitudinarian philosophy even as they derived sustenance from symbols evoking a harsh and intolerant form of secret worship.

Anthropologists have shown that the meaning of symbols is largely dependent upon the cultural context in which they are employed.[80] Nearly all fraternal symbols were clearly associated in the minds of most members with the church. Lodge members usually knelt before an altar. Without exception, American fraternal orders required that members affirm belief in God and take oaths upon the Bible. Many fraternal rituals were based on familiar biblical stories. As in church, the ceremonies of the lodge commenced and ended with songs; frequently fraternal hymns were based on popular Protestant hymns. Sunday morning's "All hail the power of Jesus' name / In whom all blessings fall" on lodge nights became "When met in friendship's sacred name / We round an altar stand."[81] Yet these common symbols —Bible, altar, cross, chalice, candles, hymns—helped conceal the deeper tension between the ideologies of church and lodge.

Lodge members and clergymen, reassured of the propriety of their rituals by the familiar symbols of the church, created and repeatedly practiced rituals which altered the context—and the meaning—of those symbols. Christians who joined orders were likely to have believed that the rites posed no challenge to their religious convictions. Symbols linked lodge and church, and, what is more, the professed purpose of the rituals—to make men mindful of ethical principles—accorded with the teachings of Christianity. With each successive degree, however, the context of the symbols changed. By the time a Mason came to the point of performing the revised version of the thirtieth degree of the Scottish Rite (Knight Kadosh), in which he drank wine and broke bread, the likelihood of his perceiving a Christian significance in that act had diminished considerably.[82] Rather, in a setting of coffins and skulls, bloody oaths and frightening scenery, the symbols of chalice, wine, Bible, and candles connoted antithetical ideas about the past, death, and divinity. By disguising the contradictory ideas of liberal Protestantism and initiatory ritual, fraternal symbols evoked the unity of church and lodge even as they refuted liberal theology.[83]

An example can be found in the interpretations of the cross bearing the letters INRI that was engraved on the Worshipful Master's chair. New Masons probably assumed that the letters stood for the Latin inscription on the cross of Jesus: *Jesus Nazarenus Rex Iudoeorum*. According to Masonic scholars, however, INRI stood for the Hebrew words *iammim* (water), *nour* (fire), *rouach* (air), and *iebeschah* (dry earth), as well as for the Latin *Igne Natura Renovatur Integra* (all of Nature is renovated by fire).[84] Similarly, the cross itself figured prominently in many fraternal rituals, but initiates gradually learned that it did not refer to Christ. The cross, Pike wrote, was a sacred symbol among the druids, Indians, Egyptians, and Arabians "thousands of years before the coming of Christ."[85] The obvious Christian meaning of these symbols merely concealed a deeper association with ancient—and pagan—religions.

Anthropologists have observed a similar "multivocalic" character to symbols in primitive societies. Victor Turner found that among the Ndembu in Africa the whiteness of clay elicited a multiplicity of associations ranging from biological referents (semen) to the abstract idea of ritualistic purity.[86] Audrey Richards, in a study of female puberty rituals among the Bemba, showed how the hoe represented both the woman's gardening duties and the husband, who makes his wife fertile.[87]

Turner went one step further. By encompassing many different meanings, he argued, symbols make it possible to express indirectly conflicts within society. Tensions between society and the individual, and between social norms and personal drives, could be condensed and unified in certain dominant symbols.[88] Although Ndembu informants repeatedly insisted that the "milk-tree" connoted the unifying principle of matrilineality on which their society was based, the same symbol in different rituals gave expression to gender tensions within Ndembu society.[89]

Fraternal ritualists and scholars acknowledged the multivocalic nature of their symbols. Pike wrote that the symbols of Masonry "have more than one meaning" and "conceal rather than disclose the Truth." "Truth had always been hidden" he added, "under symbols and often under a succession of allegories: where veil after veil had to be penetrated, before the true Light was reached, and the essential truth stood revealed."[90]

If fraternal rituals helped to disguise the tension between lodge rituals and liberal theology, the question remains: Why did middle-class Protestant men subconsciously create this theology for the lodge? Fraternal historians insisted that revisions were in response to the "desires" and "cravings" of members.[91] One can, of course, find satisfaction in austere and demanding religious beliefs; why, in particular, middle-class men in the early to mid nineteenth century would choose to create and embrace so foreboding a theology is less obvious.

❖ LET THY SACRED FIRE DESCEND ❖

As the initiation for the Chief's degree—the highest level of the Improved Order of Red Men—commenced, the Chiefs assembled around a council fire at the center of an otherwise darkened lodge. The initiate, wearing moccasins and a loincloth, was silently escorted around the lodge four times. As he completed the final circumambulation, the council fire went out. A Prophet emerged from a tent carrying a torch that cast light upon a skeleton. "The Great Spirit," he solemnly announced,

> is offended at his red children, and has withdrawn the visible symbol of his pleasure. The spirit of darkness has gone abroad, and spread its sable mantle over the once smiling bosom of creation. The azure heaven above; the green earth beneath; the pleasing foliage of the forest; the shiny bosoms of the lakes; the rippling waters of the swift-running rivers, and the variegated hues of the angry waves of the great ocean which surround our land—all, all have merged into darkness and disappeared. The beasts of prey have gone forth; the stealthy panther utters his piteous but deceptive cries; the ravenous wolf breaks the dismal gloom with his sanguinary bark; all, all is darkness and desolation.

The Prophet faced the candidate and invoked the "almighty power" of the Great Spirit:

> Oh, let Thy sacred fire descend. Inspire our brother's heart with truth, sincerity, benevolence and charity—the sacred mystery of every Red Man's love.

Following a series of incantations, the Prophet ignited the Chief's sticks, which were used to relight the council fire.

The eighteenth degree of the Scottish Rite was similar to the Royal Arch ritual. But whereas the Royal Arch focused on the rediscovery of the name of God, the eighteenth degree was primarily concerned with the rebuilding of Solomon's temple. The initiate learned that the first temple of Jerusalem had been destroyed and that efforts to rebuild it had ceased. "Confusion has come upon our works," the Master lamented, "and it is no longer in our power to continue them. You must perceive from our looks and the consternation which prevails among us, what confusion reigns on the earth. The veil of the temple is rent, the light is obscured and darkness spreads over the earth . . . the sacred word is lost." The candidate pledged to help find the sacred word. Whether the temple would be rebuilt was left in doubt.

The temples had a double symbolic function. At the beginning, lights were extinguished and the furniture was placed in disarray. The lodges became wastelands, ruins, deserts, hells. To dispel the darkness and regenerate the world was the member's sacred duty. This he might accomplish through the proper configuration of mystic rituals, incantations, and symbols; God's temples must be rebuilt, and His proper worship practiced. Those whose knowledge encompassed the wisdom of the ancients, or who had experienced the transcendent knowledge that attended death, might be able to invoke the aid of God to regenerate mankind and to restore the Light that would illuminate His glorious temples.

Historians of American Protestantism have described the years following the Civil War as the "summit of complacency," or, more positively, as a "golden age" of liberal theology.[92] What has not been considered is the possibility that American men unconsciously invented and repeatedly practiced in the lodge a faith whose appeal was deep-rooted, and whose implicit theology was antithetical to the liberalism preached in most middle-class pulpits.

If middle-class men built new temples, it was because existing ones had proven deficient; if they created strange new gods, it was because the ones with which they were familiar had failed them; and if they chose to evoke spiritual wastelands, it was because such representations in some way resembled the world in which they lived. To understand these underlying discontents, it is necessary, as Mackey advised, to descend further into the shadowy labyrinths of the rituals themselves.

CHAPTER III

Darkness

"Saved in the Lord's Own Time and Place"
Finney wrestling in prayer during his conversion
in the woods near Adams, New York
From an anonymous woodcut.
Courtesy of Keith J. Hardman.

"Finally, I found myself verging fast to despair. I said to myself, 'I cannot pray. My heart is dead to God, and will not pray.' When I came to try, I found I could not give my heart to God. My inward soul hung back, and there was no going out of my heart to God. I began to feel deeply that it was too late; that it must be that I was given up of God and was past hope. . . .

"Just at this moment I again thought I heard some one approach me, and I opened my eyes to see whether it were so. But right there the revelation of my pride of heart, as the great difficulty that stood in the way, was distinctly shown to me. An overwhelming sense of my wickedness in being ashamed to have a human being see me on my knees before God, took such powerful possession of me, that I cried at the top of my voice, and exclaimed that I would not leave that place if all the men on earth and all the devils in hell surrounded me. 'What! I said, 'such a degraded sinner as I am, on my knees confessing my sins to the great and holy God; and ashamed to have any human being, and a sinner like myself, find me on my knees endeavoring to make my peace with my offended God!' The sin appeared awful, infinite. It broke me down before the Lord.

"Just at that point this passage of Scripture seemed to drop into my mind with a flood of light: 'Then shall ye go and pray unto me, and I will hearken unto you. Then shall ye seek me and find me, when ye shall search for me with all your heart.' I instantly seized hold of this with my heart. . . .

"By evening we got the books and furniture adjusted; and I made up, in an open fire-place, a good fire, hoping to spend the evening alone. As I closed the door and turned around, my heart seemed to be liquid within me. All my feelings seemed to rise and flow out; and the utterance of my heart was, 'I want to pour my whole soul out to God.' The rising of my soul was so great that I rushed into the room back of the front office, to pray.

"There was no fire, and no light, in the room; nevertheless it appeared to me as if it were perfectly light. As I went in and shut the door after me, it seemed as if I met the Lord Jesus Christ face to face.

"I must have continued in this state for a good while; I returned to the front office, and found that the fire that I had made of large wood was nearly burned out. But as I turned and was about to take a seat by the fire, I received a mighty baptism of the Holy Ghost.

"When I awoke in the morning the sun had risen, and was pouring a clear light into my room. Words cannot express the impression that this sunlight made upon me. Instantly the baptism that I had received the night before, returned upon me in the same manner. I arose upon my knees in the bed and wept aloud with joy, and remained for some time too much overwhelmed with the baptism of the Spirit to do anything but pour out my soul to God."[1]

❖

Charles Grandison Finney's account of his conversion in 1821, from which the quotation above is taken, is one of the classic documents in nineteenth-century evangelism. From this wrenching experience he formulated the principles that sustained American evangelism for the remainder of the century.[2] They served as the foundation for his rise as the most important American revivalist of the nineteenth century. By informing him that salvation was "an offer of something to be accepted," the inward voice delivered him from a crippling fear of an offended God, whose wrath would pull him down to hell. He now realized that all who were willing to give up sin could find salvation in Christ.[3]

Finney's theology was an amalgam of orthodox and liberal tenets. He did not believe that man was innately good. He ridiculed the notion that sinful man could discern God's intentions by studying the Bible or contemplating nature. Yet he agreed with the liberals that believing in man's utter depravity and his complete dependence upon God had caused Christians to become lethargic in their devotions. Millions of souls had "gone down to hell while the church has been dreaming and waiting for God to save them."[4] He hoped to reconcile Jonathan Edwards's doctrines of human depravity and God's "otherness" with an activist approach to salvation. His own conversion had suggested a solution: The enormous gap between sinful man and a distant God could be bridged through a cataclysmic emotional experience.

Seventeenth-century Calvinists had also associated conversion with emotional turmoil. They believed that the infusion of God's grace into the souls of the elect would precipitate a conflict with Satan, embodied by man's sinfulness. Prospective church members were obliged to describe this turmoil to prove sanctification. Finney, however, conceived of a different psychological process. Though spiritually "sluggish" and inclined to complacency in religious matters, man unfortunately was easily diverted by "worldly excitements." The revivalist would redirect these unstable emotions toward issues of the soul.[5] Thus Finney savagely attacked listeners for persisting in sin, commanding them to come forward to the "anxious seat," a special bench where penitents received a blast of his "denunciatory" preaching. Such practices often triggered wild and even violent emotional excesses, but Finney insisted that these measures were necessary to "break the chains of pride" and "uncover the delusions of the human heart."[6] Before one could truly accept Christ, he must undergo a shattering of the self.

Fraternal ritual shared some characteristics of Finney's brand of evangelism; indeed, his own conversion experience was similar in certain respects to the Master Mason degree. Much as the initiate circumambulated the temple, Finney set himself in motion to find places to pray, traveling first to a "kind of closet" in the woods and going later into a back room in his house. Masons, after journeying around the lodge, searched for their departed master, Hiram Abiff; Finney received as revelation a passage of Scripture concerning a similar quest: "Then shall ye seek me and find me, when ye shall search for me with all your heart."

The Master Mason degree superimposed upon the search for Abiff a metaphysical journey: The initiate was repeatedly asked, "Why do you leave the west, and travel to the east?" and "What do you now most desire?" Each time he answered that he was seeking "more light." The ritual reached its climax when the Worshipful Master responded, "And God said, 'Let there be light,' and there was light." The blindfolds were then removed.

Finney was also preoccupied with light—and with secrecy. He went into the woods to be "away from all human eyes and ears" so that "no one might see me" (a phrase he repeated three times). That evening, after he made a fire, he rushed into the back room where, although there was "no fire and no light," it appeared "perfectly light." There he saw Jesus Christ, whose stare caused Finney to break down in tears. The next morning, after he had told a church elder that he was quitting the practice of law and joining Christ, the man began to laugh. A kind of darkness came over Finney, and a "cloud seemed to shut in." He went to bed unsettled, fearful that the incident that morning had obscured his path. When he awakened the following morning the "sun was pouring a clear light" into the room. The "baptism" of the previous evening had made Finney a new man.

This Masonic reconstruction of Finney's conversion as an allegory for fraternal initiation would be preposterous were it not for the fact that Finney had joined the order in Connecticut eight years earlier (1813) and by his own account had taken the "sublime degree" of Master Mason. When he moved to New York in 1818 he joined the local lodge, became its secretary, and attended meetings regularly. He "paid the strictest attention" to the rituals and committed them to memory. Shortly after his conversion to Christ he was called upon to give the opening and closing prayers at the lodge. But as he left he became depressed. "I soon found that I was completely converted *from* Freemasonry *to* Christ, and that I could have no fellowship with any of the proceedings of the lodge."[7]

Finney later wrote that when he went to study law at Adams, New York, in 1818 he was "almost as ignorant of religion as a heathen." There he attended the church of the Reverend George W. Gale. Finney complained that he was unable to learn from this stiff and uninspiring young preacher.[8] From the time he was twenty-one until his conversion at twenty-nine, Finney's only satisfying involvement with religion was a consequence of his participation in Masonic rituals.

There is no evidence that Freemasonry prepared him for conversion, but Finney's early experiences with ritual made him acutely conscious of its threat to evangelical Christianity. Finney perceived, better than anyone else (excepting, perhaps, the Mormon prophet Joseph Smith) that fraternal initiation could serve as a substitute for religious conversion: Both revivalism and fraternal ritualism depended upon an agency outside of the individual to generate a personal transformation; both depicted man as inherently deficient; and both evoked grim visions of death and hell to precipitate an emotional response that could lead men to an unknowable and distant God.

Oddly, Finney did not seek to leave the Masonic order until just prior to his ordination in 1824, some two and a half years after his conversion. During the commotion following the disappearance of William Morgan in 1826, Finney was silent. He later wrote that he did not attack the order because he still considered himself bound by the oaths of secrecy. Probably he also thought it prudent to remain quiet lest Antimasons wonder why he had remained in the order for nearly nine years. In any case, the extraordinary growth of the orders at mid-century reawakened Finney's fears that they imperiled evangelical Christianity. Shortly after the Civil War he publicly renounced the "horrid oaths" he had taken more than a half-century earlier. He resigned his long-standing position as president of Oberlin College. In 1869, now seventy-seven years old and secure in his preeminent position in American evangelism, Finney published his indictment of the order, *The Character, Claims and Practical Workings of Freemasonry.*[9]

Other evangelical ministers had noted that fraternal ritual provided a kind of "counterfeit salvation," and, like Finney, they were appalled by the proliferation of the orders. In October 1867 nearly a hundred ministers and laymen from ten denominations met at Aurora, Illinois, to hold the first convention since the 1830s met to oppose secret societies. There, and at the National Christian Association's national convention the following May, veterans of the earlier Antimasonic campaign proudly recounted their achievements. Younger evangelicals were less optimistic. If the battle had indeed been won in the 1830s, why had it proven necessary to create the NCA now? Jonathan Blanchard, a Congregationalist clergyman who in 1860 founded Wheaton College in Illinois as an anti–secret society citadel, noted that the recovery of Freemasonry was "without parallel in the history of human error and folly." "What seemed a dead carcass," Rev. Richard Horton observed, "is again raised to life."[10]

Many of the evangelical leaders of the National Christian Association had been prominent in antebellum reform movements.[11] Under Finney's leadership Oberlin College became the "seedbed of American Christian radicalism," a gathering place for activists in causes ranging from racial justice and antislavery to women's rights, peace, and prohibition.[12]

The NCA's abolitionist roots were especially deep. Finney had converted Theodore Weld and admitted blacks to his Chatham Street Chapel, which had been built by the abolitionist Arthur Tappan.[13] Blanchard had served as an official at the World Anti-Slavery Convention in 1834. Benjamin T. Roberts, president of the NCA Convention of 1874, had been expelled in 1857 from the Genessee Conference of the Methodist Episcopal Church for his strident abolitionism; in 1860 he organized the Free Methodist Church, which opposed slavery. John G. Fee, founder of an abolitionist school, and Henry Cheever, secretary of the Church Anti-Slavery Society, were co-chairmen of the 1874 NCA convention at Worcester. Gerrit Smith, who spoke frequently at NCA conventions, had helped finance John Brown's raid. Wendell Phillips and Samuel Pomeroy, the famous abolitionists, also were featured speakers. The organization's first platform opposed slavery and called for the preservation of the Thirteenth, Fourteenth, and Fifteenth Amendments to the Constitution. The NCA compared its broadsides to *Uncle Tom's Cabin* and ended its sessions by singing Julia Ward Howe's "Battle Hymn of the Republic."[14]

These evangelical activists were troubled that the prewar enthusiasm for reform had suddenly disappeared. Their plans to transform America into a "Kingdom of God" had been undone by public apathy. And this had been caused, they asserted, by the resurgence of the orders.

Speakers at the conventions complained that a "dark flood" of secret influence was "pouring into the church" and even carrying away sober ministers.[15] In an open address to American pastors one minister warned that the lodges were emptying the churches. Another said, "The Christian who adheres to the lodges usually loses his spirituality, if he ever had any, and is lost to the church on earth, if not in heaven."[16] Another speaker warned, "He who attempts to love the church of God with one half hemisphere of his heart, and the secret society with the other, will speedily find that he is very much more of a lodgeman than a churchman. This is my first and most emphatic objection to the secret lodge: That it alienates the hearts of Christians from their allegiance to the church of Christ."[17]

It even appeared that fraternal members preferred the "false doctrines" of lodge rituals to Protestant dogma. "Their eyes are darkened," a Lutheran minister said of fraternal initiates, and "they are . . . turned off from the word of God and the church, become more indifferent to the preaching and the sacraments . . . and so they are gradually, without knowing it, converted to the doctrine of the order."[18] Jonathan Blanchard told the NCA, "There is something in the lodge rites which destroys all relish in those who practice them for the rites appointed by Christ."[19]

Leaders of the NCA added that the orders threatened to destroy the financial underpinnings of the church. One Methodist minister complained that three prominent members of his church had donated a total of $650 to their lodges but only $90 to the church.[20] Another observer noted that while the churches went begging for money, fraternal orders effortlessly raised millions of dollars for sumptuously appointed temples.[21]

The NCA was especially shaken by the large number of Protestant ministers who joined the Freemasons, Odd Fellows, and Pythians, and who even served in the offices of High Priest, Chaplain, or Prophet.[22] At the 1870 conference of the Methodist Episcopal Church in Detroit, a resolution condemning ministerial affiliation to secret societies went unseconded. When the author of the resolution attempted to speak in its favor, he was hooted down.[23] By 1875 only a handful of Protestant churches prohibited ministers from belonging to these orders.[24]

Veteran Antimasons proposed to dust off their tracts and mount a new campaign against secret societies, but some NCA leaders were not optimistic about its prospects. Blanchard observed that secret societies had changed considerably since the 1820s and 1830s and were now a more formidable foe. The antebellum fraternal orders had functioned for the most part as drinking clubs, he noted, but during the 1850s and 1860s the secret societies had downplayed their social aspects and emphasized long and quasi-religious initiatory rituals. Odd-Fellowship had become infused with a "spirit of idolatry." Other fraternal organizations, by attaching themselves to popular issues, introduced members to rituals and created a "thirst for sham mysteries and harlot rites." That members of these groups would eventually find their way to the more elaborate rites and even greater sacrilege of Freemasonry seemed inevitable.[25]

The evangelicals believed that the mysterious force behind these rituals was Satan: "We go into the lodge one degree after another, as a charmed frog goes into a snake's mouth," one renouncing Mason reported.[26] "These dark orders," Blanchard noted, "never grow and spread rapidly till they begin to worship—that is, till Satan enters them." The Masons and Odd-Fellows had been "semi-occasional drinking frolics" until they set up worship, he asserted. "Then they grew."[27] Men were drawn to the lodge by ambition and curiosity, but then became "bewitched by her sorcery." He elaborated, "She hides her claws in her fur . . . till she sucks out the breath of their manhood and turns them into cunning beasts like herself."[28] If Satan could take the form of an angel of light, Blanchard told the NCA, well-meaning people, even ministers, could be deceived into so perceiving him.[29] A variant of this theme viewed Freemasonry as the successor to the Roman Empire, the Inquisition, or the Jesuits. Some ministers saw Freemasonry as the culmination of all three, the "highest degree of spiritual wickedness ever attained by man."[30]

The NCA determined to reinvigorate the Protestant church by depriving the rituals of their mysterious power: It sponsored some thirty traveling lecturers who performed—and ridiculed—the initiations of the various orders. It published the *Christian Cynosure*, a four-page biweekly—later a sixteen-page weekly—that featured exposés of the rituals. It also published book-length exposés.[31] The NCA contended that publication of the rituals would abate the "itching curiosity" that "now lures our sons into the lodge."[32]

The fraternal movement did little to allay the fears of the churchmen. Pike and Mackey claimed that the orders flourished because the theology of the Protestant church was itself "overlaid with errors" and the church had so many competing structures. By dissolving these untruths the universal religion of Freemasonry would restore the pristine Christianity of antiquity.[33] At the 1876 meeting in Chicago of the Masonic Grand Lodge of Illinois, the Grand Orator took note of the criticisms of the order by the Chicago-based NCA.

> If the church fully and justly discharges the duties of its trust, there will be no occasion for any other force to undertake their discharge . . . [but] if the church, I say, occupying this [sublime] vantage ground and armed with [a] divine commission, still allows itself to be elbowed out of its own field by an organization claiming no divine sanction . . . then manifestly either the church's claims are false, or [it] itself is unequal to its appointed work or recreant to its obligations; and in either case, the sooner it is supplanted by something stronger, the better for the well-being of the race, and the love of God among men.[34]

Evangelicals were little consoled when Masonic writers reminded members not to say that they belonged to "the Masonic Church."[35] William Rounseville, editor of the *Voice of Masonry*, exhibited a comparable lack of diplomacy when, after he had insisted that the lodge did not compete with the church, he related the tale of a young revivalist who tried to gain fame by attacking Freemasonry. In a short time his church became insolvent as Masonic members refused "to furnish a rod for their own backs." Then the young pastor's "moral purity" was called into question. Shortly thereafter he was dismissed.[36]

By the 1870s fraternal leaders generally conceded that their initiatory ceremonies were of a religious character. "Every Masonic Lodge," Pike insisted, "is a temple of religion; and its teachings are instruction in religion."[37] In 1871 the Reverend F. H. Johnson, a Mason, published a long book with the subtitle "Proved by Tradition, History and Revelation . . . that Masonry and Religion Are the Same." He chided members who sought to mislead the public into thinking that the rituals were not religious.[38] In November 1891 the *Voice of Masonry* acknowledged the obvious: "Masonry is a religion, a handmaiden of Christianity, if you will, but still a religion."

The conflict between the NCA and the lodge was characterized by intemperate language and emotional intensity. The NCA did not mince words when attacking the work of Satan. And Masonic writers, who often prided themselves on an indifference towards critics, nonetheless described Blanchard as an "imbecile old man" and an "addle-headed old pedagogue."[39]

Significantly, the vicious charges and counter-charges were often couched in the rhetoric of gender. Blanchard was not merely stupid, but old, feeble —and, implicitly, unmasculine. The NCA was said to be composed of "old men, women and children, with a slight sprinkling of vigorous blood in the person of a few middle aged reformers."[40] On the other side, the evangelicals described the fraternal orders as reversions to a primitive era of masculine aggression. It was little wonder, they charged, that the secret societies derived their rituals from the "savage warriors of the dark ages," the militaristic institutions of the Roman Empire—or from the Beast of Darkness himself.[41] Rev. Woodruff Post specifically indicted the orders for excluding "angelic, pure minded woman." He saw the religion of the lodge as the work of a "strong, steel-hearted, iron-nerved, robust, selected few of the masculine order."[42]

In their less-guarded moments fraternal leaders confirmed that the tensions between church and lodge often were rooted in the differing religious sensibilities of women and men. In 1888 Warren C. Hubbard, rector of St. Paul's Protestant Episcopal Church and a Masonic chaplain, complained to Masons in Brooklyn that whereas men cursed, pursued money relentlessly, and neglected religion, the "average woman," though overburdened with domestic chores, found time to go to church: "Men seem to think that religion is meant for women and children." As for the members' complaints that the Sunday services were "tame and uninteresting," Hubbard suggested that many Masons had failed to give their churches a chance.[43] In 1872 the *Voice of Masonry* praised an editorial in the *Chicago Tribune* that asserted that woman was naturally religious and man "naturally the reverse." The *Voice of Masonry* added that because churches were attended mostly by women, they should be given a greater voice in church governance. Men, on the other hand, should rest content with their exclusive dominion over the religion of the lodge.[44]

The NCA further charged that the lodge "emasculated" the Protestant church: "Are not the young and middle-aged men in the secret fraternities, and not in the army of Jesus?"[45] Ministers who scheduled church meetings in the evening found that most men preferred to attend the lodge.[46] The Reverend Edward Anderson of Quincy, Illinois, told the State Association of Congregational Churches that in his town 4,952 men, most of them young, belonged to fraternal orders, but only 1,813 men were members of Protestant churches. Was it any wonder, he asked, that throughout the Protestant churches of the nation women outnumbered men by a two-to-one margin?[47]

Anderson's statistics were correct, but his understanding of causation was less sound. He assumed that men converted to the religion of the lodge and then abandoned their church. However, the disproportion of women to men antedated the growth of the fraternal movement. By the early 1800s women already outnumbered men by a two-to-one margin in many denominations, and in some communities their proportional representation was even higher.[48] The orders, the total membership of which was then minuscule, did not cause the "feminization" of Protestant churches.

Early in the nineteenth century many men began to distance themselves from evangelical Protestantism precisely because it was becoming so closely associated with women and their concerns. The reverse side of the church's "emasculation" was its dependence on women. Finney's spectacular revivals in Oneida County would not have been possible without the aid of an existing network of women's associations, which organized and publicized the revival and conducted prayer meetings and visitations for new converts.[49] Finney's linkage to this female network was greatly facilitated by his wife, Lydia, a devout woman who belonged to the First Presbyterian Society in Oneida, the founding group for the Oneida Female Missionary Society.[50] Finney's endorsement of women's right to speak during religious services was an acknowledgment of their indispensability to the evangelical cause.

The alliance of women and ministers was born of necessity for, as Ann Douglas has observed, both groups were experiencing forms of "disestablishment" during the early nineteenth century. As family farms gave way to commercial farming, and household manufacturing to factory production, middle-class women no longer had a direct role in producing goods. The specialization of the nation's economy intensified sex-role distinctions: Men generated wealth and created the economic and political institutions on which civilization depended; women raised children and cultivated moral and religious values, so that civilization would retain a modicum of civility.[51]

Ministers were similarly cast aside in the rush for material prosperity that gripped the nation in the early 1800s. They watched helplessly as their salaries declined, their tenures became less stable, and their campaigns against disestablishment and secularization failed. But whereas women's exclusion from economic matters was a function of their gender, and thus beyond criticism, the minister's decision to occupy himself with womanly concerns seemed almost a conscious abdication of manhood. Denied access to the masculine world of business and politics, ministers settled for the companionship of women.[52]

Revivalists such as Finney preserved their sense of masculinity, and perhaps their standing among men, by adopting an aggressive and energetic preaching style.[53] During the mid-nineteenth century, however, their predominantly female congregations reacted against the energetic excesses of the earlier evangelicals; subsequent revivals, as Sandra Sizer has shown, adopted a feminine rhetoric and consigned religious fervor to the domestic sphere.[54]

Clergymen thus had little choice but to accept women's predominant influence in the church. Justin Dewey Fulton, a Baptist, growled that women had virtually taken over the Protestant church:

> Within, in her lowest spiritual form, as the ruling spirit she inspires, and sometimes writes the sermons. Without, as the bulk of his congregation, she watches over [the minister's] orthodoxy, verifies his texts, visits his schools, and harasses his sick. . . . The preacher who thunders so defiantly against spiritual foes, is trembling all the time beneath the critical eye that is watching him with so merciless an accuracy of his texts. Impelled, guided, censured by women, we can hardly wonder if, in nine cases out of ten, the parson turns woman himself.[55]

Ministers and their vigilant female congregants transformed the theology of Channing into a religion of consolation.[56] Liberal theology and its evangelical variant proved readily adaptable to the needs of middle-class women.[57] The liberals' insistence that proper feeling was more important than sound doctrine undercut the ministers' authority with the implication that a good woman, though unschooled in theology, could better discern the will of a loving God than could a hard-hearted doctor of divinity. The liberals' conception of death as a casual stroll into a domesticated heaven further suggested that if woman did not inherit the earth, she would at least hold sway in heaven. And by focusing on a femininized Christ the Redeemer, the liberals escaped the need to engage in anguished speculations on the nature of God the Father.

Many men resented woman's increasingly dominant role in religion and the moral authority it conferred upon their actions within the home. After Finney had visited one couple, the husband fumed that the revivalist had "stuffed my wife with tracts, and alarmed her fears, and nothing short of meetings, night and day, could atone for the many fold sins my poor, simple spouse had committed, and at the same time, she made the miraculous discovery, that she had been 'unevenly yoked.' From this unhappy period, peace, quiet, and happiness have fled from my dwelling, never, I fear, to return."[58]

❖

Fraternal members built temples from which women were excluded, devised myriad secrets and threatened members with fearful punishments if they should "tell their wife the concerns of the order," and created rituals which reclaimed for themselves the religious authority that formerly reposed in the hands of Biblical patriarchs.

The rituals' exclusion of references to Christ and their implicit refutation of liberal theology can best be understood as an indirect assault upon women and women's role in the church. Although most members were unfamiliar with theological issues, they could identify rituals which, though appropriate in a church filled with women, did not belong in temples reserved for men. Those rites that initially referred to Christ, that depicted death as a gentle stroll, or that spoke of "God's love"—the White degree of the Odd Fellows, for example—were soon discarded as being "formal" and "unmeaning." The hideous "emblems of mortality" and the dramatic journeys in search of a distant god were substituted because they refuted the feminine theology of the liberal church.

These gender antagonisms first surfaced during the Antimasonic crusade. Because women operated from the confines of the domestic sphere, their role in this Antimasonic campaign is difficult to document, but Dorothy Ann Lipson found that women spoke against Freemasonry during church meetings and acted in concert to publish Antimasonic resolutions—this at a time when women's involvement in public affairs was rare. Women served as the most effective agents of what Lipson calls a "silent and unorganized" Antimasonic movement that helped "cripple" the order for nearly a generation. Women also insisted that the secret rituals rendered men less pious.[59] Decades after the first Antimasonic campaign, elderly Masons confirmed that the "gentler sex" was largely responsible for crushing the order during the 1820s and 1830s.[60]

The fraternal movement that emerged at mid-century, purged of alcohol and imbued with a sobering religious ritualism, posed a greater challenge to evangelical women. By offering religious guidance and an ideology of personal transformation, the reformed orders further encroached upon woman's role of Christian nurture. The NCA appealed "to the home-loving, true-hearted women of this land," especially ministers' wives, to save the nation from the baneful influence of secret ritual.[61] Those attending NCA conventions were warned that fraternal members shielded each other in legal proceedings, especially divorces. The real purpose of fraternal orders, declared the women's suffrage leader Matilda J. Gage, was to "set one sex against another." The "great tragedy" of her life, she added, was her husband's steadfast refusal to leave his lodge.[62]

The participation of Gage reflects the NCA's identification with women's issues. In 1827 Finney had been one of the first ministers to encourage women to pray and speak in public; the New Lebanon Convention, which that year sought to reconcile Finney and his followers with the more traditional evangelism of Lyman Beecher and Asahel Nettleton, broke up over Finney's rejection of the Biblical injunction that women remain silent in church.[63] From the beginning Blanchard urged reform societies to accept women; his church in Cincinnati was one of the first to allow women to vote.[64] Many NCA speakers supported the ordination of women, and in 1874 the NCA debated whether to endorse woman's suffrage. (The proposal, though supported in principle, was rejected as inexpedient.)[65] When Blanchard was nominated by the NCA to run for President of the United States on the ticket of the American Party (not to be confused with the earlier American [Know-Nothing] Party), he tried to include a woman suffrage plank in the platform. In 1888 he met with Frances Willard, president of the Women's Christian Temperance Union, to combine anti–secret society and prohibition forces. (Willard, who welcomed the alliance in principle, could not agree because the Knights of Labor and the Good Templars, major WCTU supporters, employed secret rituals.)[66]

The NCA's identification with women was so strong that one suspects they formed its main constituency. A historian has found evidence that the NCA had a "disproportionate share of feminine followers" and that NCA lecturers suppressed information demonstrating their lack of support among men.[67]

The NCA's hopes of vanquishing the orders rested squarely upon the shoulders of evangelical women. As fraternal membership mushroomed, newspaper editors and politicians became ardent supporters of the secret societies. Church members realized that it would be impossible to rekindle a political controversy such as had swept the nation in the 1820s and 1830s. Protestant ministers were responsive to their female congregants, but many fraternal members who belonged to a church still contributed the money on which it, and the minister's salary, depended. The fate of the fraternal movement—and of the evangelical war against the "works of darkness"—would be determined by the solitary actions of hundreds of thousands of women: Would they again press their husbands to leave the secret societies?

❖ DECEIVING THE LADIES ❖

Even before the NCA mounted its assault upon the secret societies, fraternal leaders recognized the need to forestall the opposition of women, no easy task, given that they explicitly excluded women. The problem was further complicated by the new rituals. How could members explain to their wives why they spent time and money reenacting Old Testament battles, voyages through Hades, or Indian rites?

Although secrecy remained the lodge's main defense, by the 1850s and 1860s leaders developed new ways to allay women's fears. The editors of the fraternal monthlies published by scores of state grand lodges or freelance organizations began to address a female audience. Thus the *Voice of Masonry* in the late 1860s changed its name to the *Voice of Masonry and Family Magazine*. Subsequently it began a "Ladies' Department."[68] Interspersed among the recipes and the fashion accounts were articles explaining how Freemasonry accorded with the sentiments of evangelical women. Leaders also began to invite wives to attend lectures and banquets at the lodge, a practice to which many members strenuously objected.[69] Most important, the societies embarked upon a proposal to introduce women to the lodge through the creation of what they called ladies' auxiliaries.

Journal editors reminded women not to criticize that which they did not understand.[70] A story in the *Masonic Review* entitled "Too Late at the Lodge" described a young married couple who grew cold to each other after the husband had joined the Masons and begun to spend several evenings each week at the lodge. In a final attempt to save their marriage, the Mason allowed his wife to accompany him on "lodge business." The woman learned to her amazement that on lodge nights her husband had been delivering medicine to sick Masons and their families, doing chores for widows and orphans, and taking books to a cripple.[71] The story neatly inverted the gender associations of the evangelical groups: The woman's unchristian suspiciousness and possessiveness were confuted by the example of the Mason's charity and missionary zeal. His secrecy only confirmed his Christian selflessness.

But women could well wonder why they should be expected to trust husbands about the propriety of evenings at the lodge if husbands refused to share its secrets. One woman expressed the issue succinctly in verse:

> If the Masons to us will their secrets impart,
> We'll embrace the dear Rite with all of our heart:
> If they all their secrets with us will but share,
> We will love them and trust them wherever they are;
> The cause we'll uphold all the days of our life,
> And be happy and thankful we're a Freemason's wife.

As matters now stood, however, she intended to advise friends *not* to marry Masons.[72]

Many editors suggested that leaders pull the veil of secrecy back just far enough to allay women's fears. The *Masonic Review* in the mid-1850s proposed such a strategy through the letters of a contributor named Mary. (Whether any such woman actually corresponded with the *Review* seems doubtful. Unlike most contributors, Mary did not give a surname, and her letters, which reflected the views of the editor with an uncanny consistency, appeared with the regularity more commonly associated with the writing of magazine editors than of mail correspondents.) Mary confirmed that secrecy was at the heart of women's opposition to Freemasonry, but she insisted that they wanted to be "enlightened just so far as will remove prejudice" against the order. They did not wish to know all the secrets or to discourage members from their "great 'work'."

Several months later Mary wrote that she had toured a lodge room and been struck by its somber religiosity, in particular by the prominent display of the Bible upon the altar. "What *good*men must Masons be, I thought; so much like *ministers*" [Mary's emphasis]. Yet she wandered away from the tour group, crept along a dark passageway, and discovered on a stone wall a mysterious iron ring, which she couldn't resist pulling. The ring, she learned to her dismay, entombed a hornet's nest.[73]

Fraternal leaders assured women that the lodge now posed no threat to the domestic sphere. They conceded that, when lodges had been based in taverns, their predecessors had from time to time engaged in drunken revelries, but those days, they insisted, were long gone.[74] Fraternal orders now promoted moral development. The death benefit and insurance provisions guaranteed the financial security of the family. The lodge "throws its mighty arms" around the home, orators proclaimed.[75]

Another strategy was to extinguish women's opposition with gusts of flattery. The *Voice of Masonry* asserted women's right to preach in church for the simple reason that "woman is better than man."[76] Many writers also affirmed the order's commitment to the ideals of True Womanhood, a constellation of values that counterposed the purity of woman to the baseness of man.

This was particularly apparent in fraternal novels, most of which were serialized in the monthly magazines. *The Signet of King Solomon* (1866) was typical of the genre: A member of the Knights Templars comes before the lodge and confesses to an illicit sexual liaison. The Grand Commander sentences him to "march in the path of penitence" for a year and a day; during this time he is to "watch over the defenseless and helpless" and to "frustrate the evil machinations of the wicked, who seek to despoil the widow and the orphan." The Knight-errant soon discovers an ample supply of heroines in need of deliverance. A wealthy merchant imprisons one maiden and attempts to have his way with her. Later a jealous couple murders an infant and blames the hapless maiden. The order intervenes—repeatedly—to save the damsel. Several Knights, after recognizing the order's secret passwords and signals of distress, help the lodgeman rescue the heroine from these and sundry other conspiracies. The novel ends when the maiden is appropriately consigned to a permanent male protector—a husband. He belongs, of course, to a lodge.[77]

These novels often commenced with the disruption of the family, usually through the death of one or both parents, and described the calamities that ensued when children were prematurely exposed to the world of men. In *Sunshine in Shadowed Lives* (1892), the Reverend Richard Martin's paean to the insurance order called the Royal Arcanum, two orphans, separated after their father's death and cheated of his insurance, are cast amongst forgers and murderers. Nature itself is tainted with evil and assails the children with storms and rockslides. Resolutely opposing this relentless dark tide are the members of the Royal Arcanum. After nearly twenty years of effort, they reunite the orphans, restore them to prosperity, and, by arranging a double wedding, return them to the safety of the home.[78]

By their virtue, women protected the home from masculine aggression and materialism. But fraternal writers repeatedly warned women against wandering too far from the domestic sphere. The traits that made the heroine of *The Signet of King Solomon* so appealing to fraternal readers—she was beautiful, "meek," and "artless"—rendered her vulnerable outside the home. Imperiled by unregenerate men, True Womanhood required the assistance and protection of the lodge.

Since women presumably were predisposed to goodness and domesticity, fraternal writers were obliged to account for those who fell short of the ideal. The author of *The Signet of King Solomon* took pains to explain that the female villain's deviance stemmed from childhood. Her mother was weak and ignorant, and "poorly calculated to discharge a mother's duties toward the tender children which God had given to her care." Her father, "a dark stern man" who hated the institution of Freemasonry, intimidated his wife and usurped her natural authority in the home. Raised in a "pestiferous atmosphere" of masculine aggression, the girl eventually fell prey to a young man who aroused her "baser passions" and set her upon a path of crime. Had she been "reared under different influences" she might have become "one of the most beautiful ornaments of her sex."[79] The implicit argument was that female intervention beyond the proper woman's sphere—including in institutions such as the lodge—could be dangerous.

Fraternal writers blamed men for much that was wrong in the world.

Wherever maidens or children trod, there lurked unregenerate men intent on committing nefarious deeds. But the recurrent message was that men, though bad, were not irredeemably so. Had not the worthy crusader in *The Signet of King Solomon* blotted out the stain of an illicit sexual escapade? And even the grave sins of the merchant did not prevent his eventual moral salvation: He had attempted to rape a maiden, and left his wife and children ill and penniless; but at the sight of his returned wife's beautiful face he felt the "spirits of impurity" fleeing from his heart.[80]

The heroes of Robert Morris's *Life in the Triangle; or, Freemasonry at the Present Time* (1854) undergo an even more remarkable transformation. One has resolved to rape a woman who has rejected his marriage proposal, another to become a thief, the third to murder a rival. Each is on the verge of committing his crime when an earthquake changes his "whole turn of thought and action." The men successively become Freemasons, philanthropists, and the pillars of local society.[81]

Fraternal acceptance of True Womanhood provided an ingenious excuse to exclude women from the lodge. If, in Masonic parlance, man was a "rough ashlar," requiring the intellectual and spiritual polishing of initiatory ritual, woman, already a jewel, had no need for the rites of the lodge. In woman "benevolence and humility are spontaneous," Grosh wrote, but men needed to band together to "stimulate their better affections." The leading principles of Odd-Fellowship, Rev. Beharrell claimed, were "but the innate principles of woman's nature."[82] One character in a story about Freemasonry tells women, "You were *born* Masons; any initiation or ceremony would be superfluous; therefore we do not insult you by any such propositions."[83] The purpose of Masonry, an orator told the wives of members, was to "soften and humanize the rough, rude nature of man" and to "render him mild, gentle, patient, charitable, and tender as a woman." Woman, representing the highest type to which men aspired, had no reason to experience ritual. Moreover, if a woman were to belong to the lodge and associate with men, she might be dragged down "from the lofty pedestal" she occupied.[84]

This argument was easily refuted: How could the lodge teach men to behave more like women if women were not allowed in as examples? And if unregenerate men might corrupt female members, was it not equally probable that groups of men, in the absence of woman's ennobling influence, would reinforce each other's worst traits? The orders could offer no satisfactory response, nor could they again risk the wrath of women. Some leaders proposed to let women into the temples, where they would participate in secret ceremonies written for the auxiliaries—but not in fraternal rituals.

The arguments against allowing women into the order were legion; some were ridiculous, such as a Masonic scholar's objection that woman's delicate hand, "tapered and whitened for the ministry of love," was ill suited for work in the quarries of King Solomon.[85] The Grand Prelate of Tennessee worried that the fair newcomers would cause members to "worship at Cupid's altar instead of paying homage to a higher, nobler deity"—a speculation that had not been confirmed in the case of women's presence in church.[86]

Nearly all such arguments were disingenuous: Virtually no one wanted women to take part in lodge rituals. When Schuyler Colfax, a leading Odd Fellow, first broached the subject of instituting the Degree of Rebekah he conceded that it might "excite a smile" among members. He proposed this "Ladies' Degree" to "lessen and ultimately destroy the prejudice felt against the Order by many of the fairer sex."[87] He also wrote the ritual for the Degree of Rebekah, which slyly induced women into a defense of the order. After the Vice Grand had praised women for their willingness to "mitigate the vast amount of suffering and pain in our world," he invited those who did not wish to persist in this noble task to retire. Since few took this opportunity to skulk out the back door, the Vice Grand could commend women on their dedication to the cause of humanity. Rewriting the history of the Antimasonic crusade of the 1820s and 1830s, he explained how women had defended the order against the slanders of bigots. He conceded, in a clever inversion of the gender and religious dynamics of Antimasonry, that some "few women" had "joined those Pharisees, who declared that no good thing could come out of our Nazareth. But woman, as a sex, true to herself, her instincts and her impulses, smiled upon our labors, rejoiced as we prospered, defended our principles and honored our name." The Vice Grand went on to contend that the Degree of Rebekah was established in gratitude for women's assistance in warding off Antimasonry.[88]

By the 1860s and 1870s most orders followed the lead of the Odd Fellows in devising some form of auxiliary organizations or ladies' degrees. Masonic grand lodges did not formally recognize the Order of the Eastern Star (1869), but individual Masons sponsored and supported its activities.[89]

Many fraternal leaders were appalled by the barefaced deceit entailed by the creation of the ladies' degrees. In 1869 the Grand Lodge of Ohio reaffirmed an 1851 ordinance expelling Masons who officiated at such ceremonies: "The conferring of said degrees on women is calculated to deceive and mislead them, and is therefore improper."[90] The *New England Freemason* similarly derided the women's auxiliaries as attempts to "humbug" the wives, sisters, and daughters of Masons.[91]

The charges were true. Unbeknownst to female initiates, the differences between the ladies' degrees and the rituals of the male orders were profound. Even the term ladies' degree was a misnomer. The Degree of Pocahontas, for example, existed "only by virtue of the Great Council" of the Improved

Order of Red Men, which was composed solely of men. A woman's status in most auxiliaries was entirely dependent on her husband or father.[92] Female membership in the Degree of Rebekah or the Order of the Eastern Star was limited to the wives and daughters of Scarlet Degree Odd Fellows or of Master Masons; if the male relation were expelled from the order for any reason, the woman was forced to leave the auxiliary. If the daughter of a member married a "profane" (nonmember), she thereby "expelled herself" from the Order.[93]

The most striking contrast between the orders and the auxiliaries involved the degree of sexual segregation during initiations. All orders banned women from the initiation of men; many of the injunctions on secrecy were obviously framed to prevent women from learning about male rituals. On the other hand, the meetings and initiations of the Degree of Rebekah and of the Order of the Eastern Star were presided over by the Noble Grand or the Worshipful Master of the men's lodge. Men were required to be present at the initiation of their female relations. When they asked lodge officials, female members of the Order of the Eastern Star were given no explanation for this practice.[94]

The ladies' degrees steadfastly affirmed True Womanhood and Victorian gender roles in general. Initiates for the Degree of Rebekah were asked whether they were willing to "mitigate the vast amount of suffering and pain in our world" and were instructed to perpetuate the legacy of self-effacing Biblical heroines. Eastern Star initiates were told to emulate Ruth, who submitted to "whatever lot she might be called upon to endure"; and Esther, who used her "matchless beauty" to persuade her husband, a Persian king, not to exterminate the Jews. The Odd Fellows' Noble Grand warned female initiates not to encroach on traditional male pursuits, and to forswear as role models women such as Cleopatra and Queen Elizabeth: "Such we do not cite for your emulation and imitation, but rather the record of those whom the Bible commends: who signalized their lives . . . in vindicating the true modesty and worth of woman's natural character, in pouring the oil of consolation into the wounds of the afflicted, in whispering the words of sympathy in the ears of the heartstricken."[95]

These ceremonies also lacked the dramatic ritualistic structure and content of the male initiations.[96] The ritualists intuitively understood the flaw in their own logic of instituting women's rites: If woman was predisposed to goodness, then she hardly needed the dramatic encounters and powerful symbolic magic of the initiations. Female ceremonies, usually written by men, therefore consisted of dull recitations of biblical parables. Women merely affirmed their commitment to those ideals. In 1877 the *Voice of Masonry* noted the disappointment of many Masons in the rituals of the Order of the Eastern Star: "There is little of that simple strength which is found in the terse and incisive expressions of the grand old Masonic ritual." The criticisms, again, resonated with the nuances of gender. The ladies' degrees, lacking the perilous journeys, the heroic encounters, and the stark representations of death and an awesome God, were emasculated.[97]

A comparison of the Adoptive rite of the Order of the Eastern Star and the Patriarchal degree of Odd-Fellowship illuminates these differences. Both took as themes a father's decision to sacrifice a child in order to fulfill a commitment to God. In the Patriarchal degree this builds to a dramatic climax as the initiate—representing Abraham's son, Isaac—is bound, blindfolded, placed upon a sacrificial altar, read the Thirty-third Psalm, and unnerved by gongs and clattering sounds. God intervenes at the last moment to save him. In the Adoptive rite the female initiate simply listens to a narration of the story of Adah, the daughter who was sacrificed by Jephthah in return for God's favor in battle. Whereas Isaac was strengthened by his brush with death, Adah's life reached its culmination at the moment of her demise. The Masons improved upon the Old Testament by inventing a final scene in which Adah insisted that her head be uncovered during the sacrifice.[98] She could have avoided her fate, as the ritual makes clear, but she understood that her martyrdom would redeem others.

Adah served as a transparent symbol for Christ; often the ladies' degrees specifically charged women to follow His example. The Adoptive rite of the Order of the Eastern Star, for instance, commenced after officers stood to form a "Christian Star." Initiates were asked to pray to a "Holy and Merciful God" who revealed Himself through Jesus Christ.[99] These references to Christ are significant because the Masons and Odd Fellows had recently excised similar references from the male rituals, insisting that the universality of their orders did not permit sectarian exclusivity. That this principle was not applied to the ladies' degrees suggests that it was never as important as the leaders had claimed. Sensing that the masculine religion of the lodge was inappropriate for women, the authors of the ladies' degrees intuitively resorted to the tenets of liberal theology and True Womanhood. Men could ignore the role model of Christ; for women to do so was inconceivable.

Fraternal scholars made little effort to conceal the differences between the ladies' degrees and the male-only rituals. Mackey forthrightly told the woman who planned to join the auxiliary of any Masonic group that she would come "no nearer to the portals of Masonry than she was before." As long as everyone understood that the auxiliaries bore no other relationship to Masonry than an institutional one, he saw no harm in them. "But all attempts to make Masonry of them," he maintained, "and especially that anomalous thing called Ladies' Masonry, are wrong, imprudent, and calculated to produce opposition among the well-informed and cautious members of the Fraternity."[100] A prominent Odd Fellow sought to correct the impression that women would be introduced into the lodges through the Degree of Rebekah. He wrote, "The simple truth is this: Woman is not entitled to and seeks not a place among us. Our institution was originally intended and framed exclusively for men, and the various modifications it has undergone have not adapted it to the other sex."[101]

Fraternal scorn for the ladies' degrees, and for women who seemingly failed to apprehend the obvious deception, was widespread. Often the editors of the magazines of the order described women who belonged to the auxiliaries as vain and superficial, preoccupied with fashion and foliage.[102] Many thought it possible to placate them by letting them fix up the halls, arrange the curtains, and form sewing circles.[103] Members taunted brethren who participated in the auxiliaries. "Build a Temple, not a cob-house. Be men, not children," one critic sneered.[104] Leaders who had earlier insisted that women could not be trusted to keep secrets now invented "secrets" devoid of meaning; spokesmen saw no irony in plans to let women know "everything" about the secret society "save its mysteries."[105] Even the extravagant flattery of "True Womanhood" degraded real women, who could hardly conform to the ideal.

Although the entire enterprise was founded upon an elaborate but seemingly transparent deception, the ladies' degrees proved remarkably popular. By the 1890s approximately half a million women had joined the auxiliaries.[106] Surely few women were fooled by the orders' elaborate public relations campaign. Instead, no doubt, they were heartened by the support of other women beyond the familiar contexts of home or church.[107] Those not deceived about the differences in lodge rites probably assumed that husbands who nodded off during church did not take fraternal ceremonies seriously. Wives no doubt sensed that some sort of deception was afoot; they must have known that their husbands typically did not deliver books to cripples on lodge nights. Perhaps they reasoned that the magnificent temples, the supposedly somber rituals, and the earnest talk about "work at the lodge" merely disguised evenings spent in convivial entertainments.

The National Christian Association was appalled that hundreds of thousands of women joined these auxiliaries, the purpose of which, Matilda Gage told the NCA in 1874, was to silence troublesome female critics of the orders.[108] Without the support of women, the NCA's war against the lodges failed miserably. Subscriptions to the *Christian Cynosure* declined steadily.[109] Exposés of the rituals continued to sell, but many copies were bought by fraternal members to help them memorize their parts in the rituals.[110] Speakers for the NCA increasingly reported difficulty in finding lecture halls and attracting audiences. And local newspaper editors, many of whom belonged to lodges, ridiculed the sparsely attended anti–secret society lectures.[111] The NCA's candidate for president of the United States in 1880, Gen. John Wolcott Phelps, polled seven hundred votes.[112]

The NCA's fears of the orders' threat to Protestantism were realized. By the early twentieth century, lodges outnumbered churches in all large cities.[113] In 1891 a Methodist minister reported that nine-tenths of the preachers in the nation had been "captured" by the secret societies.[114] If the war against the fraternal movement was lost, another minister bitterly complained, it was because the "great divisions of the Lord's army" had defected to the enemy. Temporarily, at least, the forces of darkness had prevailed.[115]

❖ LUX ET TENEBRIS ❖

The triumph of the orders was not, as the NCA believed, the work of Satan. Freemasonry gained legitimacy during the last half of the nineteenth century by reiterating middle-class values and by preaching an unexceptionable doctrine of brotherhood. At the same time American society was becoming more tolerant of religious diversity. As the distance between the public values of Freemasonry and of the larger American society diminished, Antimasonic sentiment shrank.[116]

Fraternal ideology, however, was a mixture of publicly avowed precepts and secret meanings. This duality was expressed in the predominant symbolism of the rituals: the opposition of light and darkness, of public and private, of God and Satan. The "working hours" of the lodge were said to be from seven to ten P.M., "*after dark.*" And the rituals themselves evoked deathly shadow worlds where participants were often plunged into darkness. In the last chapter of his tirade against Freemasonry, Finney invoked this imagery of light and darkness more than twenty times: The "works of darkness," Finney insisted, must be "dragged to the light." [117]

Finney's focus on this point reflected his understanding of a crucial tenet of fraternal ritual. Mackey explained that Freemasonry "taught that there are two principles from which all things proceed; the one is pure and subtile matter, called Light, and the other a gross and corrupt substance, called Darkness. . . . The being who presides over the light is called God; he that rules over the darkness is called *Hyle*, or *Demon*." God could not triumph if there were no Satan; truth, without the example of error, would be unimpressive; light, without darkness, would seem dull. Initiation taught the lessons of death and of darkness, from which emanated the "full blaze of masonic light." [118]

Finney and the evangelical critics believed that the references to darkness and light proved that the conflict ultimately pitted Satan against Christ. A less apocalyptic explanation is that the counterpointing of paganism and Christianity, of primitivism and civilization, of death and love, and of darkness and light, underscored a more fundamental opposition in the minds of mid-Victorian American men: a tension between men and women. This, men endeavored to keep secret from women—and from themselves.

Fathers

Victor A. Searles. 96.

Morgan and Parker walked toward the lodge, stepping around puddles which the sun, filtered through the high oak trees, had not yet diminished. A woman gathered her children, who had been fishing in the stream. The youngest girl squeezed the water out of her hair and joined the group that was silently crossing the bridge toward the lodge.

A shout came from inside, followed by a long mournful chant. "The lament for the burial of the dead," Parker said. "It's Captain Frost singing." Morgan was about to ask who had died when Parker went on, imitating Frost's flat intonation:

> My forefathers,—what they established!
> My forefathers,—hearken to them!

Morgan hurried on to the lodge.

They entered and took seats up front near the Fathers; across from them were the Children, who were concealed by blankets that had been stretched across the room. Frost was walking past the fire and toward the Children. He began to speak softly. "He's telling the Children how to console the Fathers on their loss," Parker whispered. Frost raised his arm high, uttered a shrill cry, and motioned for the blankets to be lowered. The Children began to whimper, in unison.

"But they're not children!" said Morgan. Parker smiled. "If you have fathers, you must have children."

Frost paced back and forth between Children and Fathers, gesturing constantly as he spoke. Morgan could not follow much of what he was saying. Parker explained: Their grandfathers had warned league members that if they continued to fight amongst themselves a dog with white eyes would come from the East—"a dog that loves blood." Parker smiled again. When that dog came, they should look for a deep-rooted tree, gather their children and grandchildren together, and hold onto it for dear life. If they didn't, the white-eyed dog would destroy them root and branch, and leave not a single human twig to sprout and grow.

Frost turned to the Fathers, picked up the sacred beads and read: "Our ancestors have ordained that you tell your children of these laws." He then placed the beads before the Children: "You must communicate these truths to your children, and so should they be handed down from generation to generation."

Frost sat down. Jimmy Johnson, nearly seventy, a tall and stately High

Priest, came forward. "Listen to the will of the Great Spirit, who commanded us to cherish the religion of our fathers and to renew old things," he said. All the while he fingered his medal of Washington, the great departed leader. Morgan understood why no one interrupted him, for he was a living bridge to a heroic and nearly vanished past.

Then Blacksmith, a powerful man with a heavy face and a fringe of grey hair, began speaking, his voice soft and musical. Long ago, he said, he had warned them to heed the fathers, but no one had listened. Blacksmith's lugubrious message was incompatible with his singsong voice, which, like some potent drug, induced members into an even deeper trance. When Blacksmith finished, he turned and walked out.

Frost again stood up and expounded on the duties of the Children. Morgan looked around the lodge. The flickering red light of the fire streaked the faces of these all-too-civilized "savages." Some kept their eyes fixed before their feet; others held their heads, absorbed. Parker now seemed pensive, even irritated, and he ceased to talk. Morgan knew—as did everyone else—that this would be the last such ceremony.

As Morgan pondered the scene, this desperate attempt to amend that which could not be undone, he looked around, furtively, hoping that no one sensed his exhilaration.[1]

❖

Lewis Henry Morgan's trip to the Tonawanda Reservation of the Seneca Indians on October 1, 1845, marked the beginning of American ethnography. The purpose of the first ceremony he witnessed was to fill vacant chieftain positions (life sachems) at the Six Nations Council of the Iroquois. It was largely symbolic; most of the tribes had lost their lands to white speculators, and the Iroquois had been dispersed to reservations in Ohio and Michigan. The advice of sachems such as Blacksmith, Johnson, and Frost, who called for a return to the ways of their ancestors, had come too late.

At the time of his visit to Tonawanda, Morgan had no scholarly interest in ethnology. A twenty-seven-year-old lawyer from Aurora, New York, he had few clients and devoted his ample spare time to a literary society, the Order of the Gordian Knot. In January 1843 Morgan had become intrigued by Washington Irving's "irresistably agreeable" portrayal of primitive society in *Columbus*.[2] Soon afterward he proposed to transform the order into a secret society based on the "whole history, customs, exploits, dress, and mythic lore" of the Iroquois.[3] Morgan told members of the romantic possibilities in the situation of the vanquished Iroquois; he perceived "something impressive, even melancholy" in their traditions and their fatalism, which sprang "from deeper impulses of mind than we are aware."[4] That summer members agreed to reinstitute their organization as the Order of the Iroquois. They named Morgan their Grand Sachem.[5]

Morgan reasoned that the best way to share in the romantic meaning of Indian life was to experience Indian rituals. Therefore, a year before he had set foot on a reservation, he superintended the creation of the order's first induction ceremony, which he called an "inindianation."[6] The ceremony bore no relation to any Seneca ritual.

A "prophet" commenced the proceedings by describing the lamentations of an Indian maiden grieving that her mother's grave had been desecrated by farmers' plows. He told of how the spirits of ancestral warriors ascended from the burial grounds and danced over their own dry bones. Elsewhere a chorus chanted:

> We cannot rest. We rise to ask our children why they forget their Fathers' ways; but we cannot find them. Oh where, where are our children?

After the chorus had called for the complete destruction of the white man, the Great Spirit professed love for his "red children." In return the Sachem promised to preserve the memory of departed ancestors, and begged the Great Spirit to "receive us as your children. . . . Extend around us thy fraternal arms, on us pour forth thy love, bind us firmly together and lead us joyfully onward in the work we have chosen. Be among us to guide and to protect." The ceremony then followed fraternal conventions.

Although the ritual began as a jeremiad on the plight of the Indians, its underlying theme was the disruption of generational ties. The fathers had lost their children, and the children had forgotten the ways of their fathers. Similarly, the Great Spirit lamented the annihilation of *his* doomed children (the Iroquois) and pleaded with them to "save from oblivion" the names, customs and deeds of their fathers. The "regeneration" of initiates depended on the reestablishment of father-son bonds, a point that became explicit when the Sachem pleaded to his Father, the Great Spirit, "Receive us as your children."

Members were apparently satisfied with the ritual, but Morgan came to doubt whether they could vicariously share in the deeper impulse of Indian life through experiencing spurious rituals. Wanting to learn of authentic Indian rites, he visited the New York State archives in Albany. There he met Ely Parker, a young Seneca, who became Morgan's chief Indian correspondent and interpreter. As Morgan learned more about Iroquois customs, he grew increasingly dissatisfied with his fanciful "inindianation." In early 1845 he wrote a new ceremony based loosely on an Iroquois ritual for adopting captured warriors.

Morgan's attempt at authenticity produced an uninspired amalgman of Iroquois nomenclature and fraternal conventions: As in most orders, a blindfolded initiate knelt before a lodge officer and received the usual secret grips and passwords. Morgan's revision was similar to its predecessor in the emphasis on generational ties. The initiate, now a "young captive," was described as having wandered so long amongst the palefaces that he had "lost nearly every trace of his parentage and descent." The ritual was to regenerate lost bonds by adopting him into the brotherhood of the tribe; this was symbolized, significantly, by his receipt of an authentic Iroquois name, names having been the focus of Morgan's early research.[7]

When Grand Sachem Morgan advised initiates to rediscover their lost fathers, the order was meeting in the defunct Masonic lodge, a structure that had been built by Morgan's own father, Jedidiah.[8] In 1819, the year after Lewis Henry was born, his father, a prosperous farmer, had advanced funds to erect the Masonic temple in Aurora. In the same year, Jedidiah became Worshipful Master of the Scipio Masonic lodge and High Priest of the Aurora chapter of the Royal Arch Masons, a position he held until his death.[9] In 1823 he was elected to the state senate and befriended Governor DeWitt Clinton, the most prominent Freemason in New York State. Clinton laid the cornerstone of Morgan's Aurora lodge. In the clamor after William Morgan (no relation of Jedidiah) disappeared in September 1826 in Batavia—it was rumored that he had been hidden on the Tonawanda Reservation[10]—reporters in Albany suggested that Jedidiah's support of Clinton's handling of that incident was due to Masonic obligations.[11]

Little came of the charges, for Jedidiah Morgan died in December 1826. Lewis Henry, then eight years old, was shaken by the loss. Thirteen years later, when he was about to be married, he drew up a will specifying that he be buried beside his father. Decades later he wrote that a "child is never ready to part with a parent."[12] In the absence of a father, Morgan was raised largely by his mother and, especially, his older sister.[13] When he returned home after graduating from Utica College in 1840 as a twenty-two-year-old attorney without prospects of a practice,[14] secret societies became his regular escape from domestic duties and from the affectionate vigilance of the women in the family.

Morgan's fascination with initiatory ritual may have reflected an unconscious wish to follow in his father's steps. He could not have joined his father's Masonic lodges, which ceased meeting during the Antimasonic uproar, but he surely became aware of Masonic ritual when countless churches during the late 1820s and 1830s in the "burned-over district" of western New York featured exposés of Masonic secrets. Thus even as Morgan preserved the legacy of Indian forebears by practicing their initiatory rites, he was imitating the example of his father, the Worshipful Master of the Scipio lodge and High Priest of the Royal Arch Masons. When Sachem Lewis Henry Morgan pleaded with the Great Spirit to "receive us as your children," and to "save from the grave" the memory of departed fathers, he was conceivably "regenerating" the paternal bonds of which he had been deprived as a boy.

During the spring and summer of 1845 Morgan invited prominent Freemasons and Indian scholars of his father's generation to become honorary members of the Order of the Iroquois. It is perhaps too much to suggest that Morgan, like the sachem in his rituals, was trying to establish a dialogue with the men of his father's generation; yet the list of those who received invitations included his father's good friends Salem Town, author of *A System of Speculative Masonry*, William Leete Stone, a "high Mason" and author of *The Life and Times of Red Jacket* (1841), and Henry Rowe Schoolcraft, the famous scholar of Indian Life.[15]

Several months later Morgan made his journey to Tonawanda. Initially intent on finding materials suitable for new rituals, he was struck by the way that nearly all aspects of Indian life were translated into the language of family relations. This became evident during the "mourning council" (the first Indian ceremony witnessed by Morgan) of the League of the Iroquois, at which the elder nations of the confederation—the Mohawks, Onondagas, and Senecas—were ritualistically regarded as fathers, and the younger nations—the Oneidas, Cayugas, and Tuscaroras—as children. The death of a Seneca sachem required that the children lament the loss of their father; the fathers in return asked their orphaned children to accept the newly designated sachem as their new father.

When he returned to Aurora, Morgan dashed off a note to Schoolcraft saying that his head was "so crammed with matters pertaining to the Iroquois" that he must further examine the subject "for my own relief."[16] Soon thereafter he began his famous book, *League of the Ho-de-no-sau-nee, or Iroquois*. In this book, usually called *League of the Iroquois*, he explained that the league was "designed to be but an elaboration of the Family Relationships. . . . The several nations of the Iroquois, united, constituted one Family, dwelling together in one Long House; and these ties of family relationship were carried throughout their civil and social system, from individuals to tribes, from tribes to nations, and from the nations to the League itself, and bound them together in one common, indissoluble brotherhood."[17]

One year later Morgan asked Parker if the Iroquois would allow him to undergo the ceremony of adoption. The sachems were mystified by the request, but agreed, providing that Morgan pay for the feast afterwards. On October 31, 1846, Morgan was adopted by the Hawk clan. His new father was Jimmy Johnson, a nephew of Red Jacket.[18] Morgan offered little comment on the ceremony. Within a year he lost interest in the Order of the Iroquois and its "boyish" rituals; it disbanded shortly thereafter.[19]

Morgan, one biographer noted, was not a "born ethnologist," as some have claimed, "but was made one by a secret society."[20] Morgan never explained his early interest in initiatory ritual, and as a mature anthropologist he wrote that religious beliefs and rites, which dealt "so largely with the imaginative and emotional nature," were nearly unintelligible.[21] His reluctance to examine emotional issues may have also stemmed from concerns over his own earlier preoccupation with such rituals. The self, of course, is the most closely guarded secret.

❖

While Morgan was devising initiations based on the rites of the Iroquois, a fraternal group founded by ex-Freemasons in 1834 was also attempting to rework Indian legends into an appropriate ceremony. The early history of the Improved Order of Red Men was similar in many ways to that of the Odd Fellows. Originally a working-class drinking society, the order underwent a transformation in the 1830s as a protemperance faction eventually gained a majority in the Grand Lodge. By 1840 it prohibited "tribes" from renting rooms in taverns and expelled members who opposed this and similar measures.[22] Despite these concessions to middle-class sensibilities, the Red Men experienced little growth: By 1850 they had only forty-five tribes and 3,175 members.[23]

The order determined to replicate the success of the Odd Fellows by devising rituals comparable to the Initiatory degree of the latter. It has not been established whether the Committee on Ritual of the Red Men, which deliberated in Baltimore, were familiar with the work of their counterparts in the Odd Fellows, who met in the same city. The records of the Grand Lodge from 1850 through 1868 do reveal that the "principal work" of the Red Men was the creation of effective rituals.[24] This proved no easy matter. The Grand Lodge offered cash prizes for effective rituals; created and disbanded new committees on ritual every couple of years; and adopted new rituals in 1850, 1852, 1859, and 1864, each of which was discarded shortly after its creation for failing to generate "the general approbation hoped for." By 1865 the order was nearly destitute.[25]

In 1868 the Grand Lodge revised the rituals once more, adding an Adoption degree. This time the order immediately experienced "unparalleled growth." Before the year was out the Grand Lodge reported that the rituals were "giving excellent satisfaction."[26] By the mid-1870s, 10,000 new members were being initiated each year. Circulars describing the order to prospective members now emphasized its secret work, which was "beautiful beyond description and wholly unlike that of any other order."[27] By 1900 approximately 350,000 Red Men were finding their way into wigwams of the order each week. Its annual receipts exceeded a million dollars.[28]

The question of why the earlier rituals failed to elicit "general approbation" while the Adoption degree of 1868 gave "excellent satisfaction" is unanswerable. Outside observers can never know what any aspect of a culture means to the people who create and live with it, and fraternal leaders who had to offer monetary rewards to obtain effective rituals were obviously incapable of explaining why some were popular and others not. The question is further complicated by the fact that the Red Men destroyed the unsuccessful rituals.[29]

Forty years after the approval of the Adoption degree a student of the order, Thomas Donnalley, was talking with groups of elderly Red Men about the history of the society when one of them produced a copy of the 1864 ritual. Donnalley knew that member dissatisfaction had led to its rejection, but it seemed to him "of a high order of merit as a literary production." He could not imagine why it had been discarded.[30] In 1908 he published sections of the document.

In the Brave's degree of the 1864 initiation, the candidate was given a bow and arrow and told to bring home a hunting trophy. After he had been led around the lodge, his conductor pointed toward the ceiling and told him to shoot down an eagle. He congratulated him for hitting the imaginary eagle and told him to take a plume of feathers to the Chief as evidence of his skill. Together they hiked around the lodge to retrieve the plume and take it to the chief, who, on seeing the trophy, welcomed the new brother to the order.

The Adoption degree, a ritual created in the revision of 1868, was considerably longer than the Brave's degree.[31] It began with an invocation by the Sachem, who prayed to the "Great Spirit of the Universe" to bring harmony to the tribe, to preserve the Indians' homes, and to "shed Thy bounties upon all Red Men of the forest." The ritual's main theme was death. The Sachem called upon the Great Spirit to give each Red Man the "holy courage" to paddle his canoe safely to "that undiscovered country from whose bourne no traveler returns." During the invocation he returned to the subject of death:

> Teach us the trail we must follow while we live in this forest, and when it is Thy will that we shall cross the river of death, take us to

Thyself, where Thy council fire of love and glory burneth forever in righteousness.

Then the council fire was kindled; in the preparation room the candidate—a "pale face"—removed his shirt and shoes and put on moccasins. A Scout rapped at the "inner wicket" and motioned for the candidate to follow. They padded silently around the lodge room, avoiding a group of Indians who were sleeping at the far end. Then the scout tripped over one of the Indians. The awakened Indian shouted, "Spies! Traitors in our Camp!" and the group captured the candidate; the Scout escaped. The Indian hunters conferred around a fire.

> First Brave: This pale face is of a hated nation: let us put him to the torture!
> Second Brave: He is a squaw, and cannot bear the torture!
> Third Brave: He fears a Warrior's death!
> Fourth Brave: Let us burn him at the stake!

The initiate was informed of this decision.

The braves and the candidate proceeded to the opposite end of the lodge and were led to a tepee. Just after they were admitted, another Indian rushed at the candidate with an uplifted knife, only to be intercepted by a hunter who assured him that the paleface would soon be tortured. "Then let us proceed, pale face," the hunter said, "and unless some Chief interposes, you perish at the stake. Why do you tempt your fate? or is it your wish to become a Red Man?" The candidate was prompted to answer yes. The hunter warned: "Know, then, that Red Men are men without fear, and none but such can be adopted by our Tribe." After more questions the hunter demanded proof of the candidate's courage.

The initiate was bound to the stake, and the hunters were told to prepare their scalping knives and war clubs. The Indians commenced a scalp dance and started to light a fire. Another Indian summoned the Prophet from his tent. But the Prophet halted the execution and berated the hunters for their impulsiveness, noting that the candidate had proven his courage. He added that the family of Red Men were dedicated to their "brothers," the "children of the forest." However, he warned the paleface that the final decision on his adoption rested with the Sachem. The Prophet gave the candidate an eagle's feather (as in the earlier ritual) as proof of his courage.

After more speeches and a pledge of secrecy, the candidate was led to another tepee in the far corner of the lodge. As he approached, the Sachem threw open the flap and upbraided his guards for sleeping on duty, thereby allowing a paleface to come into his presence. The warriors did not immediately respond, and the Sachem started to throw a tomahawk at the initiate. One of the hunters then grasped the Sachem's arm. "No, Sachem, no! Thy children when on duty never sleep!" The hunter added that the initiate had passed the ordeal and had been endorsed by the Prophet. He produced the eagle's feather as proof. The Sachem, realizing his error, tossed his tomahawk aside, shook hands with the candidate, and welcomed him to the order.

The 1864 and 1868 ceremonies were both concerned with liminality, Arnold van Gennep's term for the ritual transition from one status to another.[32] But the differences between the rituals were more striking than the similarities. If the plot of the 1864 ritual was predicated upon the initiate's circuitous journey to meet the Sachem, the Adoption degree was suffused with words and activities signifying motion and transition. The "pale face," who was symbolically (and prematurely?) given moccasins, "wandered" around the lodge before he was discovered by hunters, who themselves were traveling away from camp in search of game. (The ritual included an optional "amplified form," which showed the Sachem eagerly awaiting the return of his braves, thereby reiterating the image of travel.) The initiate journeyed from camp to camp, and tepee to tepee. His crime was one of trespass, for he was twice found "astray in the sacred home of the Red Men." He compounded this error of navigation by venturing towards the Sachem's tepee, which ignited a volatile exchange. After the Sachem welcomed him to the order he added, "You have left your accustomed walks in life to range the forest with Red Men." He finally noted that "all within the Order have traveled the same trail, and passed through the same ordeal."

The ritual consistently drew an analogy between motion through the forest or across rivers and the journey of life. Prior to his adoption by the Red Men, the initiate was "wandering," "astray," and "trespassing," as if the entire course of his life were somehow wayward. To redirect his energies, and to set out on a better path required considerable effort, time—and the assistance of secret ritual.

Although it may appear that the initiate's role in all of this was passive, the ritual's underlying premise was that the initiate had *chosen* to embark on a new course of life. An ode at the closing of the Adoption degree concluded with these lines:

> Is your mind with friendship flowing,
> Freedom in your pathway showing?
> Brother's love shall never cease.

The preliminary couplet, infelicitous by even fraternal standards, implied a conscious effort to link the seemingly dissimilar themes of friendship and an unencumbered "pathway." The result, taken out of context, appears non-sensical. But if the ritual is understood as an extended allegory involving personal development, the closing phrase gains a highly compressed and cogent meaning: Men must remain emotionally free to pursue a path of friendship and to avoid any obstacles that would hinder such a course.

The Sachem was especially concerned with the final destination of this life-journey. In his initial speech he had prayed to the Great Spirit to teach each Red Man "to paddle his canoe" safely to "that undiscovered country from whose bourne no traveler returns." At the close of the speech he again referred to the metaphor: "When it is Thy will that we shall cross the river of death, take us to Thyself." On two occasions the candidate's initiatory journey nearly ended in death, and his eventual deliverance was predicated on his ability to transcend fear of death. The Prophet returned to the metaphor of death-as-journey in his final speech: "And when through life serenely you have passed, / And landed your frail bark beyond life's sea, / May your eternal lot be cast with those / Who know no sorrow, and can feel no pain."

The initiate, though twice spared from execution, had in a sense already experienced a metaphorical death: His former self had not really survived the ritualistic journey; his previous life course had been shown to be all wrong. With the help of the ritual he now chose an alternative—and dramatically different—route and destination. On the simplest level, the Adoption degree implied that the life of the paleface had come to an end. As a Red Man he would chart a more "serene" course through life.

The purpose of the ritual was not to reform the initiate, but to remake him entirely, for his errant life course was due to inherent deficiencies. Though apprehended for the crime of trespass, he was to be put to death for a failing of character: He was a "pale face" and a "squaw" who "could not bear torture." He was excluded from the Tribe, which consisted of "men without fear," because he was thought to be unfit. Through the transformatory magic of the ritual, the initiate's courage was confirmed. Now he could travel with the brethren of the Red Men.

The most important innovation of the 1868 ritual was the transformation of the Sachem into a complex character. In the previous ritual he simply expressed joy on beholding the initiate. But in the 1868 revision the Sachem's character undergoes considerable development. In the earliest scenes he is portrayed as a devout religious leader fretting over his absent hunters. The initiate sees only that the Sachem is menacing; the climax of the ritual occurs when he throws open the flaps of his teepee, glares at the paleface, shouts "in an angry tone" at his apparently negligent guards, and makes motions as if to kill the intruder.

Fraternal ritualists, though by no means skilled dramatists, could certainly detect major errors in plot development. Yet the climax of the Adoption degree was seriously flawed—at least in terms of dramatic consistency—by the awkward pause after the Sachem accused his guards of sleeping. There was no reason why the guards should not have immediately explained the situation. The incident apparently was contrived to provide an opportunity for the Sachem to display his lethal wrath towards the initiate. This dramaturgical device highlighted the Sachem's emotional transformation when he learned that the initiate had passed the ordeal.[33] The Sachem's anger dissolved and he welcomed the initiate to "our bosom." He explained, "We feel it our duty, as Red Men, to watch over and supply the wants of the afflicted of our Tribe, and to shield them from danger, as the eagle shieldeth her young and tender brood."

The paternal character of the Sachem and the filial character of the brethren of the tribe had become explicit. The father-son theme, moreover, was reinforced throughout the Adoption degree. The "beloved" Prophet, addressed in reverential terms, functioned as a paternal figure whose role was similar to that of the Sachem: He delivered the paleface from the first crisis and identified him as a "man without fear." The Great Spirit of the Universe also was characterized as a loving father. The ritual seemed to be an exhibition of paternal redundancy: The "children" of the tribe addressed their fathers (Prophet and Sachem) who in turn prayed to the father of all Red Men (the Great Spirit). And like the Sachem, the Prophet and the Great Spirit initially appeared distant and imposing, yet their essential benevolence was similarly confirmed. The use of these redundant father figures ensured that even an inattentive initiate would apprehend an essential aspect of the ritual: The authority figures of the Red Men, though they might appear threatening, were actually loving and benevolent.

The Adoption degree presented an emotionally charged drama centering on family relations. In the final lecture the Sachem explained that the degree was a pallid imitation of the actual ceremonies of the Iroquois, who made their captives run the gauntlet. Those who faltered were slaughtered immediately, "but those who passed through the ordeal successfully were adopted into the Tribe, and treated with the utmost affection and kindness. By this means all recollection of their distant kindred was gradually effaced, and they were bound by the ties of gratitude to the Tribe which had adopted them." So it was to be with the initiate, who necessarily detached himself from his previous family and became through adoption a child of the Red Men, there to receive the "utmost affection and kindness" from his newfound brothers and, especially, from his newfound fathers.

Although the Adoption degree served as a model for scores of imitators, nineteenth-century historians of the order conceded that their extraordinarily successful ritual was derived from a book generated by a quest for meaningful ceremonies for another fraternal group: Lewis Henry Morgan's *League of the Iroquois*.[34]

❖

Fraternal scholars claimed that their rituals fulfilled a "universal" need among men, although they never explained whether this was due to a common masculine physiological endowment or to a particular psychological disposition. Leaders in all orders drew attention to the resemblance of their rituals to male initiations in primitive societies. Pike and Mackey extended the Masonic pedigree well past Solomon and into the time of the Druids and cavemen. And organizations such as the Red Men and the Ancient Order of the Foresters were explicitly based upon Victorian conceptions of primitive societies. Roscoe Pound, a Masonic scholar and a Harvard law professor, remarked that it was "obvious" that Masonry was related to the "development of societies out of the primitive men's house." He proposed a cross-cultural study of initiations to help explain the contemporary fascination with such rituals.[35] The subject of fraternal ritual thus begs to be examined in light of anthropological theory on male initiation ceremonies.

Analyses by anthropologists of male initiation ceremonies have been part of a larger debate over whether cultural practices evolve from the psychological needs of the individual or the requirements of the social system. Psychogenic and sociogenic explanations are not mutually exclusive, and both rely on psychological, sociological, and anthropological theories whose application to the past is problematic.[36]

Sociogenic theory is based on the assumption that social structure generates complementary cultural forms. But as the anthropologist Fredrik Barth has cautioned, there is no compelling argument to posit a causal link of this nature. By relying on structuralist assumptions, moreover, sociogenic theorists often discount the views of the people being studied and minimize the emotional meanings such rituals may communicate.[37] The sociogenic approach is fundamentally at odds with the essentially indeterminate nature of the historian's task, which, as Johan Huizinga noted, is to show the visible operation of cultural forms in time, place, and context. Explanatory models should follow from evidence; they must never precede it.[38]

Sociogenic theory, moreover, is often unsuited to issues of cultural change. The fundamental structures of society—and thus its culture—generally remain stable. Instances of ritual origins or transformations are therefore rare. Emile Durkheim was aware of one exception: the Committee of Public Safety's creation of the rites of the Feast of the Supreme Being, which he regarded as an attempt by leaders of the French Revolution to divert Catholic religious sentiment into politically acceptable channels. For Durkheim, this confirmed the general proposition that psychologically sophisticated elites create culture to reinforce the social order. Ritual is thus firmly anchored in the bedrock of social structure. He scoffed at the psychogenic notion that fleeting emotional states could produce enduring ritual forms.

There is no evidence, however, that fraternal ritual was imposed on the members from above. The record shows that fraternal ritualists, through a maddeningly unpredictable process of trial and error, attempted to "give satisfaction" and "gratify the desires" of members; they did not respond to the voiceless dictates of social necessity.

Durkheim's guesswork on ritual origins was one of the most serious errors in his study of primitive religion. Speculations over the origins of primitive customs, A. R. Radcliffe-Brown noted, "are not merely useless but are worse than useless." Edward Evans-Pritchard considered it "extraordinary that anyone could have thought it worth while to speculate about what might have been the origin of some custom or belief when there is absolutely no means of discovering, in the absence of historical evidence, what was its origin."[39] A subsequent generation of fieldworkers relegated the study of ritual, and particularly of cultural change, to a low order among research priorities.[40]

Insofar as sociogenic theory has been enlisted to explain male initiation ceremonies, it has generally presumed that formal ritualism is a distinguishing characteristic of premodern societies. The anthropologist Robert Murphy, for example, argued that the Mundurucu Indians of Brazil practice male initiation ceremonies because such ceremonies underscore sex role distinctions necessary for preserving the Mundurucu economy. Americans do not perform initiatory rites because "our society is not structured along the simple lines that would make such rites functional. If our primitive contemporaries use techniques that seem to derive from primal experiences, it is because they are grappling with primal problems."[41] Such views are obviously inapplicable to fraternal ritual, which was created and practiced by middle-class men who built a complex urban-industrial society.

Although Murphy's comments seem far-removed from nineteenth-century America, the fraternal preoccupation with primitive rituals suggests that members may have indeed been struggling with "primal problems." These Victorians assumed that primitive society was little more than the family writ large. Morgan reasoned that all Indian social and political structures were modeled after the family, the most basic human institution. By setting their ceremonies in primitive cultures, or in an Old Testament environment of tribal clans, fraternal ritualists ensured that contemporary issues of ethnicity, work, politics, and business could not intrude upon the central concern of the ritual—family relations. Even before he witnessed the mourning council at Tonawanda, Morgan had superimposed upon his rite of inindianation a family psychodrama.

Issues of family relations are central to all psychogenic theories of male initiation ceremonies. The explanatory mechanisms can be divided into psychoanalytic and nonpsychoanalytic categories.

Historians are naturally suspicious of psychoanalytic models, which presume that crucial aspects of human character are determined during infancy, well before most historical forces can be expected to prove influential. Since intrapsychic processes are presumably universal, male initiation ceremonies should exist in all societies.[42] The relatively sudden diffusion and proliferation of initiatory rituals in America during the two to three decades after 1820 cannot readily be explained by this perpective.[43]

The most suggestive nonpsychoanalytic model has been provided by psychologist John Whiting and his associates. In a diverse sample of sixty-four societies, Whiting found that the presence of male initiation ceremonies strongly correlated with (1) exclusive mother-son sleeping arrangements and (2) patrilocal residence (the bride moved to live with her husband and his kin network). Whiting hypothesized that in societies where the father is absent or plays a minor role in child rearing, the male infant perceives the mother as all-powerful, envies her role, and then adopts a feminine identification. Yet when he begins to notice the world outside the home, at about the age of five, he will in most societies perceive that men control resources and clearly occupy an enviable position. A secondary identification with the masculine role thus becomes superimposed on the female identification. Male initiation ceremonies "serve psychologically to brainwash the primary feminine identity and to establish firmly the secondary male identity."[44]

Whiting's "cross-sex identity conflict" model is strikingly successful at incorporating many of the details of fraternal rituals. It is easy to see how the Adoption degree might have functioned to "brainwash the primary feminine identity": The initiate was labeled a paleface, a coward, and a squaw. Before he could become a member of the tribe he was sent on a long journey that culminated in death and the "effacement" of family ties. The ritual could also "establish firmly the secondary male identity": The initiate, having first been attacked and threatened by hostile father figures, finally won their approval and was "adopted" into the new family of the Red Men. He was now free to travel "serenely" through life.

The caution that applied to psychoanalytical explanations must prevail here as well: It cannot be assumed that because a cultural form could have functioned in a particular manner it actually did so. Whiting's discussion of mother-son sleeping arrangements and patrilocal residence seems even less helpful in explaining developments in nineteenth-century America than the counterfactual sociogenic assumption that modern societies do not have male initiation rites. But patrilocal residence and exclusive mother-son sleeping patterns may be seen as manifestations of larger societal character-istics. Exclusive mother-son sleeping patterns could serve as an analogue for father absence in early child rearing, and patrilocal residence for dispropor-tionate male authority in the adult world.[45]

This reformulation moves the analysis of male initiation ceremonies be-yond the primitive world.[46] In its simplest outlines, the model bears a striking resemblance to the Victorian America described by successive schools of women's historians: The first, of which the collectively authored *History of Woman Suffrage* (1881–1922) was the most influential, argued that persistent male domination led to the systemic victimization of women;[47] the second, illustrated by the work of Kathryn Kish Sklar and Carroll Smith-Rosenberg, held that women created in the "domestic sphere" a subculture of shared identity and social meaning—a realm of women and children from which men were largely segregated.[48] For these historians, male domination and paternal neglect were the salient characteristics of Victorian America.

That social structures analogous to those in the Whiting sample were prevalent in nineteenth-century America is not sufficient explanation, how-ever, for the rise of fraternalism, for fraternal ritual emerged as a significant social phenomenon only in the decades after 1830. One must establish that these two structural preconditions were not present earlier. Although im-portant shifts in economic and political power occurred during the late eigh-teenth and the nineteenth centuries, male domination of most institutions beyond the home remained essentially unchallenged throughout the period. The discussion of structural change must therefore focus on the changing role of fathers.

❖ A HISTORICAL PARADIGM OF ❖

MASCULINE DEVELOPMENT

The history of fatherhood is in its early stages, and few generalizations about the role of fathers in colonial America can be proposed with any convic-tion.[49] Yet there is considerable evidence that, for much of their lives, boys in the colonial period lived under the palpable influence and control of their fathers; this was much less true of fathers and sons in the nineteenth century.

The colonial father stood firmly at the center of a "well-ordered" Puritan domicile. Every day he was expected to lead the family in prayer, scriptural study, and the singing of psalms.[50] His dominant position within the family was affirmed by common law, which gave him custody of children in cases of marital separation. Furthermore, if he died, the family as a legal entity was dissolved; no such circumstance attended the death of his spouse. The proximity of the workplace to home facilitated his management of domestic matters. Artisans, for instance, usually worked at home or in adjacent buildings, and farmers cultivated fields near their homes and returned to the house for meals. They could be summoned easily whenever household matters required their supervision. During the long winter, moreover, farmers and other seasonal workers had plenty of time to exercise the authority that had been conferred upon them as fathers by the church, the courts, and enduring patriarchal traditions.

Although care of infant boys was provided by mothers, child rearing manuals were addressed to the father, the ultimate authority in family matters.[51] Once males had moved beyond the toddler stage and were thought capable of reasoning, fathers were expected to assume responsibility for their moral supervision. At about this age, too, boys began to help their fathers in the shop or fields. There they would learn many of the skills they would need throughout life. From ten to fourteen, boys commenced more formal vocational training. If sons were to be apprenticed, fathers advised and often dictated the choice of occupations and masters. Although boys imagined that apprenticeship would lead to a loosening of paternal authority, the domination of surrogate fathers often proved even more extreme.[52]

Once young men had completed their apprenticeship, they required their fathers' assistance to set up their own shops. Those youths who began farming remained under their fathers' direct supervision for many years. In a society where ownership of land provided a livelihood and determined status, all sons had good reason to be anxious over a father's parsimoniousness, his longevity, or both. Added to these was an even more telling concern: Sons could not marry until they possessed a "marriage portion" —their own house and sufficient land to provide for a family. This enabled a father to determine the timing of his son's marriage and even to influence the choice of bride. Because they typically needed help to cultivate their fields, fathers often considered it prudent to maintain sons in a state of dependency. Filial obedience, though commanded by God, could be more readily enforced if noncompliance carried the sanction of disinheritance.[53]

Direct evidence on the character of father-son ties is limited, and what has survived can usually be interpreted in contradictory ways.[54] Perhaps the most reasonable conclusion is that fathers and sons had ambivalent feelings towards each other. Their lives were enmeshed too tightly to allow for an

easy acceptance of either's individuality, and the points at issue were too ob-
durate to be broached without rancor. But understanding, then as now, does
not depend on affectionate letters or heart-to-heart chats. Fathers who had
themselves lived under the protracted domination of patriarchs well understood their sons' longings for autonomy and independence. And boys who
had from an early age aspired to the patriarchal role perhaps also came to
identify with the voice of authority in their own lives. Hostility and affection were complementary expressions of the strong—often stifling—bonds
of dependence between fathers and sons.[55]

John Demos has observed that young people in colonial Plymouth proceeded toward maturity in a "gradual, piecemeal, and largely automatic fashion." "In some cultures a crisis at adolescence is mediated by vivid symbolic
observances," he added.

> "Initiation rites," or other ceremonies of a less formal type, mark a cer-
> tain point in time as the boundary between childhood and maturity,
> and help to smooth the transition. (In our society graduation exercises
> might be regarded as a weak sort of functional equivalent.) But nothing
> of this kind can be traced for Plymouth.[56]

Demos's view, which is similar to the interpretation presented here, is part of
a larger debate over whether adolescence as such existed in colonial America
and whether the transition to adulthood then was less difficult and circuitous
than now. But attempts by proponents on both sides to relate the colonial experience to modern customs have obscured some important distinctions.
The prolonged dependence of sons was not analogous to the lengthy schooling experienced by young people nowadays, as Demos's critics have maintained. On the other hand, the process of emotional development was surely
not "inherently less difficult," as Demos claimed.[57] Colonial fathers stood
as major obstacles to their sons' attainment of adulthood. The transition to
adulthood entails the development of many roles and statuses; there is no
single crisis at adolescence. Thus what Demos took to be the ease of adolescent transition in colonial America was, more precisely, a direct and almost
inevitable acquisition of adult male gender roles. Colonial society lacked
male initiation rites not because adolescence did not yet exist, but because
the path to manhood had not yet become problematic.

This paradigmatic analysis, derived largely from seventeenth-century New
England, fails to account for patterns elsewhere or for differences over time.
In the Southern colonies the availability of land, the reliance on slave labor,
and a less demanding Protestant tradition gave rise to a more tolerant style
of child rearing.[58] Even in New England paternal authority eroded during
the last half of the eighteenth century as sons gained earlier control of their

fathers' estates or left home in search of opportunities elsewhere. Having attained some measure of financial independence, they could marry at an earlier age and with less paternal interference.[59] That sons and daughters found it easier to evade parental discipline was further reflected in rising premarital pregnancy rates.[60]

These changes prefigured the emergence of the modern American family from about 1790 to 1840. The American Revolution consecrated an ideology that, though inconsistent in practice, provided justification for rebellion by young men who had grown impatient with domineering fathers. Even more significant was the transformation from self-sufficient to commercial farming. The prospects of commercial agriculture induced young men to abandon family farms in droves; their search for cheaper lands in newly settled areas or for opportunities in the growing towns and cities carried them far beyond the paternal domain. Economic growth also fostered a rigid division of labor by sex, as women, no longer burdened with farm tasks such as feeding animals, spinning and weaving, brewing, and soap making, increasingly became purchasers of goods rather than producers of them; and men, enticed by the seemingly limitless possibilities of the expanding American economy, found it difficult to fasten their attention upon traditional concerns of family and faith.

The transformation of gender roles and household responsibilities greatly influenced child rearing patterns.[61] One consequence of economic growth and structural change was the physical separation of men from the home during much of the day. This was particularly evident in the growing towns and cities, where rising real estate prices and business congestion led to the displacement of middle-class residential housing. As the distance between home and workplace lengthened, the husband's departure each morning underscored his separation from the "domestic sphere."[62]

The longer commute was only part of a general extension in the husband's workday. The Puritans, as Max Weber observed, could hardly be accused of laziness, and colonial farmers surely worked long hours. But their intense labors during planting and harvesting were punctuated by periods of homebound inactivity. For the emerging middle classes of the early nineteenth century, however, work no longer consisted in completing specific seasonal chores but instead entailed a continuous commitment to enterprise of an unbounded character. Perhaps even more important, in an age when most middle-class men were self-employed and business was subject to the vagaries of volatile financial markets and competitive pressures, the precariousness of their livelihood absorbed men's emotional energies in a way that further distanced them from the home.[63]

An outpouring of advice books on family government and child rearing was one response to the withdrawal of men from the domestic sphere. Some tracts, such as Theodore Dwight's *The Father's Book* (1834), tried to persuade fathers to reassume their responsibilities within the home, but most believed that men would no longer take part in the rearing of children. "Paternal neglect at the present time is one of the most abundant sources of domestic sorrow," Rev. John S. C. Abbott wrote in 1842. "The father . . . eager in the pursuit of business, toils early and late, and finds no time to fulfill . . . duties to his children."[64]

Tocqueville remarked on the "more intimate and more affectionate" relations between fathers and sons in antebellum America, which he attributed to the spread of democracy and a consequent weakening of parental authority.[65] That paternal authority declined seems indisputable, but if fathers and sons behaved in a more equable manner, it was probably because they had less in common. Sons who sought guidance about the professions, business, or industry could learn little from fathers who had spent their lives on farms or in artisanal shops. And even when fathers owned their own business concerns, sons seemed reluctant to follow in their footsteps.[66]

As sons made their own career and marital decisions or sought the advice of their mothers, many fathers felt even less responsible for their children's destinies. Having already ceded the rearing of young children to their wives, fathers now found it difficult to assume—even if they were so inclined—an active role in the development of their older sons.[67] Women simultaneously assumed the duties of child rearing as their special vocation. Middle-class women were not the passive victims of an ideology of domesticity, but the architects of a bifurcated gender system that elevated their status even as it circumscribed their actions to the home.[68] Though they remained the legal and social inferiors of men, women acquired new status as moral guardians of the young. The courts increasingly acknowledged the supremacy of mothers in child rearing.[69] Phrenology, which was taken seriously in the mid-nineteenth century, discovered that women were unusually well endowed with bumps over the portions of the brain that determined "inhabitiveness" (love of home) and "parental love." Thus science confirmed that women should devote their energies to children.[70]

The historian Mary Ryan notes that as the idea of fatherhood seemed "almost to wither away," the bond between mother and child "assumed central place in the constellation of family affections."[71] The extent to which Americans in the nineteenth century came to equate womanhood with mothering is reflected in the fact that very few married women, regardless of their economic class, worked outside the home. J. S. C. Abbott's assumption of women's dominance in the home was reflected in his unthinking choice of pronouns in writing about child rearing: "Family government," he wrote, must "begin in the bosom of the parent. She must learn to control herself."[72]

Middle-class women imparted to the tasks of mothering a sustained intensity that would have been impossible a century earlier. The large household of eighteenth-century America, in which kinfolk and neighbors freely congregated, had been replaced by the increasingly private family.[73] Mothers could exert a more profound influence upon their children in part because they had far fewer of them: The average number of children born of a white woman of childbearing age declined from 7.04 to 3.56 during the nineteenth century.[74]

Although the private domain remained women's special preserve, antebellum mothers embarked on a crusade to infuse feminine sensibilities into institutions beyond the home. Mary Ryan has described, for instance, the process by which from the 1820s through the 1840s the women of Oneida County, New York, established infant schools, Sunday schools, maternal associations, and assorted moral reform agencies in order to heighten the importance of the conjugal family. "The mothers of Oneida," she wrote, after having reformed society as a whole, would then return to the home, "bringing with them out of the associations more intense bonds with their children."[75]

These temporary efforts presaged a far more fundamental institutional reform: the feminization of the public schools themselves.[76] In the 1840s Horace Mann, whose common-school reforms were executed by a corps of highly motivated women teachers, observed that God implanted in the maternal breast a "powerful, all-mastering instinct of love."[77] The logic and the economics of the argument (women would work more cheaply than men) were formidable. By 1890 nearly two out of three public school teachers in the nation were female, and in Northern and urban communities the proportion of women teachers was much higher.[78] These women brought to the task of teaching a sense of mission.[79] Setting aside the instruments of coercion, they attempted to order the classroom through the power of love, invoking the ungentle assistance of a man—the principal—only on those few occasions when the "large boys" went wild.

As they approached physical maturity, however, the large boys increasingly chafed at feminine control and at the apparent irrelevance of schooling to their future occupations.[80] By the age of fifteen or sixteen most left school, often at the insistence of beleaguered school authorities.[81] Mothers worried that these boys, free from extended female supervision for the first time in their lives, would succumb to the temptations that stalked the world beyond the home. That world, as child guidance writers pointed out, was not only devoid of salutary feminine influences, but was also a domain of masculine aggression and turpitude.[82] The ladies' magazines were filled with cautionary tales of young men who left home to work in the city and soon became utterly debauched.[83]

The obvious solution was to keep the young man under his mother's scrutiny for as long as possible, preferably until he could be transferred to the moral custody of an equally watchful bride. That women succeeded in implementing this strategy is indicated by the steep decline in boarding among nonimmigrant children in the middle decades of the nineteenth century.[84] By the 1870s most middle-class sons remained at home into their late twenties or early thirties. They married almost immediately afterwards.[85]

❖

With the transformation of the patriarchal family during the decades after 1770, the customary path to male adulthood almost disappeared, and for a time boys and young men were left surprisingly free to chart their own developmental strategies. Many experienced alternating periods of almost total independence and then dependence. Farmers' sons worked on the family farm during the summer and early fall, but in the winter they often left home, perhaps to work as lumberers or as clerks in country stores. Boys who went to the towns and cities also achieved a measure of autonomy by living with relatives or boarding with other families. For middle-class youths these haphazard patterns of "semi-dependence" or "semi-autonomy"[86] had all but disappeared by the mid-nineteenth century, replaced with intense and prolonged feminine nurture.

Like their counterparts in the colonial period, most middle-class men in the mid-nineteenth century did not achieve full adult status—defined as the opportunity to marry and establish their own home—until their late twenties or early thirties. If the acquisition of full adult status came equally late, however, there was an important difference in the ease with which boys became confident in their masculinity and sure of their role as adult men. Boys and young men in the colonial era remained under the domination of authoritarian masculine figures. At an early age they dressed like men, worked with their fathers and other adult men at tasks related to their adult life, and came to recognize that the familiar patterns of patriarchal authority were replicated throughout colonial society.

By the mid-nineteenth century middle-class fathers had to some extent absented themselves physically and emotionally from child rearing; even their occupational skills and attitudes toward work ceased to be of much use to their sons, whose lives were dominated by women. As mothers and as teachers, women attempted to fix into the character of boys feminine sensibilities and identification with feminine roles.

Not all middle-class boys fit into this developmental model, nor did all middle-class men join a lodge and become enthralled by its rituals. But many experienced some aspects of the paradigm; Victorian American society contained at least in some general sense the structural preconditions proposed in Whiting's cross-cultural thesis. Whether the proliferation of fraternal rituals was a manifestation of a failure among middle-class Victorian American men to free themselves from a cross-sex identity conflict is another matter.

Given its sweeping implications, Whiting's explanation and particularly his psychological assumptions warrant closer consideration. His model is drawn from theories of identification which assert that children envy those adults who control their access to food and other resources. They choose to imitate adult behavior because they observe that adulthood brings tangible rewards. If fathers are ineffective or absent, boys will envy the power of their mothers, imitate their behavioral traits, and identify with the feminine role.[87]

The psychological concept of *identification* involves distinctions and refinements far removed from historical evidence; it seems doubtful that historians could ever determine whether boys or men at the core of their being perceived themselves as masculine. Moreover, the entire concept of gender identification recently has been questioned by some psychologists. Joseph Pleck emphasizes that societies impose gender *roles*, which suppress normal variations in behavior.[88] Men and women are not impelled innately toward "appropriate" gender identification. In view of these and other criticisms,[89] I propose to replace Whiting's cross-sex identity conflict model with the less problematic gender-role perspective.

Restated in gender-role terms, the dilemma for boys in Victorian America was not simply that their fathers were absent and they were thereby deprived of psychological guides to their core masculinity, but that adult gender roles were invariant and narrowly defined and boys were taught chiefly the sensibilities and moral values associated with adult women. As adolescents, or perhaps somewhat earlier, boys perceived the difference in adult gender roles and fantasized about how they would fit into the world of men. In the absence of fathers and of adult male models more generally, they contrived a "boy culture" which in its territorial disputes, cruel pranks, and stylized aggression provided an unconscious caricature of men's roles in business and politics.[90] As young men, they were drawn to the male secret orders, where they repeatedly practiced rituals that effaced the religious values and emotional ties associated with women.

Whiting concluded that certain social structures (matriarchy or father absence) would inevitably cause "gender anxieties" in boys.[91] His cross-correlations, drawn from a large and diverse sample, constitute the most important evidence for such a proposition. In Victorian America, in addition to the structural prerequisites, there is evidence that women intended to teach boys norms and sensibilities associated with the feminine role.

This subject has been amply developed by women's historians, who have shown that middle-class women, debarred from participation in economic and political institutions, determined to redeem the nation through "moral motherhood." To the task of child rearing mothers imparted an intensity borne of religious conviction—a belief that by instilling in their children the sweet virtues of Jesus they would ultimately reshape a masculine order that had grown neglectful of His mission.[92]

Women rejected Calvinist doctrines of infant depravity and embraced the romantic conception of children as essentially good.[93] An influential synthesis of maternal and religious principles appeared in Horace Bushnell's *Christian Nurture* (1847). His view of conversion as a gradual infusion of God's spirit through maternal nurture further affirmed women's indispensability. Mothers were to "plant the angel in the man, uniting him to all heavenly goodness by predispositions from itself."[94]

Bushnell did not explain precisely how women were to "plant the angel" in men, and he disapproved of overly formal child rearing strategies. But by the time *Christian Nurture* appeared, many advisers, theologians, and parents had already established most of the details in a new approach toward childhood.[95] It was still accepted wisdom that refractory children were to be disciplined, but increasingly parents were advised that this task should be accomplished through maternal influence rather than corporal punishment.[96]

The authors of child rearing manuals insisted that a mother's love would cause children to internalize her values. In 1847 Catharine Beecher, anticipating social learning theory, espoused by W. Mischel and others in the 1960s, explained that children's minds were of a "plastic texture," ready to imitate the mother's "tastes, habits, feelings, and opinions."[97] Other writers possessed a less sophisticated but equally revealing understanding of psychology. One contributor to *Godey's Lady's Book* reasoned that much as children acquired a mother's "tastes and propensities" through breast-feeding, they could attain her moral sensibilities through intense nurture. "We do not suppose, indeed, that mind can be thus transfused from one soul to another," she explained. "But we do think that the moral character of the future man may be influenced by the treatment he receives at the breast, and in the cradle."[98] Horace Mann noted that "the true mother continues to be one with the child for years after its birth. Her consciousness embraces and interpenetrates its consciousness."[99]

Boys, however, recognized the preferential status accorded men in all arenas beyond the home. They also surely perceived that prolonged maternal nurture posed problems to their own development; for instance, the diet of moral tales they were fed as children may have proven unsettling. Consider the endorsement of maternal nurture in T. S. Arthur's "The Prodigal's Return." The story concerned a young man's desire to leave home against his mother's wishes. When the boy could be dissuaded no longer, the mother pleaded, "You won't forget your mother, William?" William went off to college and proceeded to do just that, becoming dissolute and debauched. But one evening he dreamt of his mother and instantly experienced a conversion. Immediately he returned to her—and to morality. It is doubtful that the young male reader could comfortably identify with William's triumph over sin, for once he arrived home he had nothing to do.[100] His presumed destiny as a man was at odds with the lessons and sensibilities he had learned at his mother's knee. He could fulfill his duty to his mother only by sacrificing his status as a man.

Most boys would recognize the extent of the disjuncture between maternal precepts and the values of the masculine world when they went to work, usually after they had stopped attending school at the age of fifteen or so. Boys who had learned the maxim "Time is the opportunity for doing good" were stunned by the long hours and relentless exertions of the workplace.[101] Even more disconcerting was the tension between evangelical attitudes toward money and the duties men were obliged to assume as adults. Men remained at home until their late twenties or early thirties in order to save enough money to marry and to support a family. The repeated childhood admonishment to "place less value upon the shining dollar in the pocket than upon a shining grace in the heart" must have seemed incomprehensible.[102] If they chose to adhere to the moral maxims of childhood, then they, like William in Arthur's story, could not marry and establish their own family. They could not become men.

❖ A MIMIC JOURNEY OF LIFE ❖

Fraternal magazines repeatedly published accounts of the initiatory practices of primitive or ancient peoples. Occasionally these articles were historical or descriptive, but more often they were products of imagination. Much of their appeal lay in the unstated resemblance of these druidical, Egyptian, or Eleusinian rites to fraternal rituals. A typical story, "Ancient Initiations" (*Voice of Masonry*, April 1867), described a young man's entrance into the rites of Isis in ancient Egypt.

The initiate, Adrian, encountered fearful ordeals and was eventually delivered to a darkened subterranean chamber. As priests chanted softly in the background, Adrian wondered: "Can this be death?" He then recalled his "dead mother's kiss upon his brow" and heard a voice that warned of imminent dangers. It seemed to come "from the grave." He proceeded cautiously along a path strewn with skulls, bones, and deadly snakes. Masked men with swords lurked in the shadows.

Adrian then wandered into a chamber of "lovely women." The most beautiful of these approached and offered flowers and wine. Adrian pushed past her and continued his journey. The women, enraged, taunted him as he parted their ranks. He crossed a hall of fire and a wide canal and eventually fell into a "howling abyss." Deep in the bowels of the earth, the High Priest welcomed the "brave youth" and pronounced him a "conqueror of earthly passion and of earthly fear."[103]

No women actually participated in rituals whose chief purposes were to attenuate female religious sensibilities and psychological influence. This imaginary rendering of the rites of Isis is one of the few occasions in which women were described as having a role in any initiatory drama. The story introduced two antithetical types of women: the sirens in the chamber who stood literally in the way of Adrian's ultimate purification; and his long-dead mother, whose kiss served as a talisman and whose cautionary words guided him during his ordeals. The unsubtle message was that woman's sexuality was deceitful and dangerous, but a mother's love was pure and dependable.

Fraternal attitudes were part of a more general predeliction during the 1840s and 1850s to deny or minimize women's sexuality. Carl Degler doubts that the nostrums of physicians and writers reflected women's own views on the subject. He suggests that these men, who had no selfish reason to insist that women were innately frigid, advanced such views to lessen the burdens of frequent childbearing and to improve women's status in marriage.[104] When men denied female sexuality, however, they were articulating a stereotype they had learned in childhood.[105] The disjuncture between the proper female role, embodied by their mothers, and the sexuality of their wives, which surely became apparent at one time or another, troubled many men. They had either to discard long-standing conceptions of proper female gender roles or to worry that their wives lacked the purity that should inhere in their sex.

An examination of fraternal literature suggests how difficult it was for men to break away from their mothers and to renounce the restricted gender role associated with female domesticity. Poems, guidebooks, and novels consistently endorsed maternal nurture and criticized wives, even though one purpose of such publications was to mitigate wives' opposition to the orders. In a story entitled "The Old Fashioned Mother," a Mason complained about women, especially wives, who encroached on the men's sphere by seeking to join a lodge. He contrasted them with the traditional mother, "whose life was love" and who "encircles her child, if he be on the face of the earth." She was, he added, "the divinity of our infancy," the "sacred presence in the shrine of our first earthly idolatry." [106]

The pages of fraternal magazines were filled with similar odes to mothers and motherhood. Typical was the tale of a distraught woman who after the Civil War journeyed to the Andersonville prison to await the appearance of her long-dead son. She was eventually dispatched to a lunatic asylum but escaped and returned to the site of the prison, where she wondered "why her boy did not come." The woman's madness, the narrator concluded, was characteristic of mothers, whose attachment to their sons transcended the bounds of rationality.[107] This treacle might be dismissed as an attempt to win women's support, or at least their forbearance, but it is noteworthy that few such odes were addressed to wives, whose opposition was far more formidable.

Fraternal ritualists and writers confirmed that maternal attachment had left a deep and enduring emotional imprint. One lodge member noted that even though his mother was dead, he still felt "that she is here," and "that I clasp around my heart, / Her sweet still voice, and soft caresses!" [108] Another claimed that his mother's beautiful face followed him "ever and near," with "voiceless lips that I feel, but can not hear." [109] In "To My Mother," sixty-five-year-old William Rounseville recounted his wait "through all those lengthened years" to join his mother in heaven:

> I wait the call to come, mother,
> To tread the path thou'st trod
> Which has a glorious terminus
> In mother and in God.[110]

When fraternal writers reminisced about childhood, they invariably thought about their mothers. In another poem entitled "To My Mother" (there were dozens with the same title), a Mason recalled his mother's patient guidance and care. After her death and with the onset of adulthood, life had become meaningless: "The visions of hope and fancy are gone, /

And careful I tread now life's pathway alone / Alone, aye alone, though kind ones there be, / There are none here to love me, to love me like thee."[111] Other writers longed for the "sunny days of boyhood," when they basked in the warmth of maternal love.[112]

Such reveries often contrasted childhood innocence to the sobering realities of adult life. In "Our Boy-Hood Days," a Masonic writer said he could recall no more joyous time in his life than childhood, yet he maintained that his happiness had been naive, his joy due to ignorance of "the real evils of the world." Childhood bliss had been a delusion: "In our childishness we innocently believed the most unreasonable stories, and unphilosophical narratives." With time, he noted, he began to perceive that beyond the home deception and hypocrisy prevailed.[113]

Transition to adulthood required that young men be freed of the emotional attachments and delusions of childhood and reconciled to the stern realities of the adult world. The attraction of the innocence of childhood and the unqualified love of one's mother was powerful, but if they did not become clergymen or teachers—occupations which paid little and carried a feminine stigma—men had little choice but to break away from the emotional moorings of childhood. Fraternal ritual, through decades of revision, evolved in response to this need. Nonetheless, to succeed in eradicating the emotional and ideological attachments of men to their mothers, the orders would first have to appropriate some of the tasks formerly associated with maternal nurture.

Members invariably referred to their orders with feminine pronouns and metaphors. This in itself is unexceptional; what is more significant was the extent to which fraternal members elaborated upon the simile of lodge as mother. One orator, employing language that would have been unthinkable to post-Freudian generations, described Masonry as "a divinity whose alluring graces beckon men to the grotto, where she shrouds herself in symbols to be seen by eyes, and understood by hearts." He continued, "Her robe is the mantle with which we clothe ourselves. But alas! too frequently we imagine that in thus possessing her vesture we embrace herself." The Mason's task was to "penetrate" the superficial meanings of the rituals.[114]

Fraternal scholars and authors of rituals often described the order as a "mother" and initiation as a form of rebirth. The metaphors of R. S. Dement, a fraternal orator, were by no means exceptional. Great and humble men alike, he observed, have been "cradled in [Freemasonry's] lap, have nursed at the fountain of her wisdom, have listened to her sweet songs of love, her gentle admonitions, her prayers." Freemasonry's influence upon men, consequently, was incalculable:

As well to seek to measure the influence of mothers—the mothers!—
What a world comes to us with this thought! I have sometimes felt that,
in the Hadean shades that lie between us and the eternal life, there
is a separate abode, or resting place, for the mother-souls; and that,
together, they become as one—a force of the universe, from whence
those silent chidings, gentle admonitions come, and soft, sweet breath-
ings of fond love that seem to inspire us ever and only to the good.

Dement concluded that the Mason found

no resemblance so close to this influence as that he finds in the genius
and spirit of Freemasonry. She is our mother. Her soft sweet voice
breathes only words of love; she chides us, yet, with gentle hand laid
softly on our hearts. But, oh, the gentle hand rests heaviest when we
have sinned. She speaks her admonitions lovingly, but how they burn
in after years, when we have lived unmindful of them.[115]

The rituals affirmed that, although woman gave birth to man's body, initiation gave birth to his soul, surrounding him with brothers who would
lavish on him the "utmost affection and kindness." Sometimes, as in the Red
Men's Adoption degree, the initiate's entry into a new family was explicitly
presented. All fraternal orders, however, appropriated the language of family
relations: members were brothers; officers, fathers; and initiates, sons.

Once reborn into his fraternal family the initiate reexperienced the stages
of childhood through the successive degrees. Masonic theorists pointed out
that the Blue Lodge degrees, beginning with Entered Apprentice and concluding with Master Mason, recapitulated the traditional maturational stages
of men. Likewise, Pythians noted that the degree of Page represented the
age of seven, when the child was expected to master household duties and
learn about religion. In the degree of Esquire, which encompassed the remainder of the initiate's "nonage," he prepared for manhood, the degree of
Knight. The Order of the Knights of Honor devised an even less subtle developmental sequence; its three degrees were simply called "Infancy, Youth,
and Manhood."[116]

Unlike evangelical mothers, who sought to insulate young men from the
world beyond the home for as long as possible, fraternal ritual insisted that
men must come to terms with the unpleasant realities of life. In the highest degree (Royal Purple) of Odd Fellowship, the Junior Warden recounted
the initiate's many trials in preceding degrees, concluding, "He now hopes
to find rest among the Patriarchs." The Senior Warden immediately shattered this Bushnellian notion of a gradual and conflict-free transition to
adulthood: "Rest? Knows he not there is no rest but one? Once [a man is]

launched on life's broad wilderness, thenceforth all is turmoil even from the cradle to the grave." At this point the Senior Warden seemed to lose the thread of his argument and ruminated about the pleasures of childhood, emphasizing the "careless hours" boys spent in the "beguiling" warmth of maternal affection.

If boyhood was so pleasant, one might ask, how could life's turmoil be said to commence "even from the cradle?" In his commentary on this degree, Grosh explained that a boy is not satisfied with "the sunshine of a mother's caress," for he longs to become a man. For all its security and emotional sustenance, maternal nurture stood in the way of masculine adulthood. Grosh applauded a young man's "laudable ambition" to enter into the struggle and conflict of adult manhood. But ambition would not suffice; he also required the assistance of patriarchs whose experience and powers would further his passage through this "mimic journey of life." [117]

All rituals established a hierarchy among members, and in this sense many of the simple Masonic ceremonies of the late 1700s hinted at a paternal role for Worshipful Masters or Senior Wardens. The catechisms of the early rituals of Odd Fellowship informed members that they were to regard officers "as our parents and guardians" who presided over the lodge as "the head of a family." [118] The crucial revision of 1845 transformed this simile into a dramatic exploration of the ties between father and son. [119] Initiates could not acquire manhood and gain entry into the masculine family of the lodge until they had won the approval of patriarchs.

The magic of the rituals always succeeded in dissipating the surrogate fathers' contempt or fury toward the candidate. This was particularly clear in the Adoption degree, where the hostility of the tomahawk-wielding Sachem became transmuted into affection as he eventually embraced the initiate ("his child") and welcomed him into "our bosom." The double emotional function of the ritual produced a confusing combination of roles: To cease being a squaw the initiate became a man; yet to resolve anxieties over the adult male role, he regressed to the status of a child.

The importance of father-son issues was further confirmed by the development of the Patriarchal degree, part of the Encampment (higher-degree) branch of Odd Fellowship. The success of the Initiatory degree (1845) had prompted leaders of the Encampment to rewrite their self-described "very crude and imperfect" rituals. [120] The revised Patriarchal degree, completed by the end of 1845, was an instant success. In 1887 elderly Odd Fellows recalled that the revision was "vastly superior to its predecessor." Members who had been bored with lower degrees "found their desire fully satisfied" by the Patriarchal degree. [121]

The revised ritual was similar to the Adoption degree and the Initiatory degree of Odd Fellowship in that it featured a young man's quest for the approval of surrogate fathers. The initiate, wearing sandals and a shepherd's robe and carrying a crook, traveled across a desert to meet the patriarchs of the Old Testament. As he approached a tent he was seized, bound, and taken to the camp of the patriarchs, who removed his fetters and blindfolds, offered him food and drink, and related to him their history. A High Priest finally instructed the initiate to kneel. Then he intoned: "You have toiled through the ways of doubt and error to the bosom of our Patriarchal family."

The relationship between surrogate fathers and sons was expanded in an important later revision of this ritual (1880).[122] The beginning of the rite was not much changed, but after the initiate (now called a "notiviate Patriarch") had been accepted into the family of patriarchs, he was specifically identified as Isaac, the son of Abraham. Before he could "enter upon his course of life" he was instructed to request his father's blessing. Again blindfolded, he traveled across the wilderness of Paran to Beersheba, encountering along the way the usual obstacles. Finally he reached Abraham, who exclaimed, "You give me great joy, my son." Father and son journeyed to Mount Moriah to make a sacrifice to God. After they had erected an altar, the conductor of the ceremony, speaking for Isaac, asked what the sacrifice would be. Abraham at first hesitated, then answered: "My son, Isaac, be not surprised; it is God's order that you shall be the sacrifice. The angel of the Lord shall gather and keep your ashes sacred . . . as a memorial of your submissive obedience, and of my faith in God." The candidate was placed upon the altar, and torches readied to ignite the wood. (In some lodges, the sacrifice was instead accomplished with a knife; see the illustration at the beginning of this chapter.) The Twenty-third Psalm was read. Just as Abraham commanded that the torch be applied, a muffled gong sounded, whereupon Abraham announced that God had determined that Isaac should not be sacrificed but instead should become an equal member of the family of patriarchs. Father and son were now brothers.

This recension took considerable liberties with the Old Testament. In the Book of Genesis Isaac never lived apart from his father. The son who was cast into the wilderness of Paran was Ishmael, Abraham's son by Hagar. The ritualists of the Odd Fellows thus fused the story of Ishmael's enforced separation to that of Abraham's sacrifice of Isaac. The convergence of the two themes was important: The removal of Isaac from his father made it possible for the ritual to explore the issue of disrupted father-son ties, and the episode in which Abraham offered Isaac as a sacrifice brought the issue of father-son antagonism into clear relief. The ritual resolved these psychological tensions by reassuring the initiate that his father, though distant and imposing, had always loved him. The ritual's central theme was filial obedience: Isaac's duty to obey his father and Abraham's duty to obey God. Thus Abraham's willingness to do violence to his son was not an indication of antagonism, but of paternal duty.[123] So it was with their own distant fathers, whose absence stemmed not from anger or hostility, but from a deeply felt sense of duty to support the family.

The ritualists were probably not consciously aware of the psychological needs of American men, but they did understand that certain dramatic themes could "give satisfaction" or "fully gratify" the desires of members. Creating an emotionally compelling ritual was a process of trial and error, and experience had shown that certain themes were more likely to succeed than others. Rituals such as the Patriarchal degree acted out anxieties that young middle-class men may have felt about their fathers and about the unfathomable emotional distance they had to travel to acquire the attributes of manhood. By emphasizing a surrogate father's benevolence and love, the ritual made it easier to identify with the male role; and by accepting the initiate into the family of patriarchs, the ritual made it possible to approach manhood with greater self-assurance.

Its emotional significance to the candidate aside, a successful ritual served the needs of members who witnessed or assisted in initiations. Why should mature or elderly members expend so much time and effort in performing rituals whose chief psychological benefit was to the young? Older members surely must have enjoyed the symbolic veneration accorded patriarchs, worshipful masters, and sachems. It is also possible that they found in these rituals a replacement for emotional ties to their own children: the gender bifurcation of middle-class life had produced fathers without attentive children as well as children without effective fathers.

Much as the rituals encouraged august father figures to accept callow initiates, they also urged young men to better understand their elders. In a slight addition to the Initiatory degree in 1880, the Noble Grand, who early in the ceremony had expressed anger at the initiate, explained that he would like to become better acquainted with this new friend. He even apologized for his initial hostility, pointing out, "Men are not always to be taken for what they appear. Some may have a rough and unseemly exterior, but a good, true heart within." Having learned to control their emotions and to affect a "manly" deportment, Victorian fathers may have been incapable of articulating affection to their own sons. The ritual could literally give voice to sentiments that would otherwise remain unexpressed. Its dramaturgical devices enabled elderly sachems and patriarchs to adopt and to love as their own the younger brethren of the order, who were in turn assured of paternal approval and affection.

❖

Fraternal ritual succeeded when the participant allowed his imagination to transform the figure of a patriarch into a representation of his own father, or the "rugged road" into a symbol for the travails of life. Those with lively enough imaginations could experience something like an initiation without ever becoming a lodge member. During the nineteenth century, fiction provided for boys and men another kind of encounter with the initiatory motifs of fraternal ritual.

The enormously successful stories of Horatio Alger articulated many of the emotional dynamics presented in these ceremonies. Alger's orphans or fatherless boys were, like the fraternal initiate, set adrift in a hostile big city or in the Wild West. During their initiatory experiences they encountered and ultimately defeated an evil adult male (often a cruel and greedy relative; at other times, the local squire, who held the mortgage to the homestead). As a result of the courage he showed, the hero was finally brought under the care of a kind and virtuous benefactor, usually a merchant or stockbroker.[124] The "riches" he thereby acquired were of a personal rather than material nature.

The plot of Mark Twain's *Tom Sawyer* (1875) concerns Tom's efforts to escape from Aunt Polly, an overly diligent surrogate mother who suffocates him with attention. His co-conspirator in the flight from domesticated civilization is Huckleberry Finn, the motherless son of the town drunkard. While lost in a cave, Tom confronts murderers, saves his schoolmate Becky, and, as a result of his heroism, is virtually adopted by Judge Thatcher, Becky's father (and, surely, his eventual father-in-law). Huck Finn is placed in the care of Widow Douglas. This regression to feminine nurture, as Huck well knows, cannot succeed: "The widder's good to me, and friendly, but I can't stand them ways." Tom, having experienced a metaphorical initiation, proposes to stage an actual one—complete with coffins, blood, and horrible oaths. Huck is delighted. With this the story ends.

Lew Wallace's *Ben-Hur: A Tale of the Christ* (1880), an extremely popular novel, is also the story of a boy's initiatory passage to manhood. The central conflict is between Messala, the overbearing and aggressive Roman ruler, and Judah, the sensitive Jewish hero. In their first confrontation Messala dismisses Judah: "You are a boy; I am a man." Judah immediately returns to his mother, asking, "What am I to be?" She responds, "You are to be my hero." He kisses her and explains that it is time to leave: "Thus far my life has belonged to you. How gentle, how sweet, your control has been! I wish it could last forever. But that may not be. It is the Lord's will that I shall one day become owner of myself." The maternal ties are severed and the initiatory journey commences when Judah is sent to the galleys. After a series of ordeals, he defeats Messala in a chariot race. He is then adopted by surrogate fathers: a Roman consul whom he had saved from drowning and a wealthy sheik. It is little wonder that a fraternal order (the Tribe of Ben-Hur, mentioned above) devised a ritual based on this story.

Ben-Hur anticipated Stephen Crane's *The Red Badge of Courage* (1894), which offers a similar initiatory sequence. Henry Fleming, raised solely by his mother, enlists in the army against her wishes. He joins the "battle brotherhood"—a "mysterious fraternity"—and at first is proven a coward, much as fraternal initiates were shown to be unworthy. He then wanders through a forest strewn with corpses and stumbles upon a decaying body. He endures a transformational "torture" in the form of a head wound. The dark anthropomorphized wonders of Nature (streams have a "sorrowful blackness," campfires a "hostile gleam") and the pervasive religious imagery transform war into an almost primitive rite which, by releasing his elemental fears and passions, enables Fleming to attain manhood.

Initiation is an enduring theme in literature, and almost always the initiatory pilgrimage is undertaken by men. This fact accords with Nancy Chodorow's hypothesis that the psychological development of males is different from that of females in virtually all societies. As children are reared primarily by women, boys must seek out their own path to masculine identification, while girls need only, in a less disruptive process, become like their mothers. The process of disengagement from the mother is common to varying degrees in all societies; thus boys at all times identify with initiatory literature because it provides guidance for their own emotional path to adulthood. The psychological impulse that gives rise to initiation is a human constant: Nineteenth-century fraternal ritual and a specialized literature for men developed such powerful initiatory themes because Victorian society exacerbated in this country a nearly universal distinction in adult gender roles.

❖

Fraternal officials insisted that members undergo the entire sequence of initiations provided by their order. In every major order at least one ritual developed each of the following themes: (1) an initiate at the outset of his task was portrayed as immature or unmasculine, (2) he overcame obstacles as he embarked on a difficult journey through the stages of childhood and adolescence, (3) this journey or ordeal reached a climax when he was killed (or nearly killed) by angry father figures, (4) he was reborn as a man into a new family of approving brethren and patriarchs. In this way the emotional

Deficiency of Initiate	Journey or Ordeal	Shock or Death	Rebirth
RELIGIOUS JOURNEY			
innately sinful →	need of conversion →	wrenching conversion →	acceptance of religion of patriarchs
EMOTIONAL JOURNEY			
innately unmasculine or effeminate →	recapitulation of alternative childhood →	effacement of feminized childhood →	reconciliation with fathers

orientations instilled by maternal nurture would give way to the sterner lessons of ancient patriarchs, venerable kings, or savage chieftains.[125]

In previous chapters I analyzed fraternal ritual as an implicit though coherent theology, arguing that, in contrast to a "feminized Protestantism," the rituals emphasized man's inherent deficiencies, offered the transformatory magic of a sudden and emotional conversion, and evoked an impersonal and foreboding deity. The thesis applies as well to the rite described in this chapter, the Adoption degree (1868), which demonstrated that the life the candidate had led was wrong, a consequence of inherent character failings (an analogue for innate sinfulness). He was subjected to an emotional ordeal much like a conversion experience, and after nearly facing death was reborn into a new family and into a new sense of religious understanding. Finally, he was reconciled to the fathers of the tribe. They introduced him to the saving mysteries of a pantheistic Great Spirit whose power was "displayed in the splendor of the sun, the glories of the night, the foliage of the forest."

This developmental path to religious meaning was identical in structure to the emotional quest for masculine adulthood (see table above): After (1) the initiate was shown to be innately sinful; he (2) commenced a difficult pilgrimage for religious truth; which (3) culminated, through a wrenching conversion experience, in his death; and thus (4) led him to an understanding of a distant God.

The initiate's partial nakedness simultaneously depicted his sinfulness and his immaturity; his acquisition of sacred aprons and patriarchal robes confirmed both his newfound religious comprehension and his acceptance by the men of the order. Skulls and skeletons were evidence against liberal beliefs about the salutary meaning of death at the same time as they were used to effect the initiate's death to feminine identifications. Finally, the light with which all fraternal rituals culminated symbolized the acquisition of religious truth as well as the moment of male rebirth. The highly condensed symbolic meanings of the rituals suggest that the entire sequence carried two different but closely related sets of meanings.

Turner observed that ritual symbols could express many ideas at once; this is evident in fraternal ritual. But more important than the rituals' use of symbols with multiple meanings was their ability to carry two different but coherent symbolic messages simultaneously. Perhaps it could not be otherwise, for middle-class women gave their children liberal religious truths joined to maternal nurture. Boys and young men reared in such an environment could not confidently enter the world of manhood until they had broken with both.

CHAPTER V

Secrets

From Albert Pike,
*Morals and Dogma of the Ancient and Accepted
Scottish Rite of Freemasonry*
(Charleston, S.C.: Supreme Council of the A. A. S. R., 1871?)

In the west the jagged mountains had just pierced the sun, casting long shadows upon the haze that had settled in the valley below. The Commander thought of an initiate passing through Jachin and Boaz at the lodge in Memphis, or perhaps in New Orleans, where the twin columns nearly replicated those of the Parthenon. In the scene he imagined, the initiate's unruly beard contrasted with the austere angularity of his black tunic edged with a white collar. A complicated geometric figure was at the center of his white apron.

The Commander smoothed the handful of pages he had copied years before: Inside a nonagon—representing an encampment—was a septagon, and inside that a pentagon, then a square, a triangle, a circle, and a point. Upon the sides of the pentagon was the nonsensical inscription T E N G U. He dipped his quill into the inkpot and wrote steadily:

> The camp, which is so prominent a feature in this degree, must originally have had a meaning, for it cannot be supposed that a man of intellect ever seriously occupied himself with making a beautiful figure on paper, arranging it as a camp and adopting arbitrary letters and names without any deeper meaning than that which you have thus far discovered. It is an elaborate, complicated and intricate symbol. Its meaning was no doubt originally explained, only orally, and that alone would be reason and cause sufficient why that meaning should in time be lost. For that cause alone has cost Masonry the true meaning of many, even most of its simpler symbols and substituted, strained, unnatural and common place interpretations in their place.

Haze had nearly filled the valley, and the pale tracery of the moon appeared above the mountains to the southeast. He blotted the page, leaned back against the rough wood slats, and closed his eyes.

The initiate was now to receive the ultimate secrets of Freemasonry. The Captain gave him two daggers, fastened a rope around his waist, knocked upon the door several times, and led him into the Temple.

> "Who is this that comes as if reluctantly, or as a criminal, into this holy sanctuary?"

> "It is a lover of wisdom, and an apostle of liberty, equality and fraternity. . . . He seeks to unite with those who labor for the emancipation of mankind."

"What does he desire?"

"To be admitted a Prince of this Grand Consistory, that he may the more effectually aid in the great struggle for which Masonry is preparing, the second war against the giants, in which the liberty and happiness of humanity are at stake."

The cicadas had grown silent. Darkness had engulfed the valley. The fires of his distant neighbors filtered through the haze, and he noticed a new campfire. He stroked his beard and sipped some brandy. The soldiers would be upon him soon. The apostle of universal justice had become a fugitive; he did not even know which uniforms his pursuers would be wearing.

"What means does he possess?"

"He has courage and pure intentions."

"Are they enough?"

"No! He needs further instruction to have the veil finally removed, that has so long interposed between him and the true Masonic light; to attain the summit of the mountain up whose slopes he commenced to toil as an Entered Apprentice."

Men were by nature selfish, stupid and cruel, primed to slaughter each other in senseless wars, the commander reminded himself. Had Christ not been crucified by those he meant to serve? Few could comprehend the deeper meanings of life, and even they must be carefully prepared.

"Why come you hither with weapons unfit for a judge, emblems of rude violence? For what purpose do you bring two daggers?"

"I was told that one was intended to punish perjury and the other to protect innocence."

"And you were also told that perjury was no longer punished by the dagger, and that innocence was now protected otherwise than by the poniard. Give those weapons to our brother. They suit a Prince of the Royal Secret no better than they suit a judge. In lieu of the weapons you have given up, receive this sword of a Knight and Prince of Masonry."

The Commander closed the leather-bound manuscript and turned the key. The hour had come to leave, and to resume the campaign without end against the foes of human progress, for life was but a rehearsal for the greater mysteries.

"Give your sword to the brother. A sword is a common weapon, worn alike by oppressors and their victims. Before we return yours, it and yourself must be purified."

He gathered the papers from his desk and tossed them into a trunk; then he hurried through the stacks of books, occasionally tossing one towards a pile near the door.

"My brother, we have dipped your right hand and your sword into the water to purify them; for water was an emblem of purity, both of body and soul, among all our Ancient and Oriental Masters. And we now warn you, that many eyes will hereafter be upon you."

Soon the soldiers would be rushing up the hill, their madness spurred by greed for gold and a hatred of genius. "How shall I make men pure and holy?" Zoroaster had wondered.

"In your way stands an enemy that cannot be avoided, but must be met and overcome. To succeed in that contest, you need to be still further purified, by fire and incense."

He lumbered out to the wagon and dumped a final armload of books. Carefully he harnessed the oxen and strained to lift himself onto the seat.

"Rise, Royal Princes! Present swords. Salute!"

As he made his way along the rough trails of the Ouachitas, a light brightened the eastern sky, illuminating the myriad demons who were scurrying away from his blazing cabin.

"Depart now my brother on your last campaign and we will offer up our prayers for your success."

He snapped the reins and his laugh resonated throughout the wilderness.[1]

❖ THE SUBLIME PRINCE ❖

Albert Pike, the Sovereign Grand Commander of the Ancient and Accepted Scottish Rite, barely managed to escape from the Union soldiers who pursued him in 1864 to a remote region of the Ozarks known as Greasy Cove. Hoping to find his rumored stash of gold, they tore his cabin apart, threw his books onto the lawn, and set the building afire. But Pike had already taken his most valuable possession, the magnum opus of the Scottish

Rite, his six-hundred-page draft of the twenty-nine higher-degree rituals. He also took the early chapters of his *Morals and Dogma of Freemasonry*, an 861-page exegesis of his rituals. These works were the crowning achievements of fraternal ritualism.

For well over a hundred years Masonic scholars have debated the origins of the Scottish Rite, variously attributing it to Frederick the Great, to French free-thinkers, and to even more exotic sources. (Scotland, oddly, is rarely suggested.) They have produced various and contradictory manuscripts of uncertain provenance to prove their claims.[2] All agree, however, that in America Pike was the "Second Creator" and "Moses" of the rite, the "master genius" of Freemasonry.[3]

When Pike was first initiated into the Scottish Rite in 1853, Supreme Commander Albert Mackey simply read aloud all the degrees in a single evening.[4] The ceremonies then were "mostly skeletons," containing little more than descriptions of the lodge, titles, uniforms, oaths, and catechisms. "The truth is that the Rite was nothing, and the Rituals almost nought, for the most part a lot of worthless trash," Pike explained. His assessment is shared by Masonic historians.[5] The Supreme Council in Charleston appointed Pike to a five-man committee on revision. It never met, and Pike, working alone, copied the existing fragments and plunged into the study of ancient and oriental mysteries.[6] By the fall of 1855 he completed the twenty-first through the thirtieth degrees. He retained the earlier signs and passwords but superimposed upon them motifs and symbolic themes from ancient ceremonies. He then began to rewrite the remaining degrees. By early 1857 he had completed preliminary drafts of all the rituals.

Although Mackey was delighted with Pike's work, another member of the Supreme Council had submitted alternative revisions and the council declined to endorse either effort. The issue was still unresolved in 1859 when Mackey resigned to allow Pike to become Grand Commander. In 1860 Pike packed the Supreme Council with supporters, including John Breckinridge, Vice-President of the United States, and pressed for approval of a uniform ritual, but the commencement of the Civil War brought delays. It was not until 1863 that Pike was able to resume work on his rituals, which were approved shortly thereafter.[7]

They were immediately successful. The *Masonic Review* reported in April 1865 that the dormant Scottish Rite had suddenly been "reinvigorated from some hidden source." The editor conceded he had had doubts about yet another form of Masonry, but was won over by its "beautifully impressive ceremonies."[8] From fewer than 1,000 members in the 1850s, the Rite now grew rapidly; it numbered 125,000 by the end of the century, including some 25,000 thirty-second-degree Masons.[9] Degree writers for hundreds of orders combed through Pike's *Morals and Dogma* hoping to find fresh ritualistic motifs or bibliographical sources; the Scottish Rite had become the standard for ritualistic excellence.

Few lodges could perform more than a handful of the twenty-nine pageants of the Rite. Many lodges continued merely to read most of the degrees aloud, conserving their dramatic resources for the most popular ceremonies, particularly the thirty-second degree—called the Sublime Prince of the Royal Secret.[10]

An understanding of the Masonic pilgrimage requires an examination of its ultimate destination and of the man who charted the journey to the summit of the mountain.

❖

Albert Pike was born in 1809 near Boston, Massachusetts. He was the son of Benjamin Pike, an irreverent cobbler who drank too much and scandalized the community, and Sarah Andrews, an intensely pious woman who was determined that her only son eschew his father's example. Every day she read the Bible to the boy and made plans for him to enter the ministry.

To remove him from his father's influence, Sarah Pike sent her son to live in Framingham with an uncle who agreed to tutor him for Harvard. Young Pike had a prodigious memory. He could digest large volumes and recall their contents at will; he learned Hebrew, Latin, and Greek almost effortlessly. Eight months after his arrival in Framingham he passed the entrance examination at Harvard with exceptionally high marks. He then took a teaching post to pay for his tuition and studied the classics in the evening. He passed the junior exam easily, but when the university insisted that he pay tuition for freshman and sophomore years as well, he abandoned hope of obtaining a formal education.[11]

Pike's frustration with Harvard fueled his resentment of his mother, and his rebellion against her training became increasingly pronounced. He drank too much wine, gave wild parties, and seduced several young women. His mother, though appalled, was powerless to stop him. He abandoned the classics and wrote poems in the style of Byron and Shelley, many of which were published in local newspapers and literary magazines. When he could be heard through an open window playing the violin one Sunday morning, the school board charged him with impiety; he refused to apologize and was dismissed.

Pike was eager to break with straitlaced New England, but he had no clear idea of what to do with his life until he read Timothy Flint's *Francis Berrian, or The Mexican Patriot* (1826), a tale of adventure, war, and romance in the frontier West. It is not hard to see why Pike found the book appealing.

The hero, like Pike, had been born near Boston in Puritan surroundings. At the outset Berrian adhered to his Christian training, studied the classics, and attended Harvard. But after graduation he rejected his parents' urging that he become a minister, for he longed to share in the unconstrained life of the noble savage. He set out for the West, leaving his mother in tears.

In March 1831, using savings he had earlier earmarked for Harvard, Pike left for New Mexico. His mother wept, too, and Pike's adventures in the West nearly exceeded those of his fictional hero. His wagon train was caught in a snowstorm and he nearly froze to death. He joined a beaver trapping expedition that was attacked by Indians. Pike and the trappers fled into the desert and lost their way. Their horses died and the men went without water for days.

In Byronic fashion Pike exulted in these hardships. In the midst of each crisis he pulled out his notebooks and unburdened his soul through poetry. "Dash the waves, bold Heart, that madly roll / Across thy path!" he wrote.[12] In the end, however, Pike's attempt to relive Berrian's adventures fell short. Having exhausted his savings, he was forced to teach school at Fort Smith, Arkansas, receiving payment in pigs. Subsequently he went on to edit a newspaper and study law. He began to practice in Little Rock in 1834 and in the same year married Ann Hamilton, whose money enabled him to buy the newspaper for which he worked. He became active in politics and in 1846 led a group of volunteers against the Mexicans in the battle of Buena Vista. During the 1850s Pike successfully represented Indian tribes in law-suits against the government, collecting $192,000 in gold as his fee. He built a mansion in Little Rock and became renowned for his lavish parties.

Pike's ties to the Indians led to the events that transformed his life—and American Freemasonry. At the outbreak of the Civil War the Confederacy named him commissioner of Indian affairs and brigadier general in command of Indian regiments. Over his strenuous objections, in early March 1862 his units took part in the battle at Pea Ridge, Arkansas. During the engagement the Indians mutilated some of the Union dead, an infamy that haunted Pike for the rest of his life. The *Chicago Tribune* and the *New York Tribune* denounced him; on March 15, 1862, the *Boston Evening Transcript* called its native son "the meanest, the most rascally, the most malevolent of the rebels. It is not presumed that a more venomous reptile than Albert Pike ever crawled the face of the earth."[13]

Pike was beset with even more pressing problems. After Pea Ridge his forces, white and Indian, were ordered to other commands. Claiming that his command was independent from the others, Pike ignored or circumvented these instructions. On July 31, 1862, confronted with a direct order to release his units, he resigned his command and published an open letter to the Indians indicting his superiors for ignoring treaty obligations. Jefferson Davis refused to accept the resignation and hinted that Pike might be charged with treason. In October Davis sent some two hundred soldiers to arrest him; in November, as the Confederate position in the west collapsed, they released him.

Pike's life was in ruins. He faced charges of inciting the Indians to revolt, and his property was confiscated by Union officers. He had squandered his fortune, and his marriage had disintegrated. Worried that he would be arrested and perhaps executed by the fleeing Confederate forces or murdered by Union soldiers intent on avenging the Pea Ridge atrocities, he returned to his home in Little Rock only long enough to gather up his books. Then he fled to the hills of Arkansas.

At Greasy Cove he struggled to come to terms with what he felt was the injustice of recent events. Before the Pea Ridge battle, he had formally objected to using Indians in an offensive campaign. His written apology for the crimes to the Union commander, never mentioned in the press, was the source for public knowledge of the atrocities. His insistence that the Confederacy adhere to the treaties was a matter of simple justice, yet this courageous defense of principle was now widely perceived as treason. This was, at least in his mind, an injustice of heroic proportions. Pike sought to refract his experiences through the wisdom of the ancients. To do so, he scoured classic religious texts, translating from Latin and German sources the *Zend-Avesta* and the Indian Vedas and studying the Cabala and the writings of the Gnostics.[14]

Gradually he came to believe the teaching "Whomsoever God loveth, him He chasteneth." Adversity was not an expression of evil, but an affirmation of the complexity of God's vision. The light of truth could best be perceived against a dark background. For those capable of accepting its discordant messages, life gained meaning through a reconciliation of extremes.

Fraternal ritual, Pike now realized, was philosophically unsound. By depicting man's triumph over Hiram's assassins, over injustice and ignorance, even over death itself, it inflated man's sense of his powers. Whereas the ancient Greeks recognized the futility of the contest between the gods and man, fraternal ritual presumed man's ultimate triumph. Such a notion, he understood from his own experiences, was a delusion.

Pike followed Zoroaster in believing that truth emerged from opposition and conflict. Men should strive not to efface the contradictions of life, but to internalize them. Ritual, similarly, should teach purity and contemplation as well as aggression and heroism.[15]

For Pike, the essential contradictions of life were associated with gender. Torn by the extremes represented by his irreverent father and pious mother, Pike initially pursued a quest for manly assertion, reflected in frontier adventures, the pursuit of wealth and military glory, and gastronomic and sexual excesses.[16] Yet throughout his life he remained drawn to his mother. After his father died in 1833 he wrote "Monotone," a poem addressed to his mother:

> Thinkest of me, and weepest for thy son,
> Toiling afar with the wild waves of life,
> Stricken with tempest. Shall I ever steer
> Homeward my shattered bark, and once more hear
> Thy kind, calm tones of love, and feel thine eye
> Beaming with deep affection, and the high
> And holy spirit of a mother's love?[17]

His most recent biographer even viewed Pike's interest in Oriental religions as a transmutation of his mother's wish that he become a minister.[18]

After the disaster at Pea Ridge, Pike renounced the notion of masculine assertion caricatured in frontier tales. True manliness, he believed, was corrupted by greed and selfishness and the delusion that war brings glory. Men must learn to temper aggression with submission, and human passion with religious commitment. Pike no longer sought to efface the contradictions inherent in life, and in his own nature. He was now prepared to complete the Scottish Rite. Just as he had acquired understanding only late in life, the ultimate meaning of fraternal ritual would appear in the final, thirty-second, degree of Freemasonry.

The existing thirty-second degree, Pike had concluded, was diffuse and incomplete. For it, the lodge decorations included a skull and crossbones and a skeleton. Another death's head and crossbones rested on a black altar along with a sword and a balance. The Grand Sovereign Commander, bearing sword and shield, represented Frederick of Prussia.[19] In his rite Pike retained the decorations and the geometric figure but excised mention of Frederick. The candidate was escorted around the lodge while the Commander discussed lower degrees. From this vantage point they took on new meanings; the fourteenth, for instance, preached that "God is no longer to be feared, but to be loved with all the heart, mind and strength," and the eighteenth taught that "the new law of love" was to prevail.

At the point in his speech when the Commander reached the thirty-second degree, the blindfolded initiate, who had been given two daggers at the outset, arrived at the altar. The Commander upbraided him for carrying weapons into a temple. These were taken away, and he was instead given a sword. A rite of purification ensued: The hands of the initiate and then his sword were dipped into a font of water and cleansed with a white cloth; later they were passed over burning coals.

The apparent source of these motifs was Homer's "Hymn to Demeter," an account of the Eleusinian mysteries of Greece. (Pike composed his own "To Demeter" in 1830 as part of the collection *Hymns to the Gods*.) The conclusion of the Masonic sequence with the rites of a female deity of renewal suggests a desire to redress the hypermasculinity of the earlier degrees.[20] Pike's ceremony eliminated the daggers—symbols of masculine aggression —and conferred upon the initiate the purity that corresponded with a gentler form of manhood.

Few men, whether in the nineteenth century or any other period, could have appreciated Pike's philosophy or understood his fascination for the strange religions of antiquity. On the other hand, many of his contemporaries understood his message concerning the intersection of gender and work tensions. Pike, in fleeing from New England and domesticity, had self-consciously pursued the independent manhood of the frontier legends; his failure enabled him to see the foolishness of his goal.

❖ THE HEAVEN SO LONGED FOR ❖

The dramatic potential of all fraternal initiations had been diminished by the initiate's necessarily simple and predictable responses. He could not be coached prior to the ceremony, for that would diminish its emotional impact. Some rituals had the conductor speak on his behalf; but insofar as the purpose of the ritual was to effect a personal transformation, this strategem was emotionally unsatisfactory and awkward.

The Royal Purple, the eighth and final degree of Odd Fellowship and perhaps the most admired non-Masonic ritual,[21] offered an ingenious solution: The conductor functioned as the initiate's alter ego. In all other degrees a candidate was shown to be unworthy or somehow deficient, but in the Royal Purple the conductor—described as a "sinful" man—carried that burden himself. He would explain that he hoped to atone for his sins by guiding pilgrims past the moral dangers to which he had succumbed early in life.

During their journey, guards repeatedly warned the pilgrim (inexplicably, he was blindfolded) not to trust the guide. The two nevertheless arrived safely at the patriarchal tent, and the initiate was restored to light in the customary manner. There were no skulls or skeletons. The initiate was not handled roughly, nor did he experience a metaphorical death. The real drama centered on the guide, whose moral triumph had enabled the pilgrim to complete his own transformational journey.

On the way the pilgrim learned that the guide's sins had been of a distinctly masculine character, for, saying he spoke from experience, the guide advised against one path leading to "lust, intemperance and sensuality" and another leading to battle, "a sad display of worldly glory." A third path tempted with fame and riches, but they persisted through the "wild and dismal thickets" of masculine excess, drawn onward by soft music whose sweet notes made them long for "the eternal home." Eventually they were admitted to the tents of the patriarchs—symbols, the initiate was told, of shelter and home.[22]

The last journey of Odd Fellowship, like that of the Freemasons, contravened the messages of the previous degrees: The final abode of the Odd Fellows was a nurturing and thoroughly domesticated home, an expression of "the heaven so longed for," the conductor noted, where the initiate would find safety and repose. The pilgrim had experienced vicariously the guide's transformational journey from masculine sensuality and aggression to domesticity and morality.

The Chief's degree, the final degree of the Improved Order of Red Men, similarly renounced the message of the preceding degrees. A Prophet surveyed a darkened lodge and spoke of the Great Spirit who, angered by the Indians' penchant for violence, had deprived them of fire and light. He took down the skeleton and prayed to the Great Spirit to "inspire our brother's heart with truth, sincerity, benevolence and charity—the sacred mystery of every Red Man's love." The Senior Sagamore took a tomahawk and buried "this sanguinary weapon deep in the earth's cold bosom." No more would Red Men torture their captives or inflict on them the cruel trials of adoption. Henceforth the warrior's mission would be one of peace and good will.

Each Red Man took a blazing stick from the fire and carried it to the Prophet, who united them into a single flame. This emblem of purification consumed "the sordid and grosser passions of our nature" and dispelled "the darkness and gloom from our midst." The new chief then smoked the pipe of peace and put on a white headdress, whose "virgin whiteness" was to remind the initiate that purity and innocence were among the most graceful ornaments that could adorn the character of a Chief.

As the fraternal pilgrimage approached its final destination it seemingly returned to its place of origin. Why, if the purpose of the ritual was to eradicate feminine identifications, did the final ceremonies "purify" the initiate of masculine passions and aggressions, deliver him to home and domesticity, and demand that he surrender the manly implements of war? These questions were never addressed explicitly.

By the 1870s and 1880s many of the younger members urged that the ritual sequences conclude with a rousing affirmation of masculinity, much as Whiting's model would have predicted. In 1876 James Laird of the Grand Lodge of Nebraska endorsed a Masonic war against "destructive effeminacy," saying, "What Masons want, what the world wants, is not sympathy, not cooperation, not reform, not redemption, but strength." [23]

These calls for a more muscular and aggressive ritual culminated in the demand for quasi-martial uniformed degrees with marching displays and military drills.[24] In 1898 Henry Stillson, the official historian of the Odd Fellows, explained that the enthusiasm for uniformed degrees was particularly strong among the sons of Civil War veterans.[25] Having been denied the experience of war, they believed that they could recreate it for themselves through ritual.

Governing lodges initially resisted proposals for uniformed degrees, fearing they would draw members from existing branches. After the Grand Lodge of the Odd Fellows opposed a measure to create a martial degree, disgruntled members wrote their own ritual and established the Patriarchal Circle, an independent quasi-military order. Alarmed by the exodus of young men into the Circle, the Grand Lodge of the Odd Fellows in 1882 agreed to "furnish what the boys wanted." It created a uniformed degree, the Patriarchs Militant, for which all Royal Purple Odd Fellows were eligible. The other major orders followed suit.[26]

The ritual of the Patriarchs Militant was typical of the uniformed degrees. The initiate represented a member of the House of Abram, an Old Testament patriarch, who sought to raise an army of kinfolk to save Lot, his nephew, captured after a battle near Sodom and Gomorrah. Wearing a robe and holding a shepherd's crook, the initiate traveled to serve in Abram's army. As he approached the encampment a lieutenant commented on how war had changed Abram, who in peacetime was "thoroughly engrossed in rural pursuits, and in doing good." He continued, "But in times of war all is changed. The Patriarch then becomes thoroughly armed and equipped; he submits to and aids in enforcing the most rigid military discipline." This speech prefigured the transformation of the initiate, who would soon be accused of treachery and sent off for punishment. After he had finally proven himself, he would be raised to "soldierly manhood." [27]

Whereas the thirty-second degree—the Royal Purple—and the Chief's degree renounced the instruments of war, purified the initiate, and returned him to a restful and domesticated home, the uniformed degrees toughened him through military discipline and led him upon a journey from peace to war, from "doing good" to "soldierly manhood." Older members griped that the real Old Testament patriarchs would have been offended by the battalions of the Patriarchs Militant. Others wondered how the Red Men, who had literally buried the hatchet during the Chief's degree, could justify (let alone explain!) the swords of the Chieftain's League.[28] This tension was most clearly expressed in the debate over the admission of crippled or otherwise handicapped members.

Even prior to the Civil War, Masonic officials chided members whose "mawkish feelings of sensibility" had caused them to allow disabled men into the lodge. "If he is not a man with body free from maim, defect, or deformity," the editor of the *Masonic Mirror and Keystone* insisted, then he cannot "truly learn our mysteries and practice them."[29] This largely symbolic issue became a source of real controversy during the Civil War. The "Ancient Landmarks," the written traditions of Freemasonry, held that initiates were to be "upright in body, not deformed or dismembered, but of hale and entire limbs, as a man ought to be." But during the Civil War Masons found it difficult to exclude men who had lost an arm or a leg while performing their duties as soldiers. Grand Lodges increasingly ruled that Entered Apprentice (first-degree) or Fellowcraft (second-degree) Masons who later lost a limb could be raised to the Master Mason degree; some Grand Lodges relaxed the rules further.[30]

But during the late 1860s and the 1870s the Grand Lodges gradually drifted back "to the safe anchorage of the ancient regulations and usages." Humanitarian considerations were increasingly disregarded: Applicants who lacked so much as a thumb were to be denied admission.[31] The editor of the *Mystic Star* informed a Union veteran who had lost an arm that he could not give the proper signals or assist in raising candidates with the Master Mason grip. He added that Masons who hobbled about during initiations or who were visibly disfigured would ruin the effect of the ceremony on others.[32]

This argument was challenged by an applicant, the son of a member of a Grand Lodge, who had lost a leg during the war but had been fitted with an artificial limb and was able to perform all the requisite motions. Even his petition was rejected by the Grand Lodge of Michigan, which noted that, as in Solomon's time, it was essential that "every block should be equal and perfect in its physical proportions." The "physically perfect man" was himself a symbol of "that moral and intellectual temple, whose builder is God."[33]

The insistence upon physical perfection exceeded the guidelines of the "Ancient" Landmarks, most of which dated from the late eighteenth or early nineteenth century. Thin legalistic and ritualistic arguments barely concealed a more profound justification: The Landmarks held that initiates were to appear "as a man ought to be," and during the last third of the nineteenth century officials increasingly defined manhood in biological terms. If men without thumbs and arms were allowed into the order, it would be impossible to exclude those who lacked the most basic attribute of manhood: Even women could join.[34]

The uniformed degrees and the rejection of disabled applicants anticipated what the historian John Higham has called a "reorientation" of American culture during the 1890s, as men promoted football, took part in a fitness craze, and endorsed martial virtues and bellicose foreign policies. Until then, Higham has suggested, American men had "submitted docilely" to the restrictions on their masculinity imposed by urbanization, industrialization, and the genteel and sexually repressed mores of Victorian culture.[35] Fraternal ritual can be understood as one form of psychological solace. It is less clear why, if the purpose of the rituals was to efface feminine influence, older members opposed the hypermasculinity of the martial degrees.

❖ WHERE ALL IS DARK ❖

Even when no one was to be initiated, most orders used a special ceremony to open meetings. After the guard had tested newcomers on the passwords and recognition signals, a drill team marched around the room while members sang an opening ode, for example:

> Beyond these consecrated walls
> Where all is dark and drear,
> No danger here the heart appalls,
> For all is peaceful here.[36]

The guard then announced that the lodge was secure and that members could deliberate in safety. He reminded them that the proceedings were secret and the oaths fearful because indiscretions would unleash hostile forces against the order. "Recruits" for the Grand Army of the Republic were told that the enemy were seeking opportunities to learn its mysteries. Why the Confederacy or some foreign power would care about the arcana of the order was never explained.[37] Members nevertheless accepted that the nature of the external threat warranted transforming the lodge into a castle or sanctuary.

Although concern with security was partly a legacy of the Morgan debacle, it also reflected the members' sense that the lodge was a refuge from outside dangers. Because rituals reenacted events or legends from the past, the character of the contemporary threat was not addressed explicitly. The

Beneficial degree of the Modern Woodmen of America was an exception.
The blindfolded initiate wore ragged clothes and carried a tin cup; members
placed a placard on which was written "I am Blind" around his neck. The
conductor announced that the candidate was now standing on the streets of
a "great city in the busy world" where "bankers" and "industrialists" rudely
dismissed his appeals. "This is a cold, unsympathizing world," the conductor observed as they returned to the preparation room. Several minutes
later they reentered the temple, which was decorated to represent a forest.
The conductor informed his charge: "We are now in the primeval forest,
amid God's first temples. Here, in solitude, man adores Nature, and wor-
ships Nature's God. Here humanity has scope and breathing space. Here
the uncrowded individual grows in strength and grandeur as the sturdy oak.
Among the Neighbors of this forest we will find true brotherly love."[38]

The ritual graphically depicted a transition from the emotional detachment and rigid hierarchies of the industrial city to a bucolic domain where
the initiate could live amongst loving brothers. But the sanctuary of the
lodge was strangely foreboding; it did not offer a respite from the social
pressures of daily existence. Members might sing that the world beyond the
walls was dark and dangerous and all was peaceful within, but as they turned
off the lights, prepared the "rough and rugged road," arranged the skeleton
in the coffin, and hid in the shadows, they knew better. The significance of
the lodge did not reside in its infrequent social activities, which might have
served as diversions from the heavy burdens of work and family, but in its
rituals, which brought into the lodge many of the conflicts of the outside
world, first transforming them into metaphors and symbols so that members could more effectively confront them. And one of the most important
tensions in Victorian American life concerned gender.

❖

In the 1940s and 1950s sociologist Talcott Parsons argued that gender specialization had proven beneficial to modern societies. Men, now free to focus
on the "instrumental" tasks of society, were comforted by spouses who specialized in "expressive" and nurturant skills. The psychological pattern was
replicated as young boys were taught by their mothers to expect to receive
emotional support from women and by their fathers to expect to move into
the world of business.[39] The question of whether this division of behavioral
tasks benefits society is beyond the scope of this argument, but in Victorian
America, at least, it came at a psychic cost.

Unless one assumes that behavior in men and women is determined by
biology or by invariant gender-defined psychological processes—a position

for which there is little solid evidence—[40] one must conclude that the oppositional character of Victorian gender roles forced men and women to suppress much of their individuality. These constraints were felt most acutely during childhood, as boys and girls and young men and women were urged to internalize the limitations imposed by adult gender roles. More than one generation of adolescent girls learned to "conquer themselves" by following the disheartening if plucky example of Jo in Louisa May Alcott's *Little Women*. (1868)[41] While girls were expected to suppress egoistic drives, boys were obliged to learn how to subordinate expressive and nurturing emotions and to commit themselves to a world of work and emotional restraint. Many would stumble along this difficult path; others would lose the way entirely.

The fraternal ritualists were such men. Many began as clerks and never advanced much farther. Justus Rathbone, whose rituals were credited for the extraordinary success of the Knights of Pythias, spent his adult life as an office clerk. At forty-two, he was bankrupt. He was buried in an unmarked grave.[42] Other ritualists were ministers, an occupation that paid little and carried the stigma of effeminacy. Even the life of Horatio Alger, Jr., whose stories endlessly recapitulated fraternal motifs, read like "a case study in frustration," his biographers concluded. His anxieties about masculine adulthood were surely intensified by his homosexuality.[43] Most obvious —and dramatic—was Albert Pike's disastrous failure to realize Timothy Flint's caricature of manliness.

Ineffective as leaders and organizers, the ritualists were always elbowed aside by more aggressive and competent (that is to say, "manly") leaders. Historians of the orders, unable to conceal the failed (and brief) administrations of the founders, explained that they were "idealists" or "visionaries" whose special skill was one of perception: They could see what no one else could. And they saw the difficulties along the path to manhood with such clarity because those obstacles had loomed so large in their own lives.

These marginal men retreated from the routine patterns of work and family and immersed themselves in romantic literature, history, or mystical religions. After his disaster at Pea Ridge, Pike abandoned his wife and children for his retreat at Greasy Cove. In 1868 he returned to Washington, where he lived as a recluse in a room provided by the Scottish Rite.[44] He devoted himself to ritual until his death in 1891.

This description is strikingly similar to the historian Richard Sennett's depiction of middle-class fathers in Victorian Chicago as men who had lost their acquisitive energy and their manhood. Sennett concluded that Parsons was wrong. The isolated nuclear family with its gender specialization was prone to become overburdened with psychological pressures. Lacking the emotional support they desperately needed, fathers became passive and weak; and their sons, deprived of an effective male model, identified with their mothers. They retreated from the world, and, dispirited and fearful, locked themselves inside a private, female-dominated home.[45]

Sennett's initial premise is consistent with the argument presented here, but he erred in assuming that men made no attempt to resist this psychologically destructive process. In particular he concluded—wrongly—that middle-class Chicagoans did not join fraternal orders.[46] The ritualists in a sense served as psychological lightning rods, intensifying and channeling widely shared anxieties and then discharging them harmlessly through the medium of liminal ritual.

The rise of fraternal ritual is evidence of man's ability to create cultural forms to mediate the demands of society. It suggests that human beings do not race, lemminglike, to their psychic doom. This creativity is one of the strengths—and perhaps a chief weakness—of the species, for it gives us strength to endure, even when endurance may be a fault.

❖ THE SUBLIME SECRET ❖

At the outset of the final pilgrimage in Masonry, the Commander conducted the candidate to the west end of the lodge, where the members stood along the sides of a nonagon, symbolic of an encampment of the Masonic army. As the initiate was led around the camp he was told that he would finally learn the esoteric meaning of the order:

> You will then perhaps see that whatever in Masonry seems arbitrary or incongruous; mere empty words, and idle images and pictures, has in reality a profound meaning; that a great idea is embodied in this degree, of which its organization, and the disposition and details of the camp are the utterances, scientifically and skillfully arranged, and that in every thing it proceeds with precision and order to develop the idea, and insure the success of the noble and holy cause for which it is armed and organized.[47]

The initiate made two circuits around the nonagon, which was surrounded by flags. As he passed each flag, the Commander explained the meaning of another of the first eighteen degrees. He then invited the initiate to pass through the sides of the nonagon. The Commander displayed a drawing. Inside a nonagon were inscribed several smaller geometric figures. The initiate was told that the septagon represented the nineteenth through twenty-fifth degrees, and the pentagon the twenty-sixth through thirtieth. Within the pentagon was a triangle, then a circle and a point; these latter symbols were not explained. The initiate was advised to remember what he had just learned so that he could better understand what was to follow.

The final lecture was long and oddly inconclusive. Of the relationship between the geometrical shapes and the number of degrees, the Commander explained that little could be determined because the original meaning had been obscured by modern innovations. He also confessed that many symbols had still deeper meanings and ties to ancient mysteries, but that he had "succeeded in obtaining but a few hints" and could therefore "communicate no more to you."[48]

This degree, the ne plus ultra of Masonry, must have been a disappointment, for it raised more questions than it answered. Why had the dramatic structure of the earlier ceremonies been replaced with these benign rites of purification? Why, if the initiate was to travel to the inner chambers of the mysterious geometric figure, had the ritual come to an end when he reached the triangle? And what was the Royal Secret?

Those who were troubled by such questions surely consulted Pike's *Morals and Dogma of Freemasonry*. Four pages from the end of this lengthy tome, he explained that the Royal Secret was related to what the Sohar, the sacred Zoroastrian text, termed the "Mystery of the Balance" or the "Secret of the Universal Equilibrium." Good and Evil, Light and Darkness, indeed, all aspects of the universe emanated from a single loving god. Pike illustrated the point with an analogy to the movement of planets, which are held in orbit by gravitational and centrifugal forces. Though opposed, these forces together produce Harmony.

Pike referred the reader to an etching (dated 1613) by the Hermetic philosopher Valentinus. (See beginning of chapter.) Valentinus' figure was nearly identical to the center portion of the thirty-second drawing: A triangle was placed upon a square, both of which were contained in a circle. At the center of this device was a point and, above, a person with two heads —one male, the other female. By the male head was the sun, and by the female head the Moon. The hand on the male side held a compass; that on the female side a square.

Pike explained that the pointed compass, which was used to draw arcs connoting the heavens, symbolized things male, while the square represented the level earth—"the great, fertile, beautiful MOTHER [Pike's emphasis]—that produces . . . everything that ministers to the needs, to the comfort, and to the luxury of man."[49]

Pike added that the bisexual character of the human was reiterated by the geometric figure upon which it rested. The triangle, representing divinity, was bisected into two right triangles, symbols of sexual generation, as Pythagoras illustrated: The perpendicular stood for the male; the base, for the female. Together they produced the hypotenuse. Creative union, and ultimate truth, emerged from the conjunction of opposites. As in nature, moreover, the interaction of opposites in man was evidence not of a struggle between God and Satan, but of the necessary opposition that ultimately generated beauty, truth, and meaning.

The principle was further expressed by the symbol of the point within a circle. Entered Apprentices were told that the point represented the individual brother and the circle the boundary line of his duty to God and man. But Adepts—those initiated in the thirty-second degree—learned that this "trite and meager" interpretation concealed a greater truth. Almost universally, Pike noted, ancient and primitive peoples used the point within a circle to denote the joining of the phallus to the female receptacle.[50]

And so it was with the other symbols. The male sun emanated points of light which were received by the female moon (recall again Valentinus' figure). Jachin and Boaz, the great columns outside the Masonic hall, no longer stood for strength and establishment, as Fellowcraft Masons were told, but were seen to symbolize the phallus; and the globes upon the columns, which had been said to illustrate the universality of Masonry, in fact represented female sexuality.

Pike and Mackey noted that ancient philosophers believed that this union contained the secret of divinity. The many deities of pagan antiquity could be reduced to two different forms: the active, or male (Jupiter, Bacchus, Osiris), and the passive, or female (Juno, Venus, and Isis). But the more thoughtful philosophers realized that these generative principles existed within the same deity. Upon formulating the theorem of the right triangle, Pythagoras was supposed to have exclaimed, "Eureka, I have found it," for the perfect union of male and female established the hermaphroditic character of divinity. Similarly, Plutarch ("On Isis and Osiris") identified God as a "male and female intelligence."

Pike insisted that the vengeful and threatening images of God in the earlier degrees were not wrong, but rather were incomplete, for they neglected the female aspects of God's character. The tetragrammaton—the ineffable word denoting Deity prominent in many Masonic rituals—consisted of four Hebrew letters: yod, heh, vau, and heh. They produced the word IHOH, which made no sense in Hebrew. In the Cabala the true meanings of important mysteries were often disguised by reversing the letters; if the tetragrammaton were divided and read backwards, it would produce the word HO-HI. In Hebrew HO was the masculine pronoun; HI, the feminine. The reordered tetragrammaton was translated into English as HE-SHE, further confirmation of God's bisexual character. One of the most puzzling passages in the Old Testament now became clear: "So God created man in His own image, in the image of God created He him; male and female created He them" (Genesis 1:27). God created male and female in His own image because He/She was a union of both.[51]

Both Valentinus' figure and the thirty-second degree of Freemasonry embodied the cosmic opposition of heaven and earth, spirituality and sensuality, male and female. But, Pike noted, it was in man himself that the "strong currents of adversity" proved most contentious. The soul (symbolizing the male principle) sought to be reconciled with the "baser" female principles of sensuality and earthly desires.

In the final sentences of his analysis Pike explained that man was of a "double nature." His intellectual and moral sense was always at odds with his earthly and material nature. He attained the fruits of his destiny "only when the two natures that are in him are in just equilibrium; and his life is a success only when it too is a harmony, and beautiful, like the great Harmonies of God and the Universe. Such, my Brother, is the True Word of a Master Mason."[52] Pike's final sentence was in Latin: "*Gloria Dei Est Celare Verbum* —Amen." He offered no translation of the phrase, which means "God's glory is to conceal the word."

❖

At their first initiation lodge members were told that the secrets of the order were important to all men and that these secrets were concealed and yet revealed by the ritual symbols. Many of the oddities of the movement turned on this paradox: A mass secret society was a contradiction in terms, for several hundred thousand members could hardly be expected to keep a secret. On the other hand, if all men could benefit from the truths of the rituals, why were they concealed at all?

The implicit meanings of the symbols suggest that many men were deeply troubled by the gender bifurcations of Victorian society, which deprived them of a religious experience with which they could identify and of a family environment in which they could freely express nurturing and paternal emotions. The Royal Secret, like all the final degrees, contradicted the assumption that men were innately impure, aggressive, and unemotional. By affirming that men possessed traits socially defined as female, the symbols conveyed a message expressed nowhere else in Victorian America.

These ideas and emotions could not be stated publicly. If men had acknowledged that the orders were an alternative form of religion, of family, and of social organization, the forces that had crushed Masonry in the 1820s might have again besieged the fraternal movement. The Royal Secret alone would have precipitated a major scandal.[53] There was another, far more important, reason for concealment: Few Victorian men could have admitted to themselves the truth of the Royal Secret—that they, too, were of a "double nature": a unity of assertion and nurturance, of aggression and conscience, and of male and female.

❖ EPILOGUE ❖

❖ THE DECLINE OF ❖
FRATERNAL RITUALISM

The institutional foundations of the fraternal movement collapsed during the depression of the 1930s. Few orders could retain the millions of members who fell behind in their dues. From 1925 to 1940 the Improved Order of Red Men lost over 300,000 members and the Knights of Pythias 550,000. Freemasonry and Odd Fellowship survived the Depression, but taken together they lost nearly a million members. Hundreds of smaller orders passed out of existence entirely.[1] Thousands of lodges, unable to meet mortgage payments, went bankrupt. Sociologists concluded that the fraternal movement was all but dead.[2]

The demise was not caused solely by hard times, for the orders clearly had been in trouble even during the prosperous decade of the 1920s. "Never did I realize until last year the apparent lack of interest in Masonry shown by many lodges," one Masonic official commented in 1920.[3] In their study of Muncie, Indiana, in the 1920s Robert and Helen Lynd reported that "the great days of the lodges have vanished."[4] Officials even then worried that the lodges were becoming the "patrons of the mediocre" as middle-class and better-educated men flocked to recreational clubs and service organizations.[5] Aggressive recruitment policies and relaxed admission standards for a time masked weaknesses that became all too evident with the onset of the Great Depression.[6]

Critics within the movement explained that men were no longer interested in the "unadulterated diet" of ceremony and symbolism.[7] "The time is past when the mere ritualistic conferring of the Order can be regarded as the sole mission of Templary," the Grand Master of the Knights Templars concluded.[8] "We have tried to fool ourselves into believing that the conferring of degrees should attract intelligent busy men as a regular thing," a Masonic editor observed in 1921.[9]

The more enterprising lodges hosted dinner dances; sponsored club nights with billiards, card games, and movies; and organized baseball teams, bowling leagues, and recreational trips. Others sought to replicate the success of service organizations such as the Rotary and Lions by undertaking charitable projects.[10] But the rituals impinged on these activities. Men who wanted primarily to enjoy themselves or to serve their community soon realized that organizations committed to long rituals were not suited to their purposes. Some orders truncated the rituals or even abandoned them entirely.[11]

Traditionalists were appalled by proposals to transform the lodge into "just another kind of club." An organization based upon ritual, they added, could not expect to be as effective in promoting recreation as the clubs created solely for that purpose.[12] "Let us have a real revival of the old-fashioned ritual work," one official told the Grand Lodge of Connecticut Odd Fellows in 1924.[13] According to the traditionalists, the current apathy was caused by recent modifications, abbreviations, and deviations in the rituals. The somber religious tone of the nineteenth-century lodge had been shattered by the "non-observance of proper decorum."[14] Liquor, banned for nearly a century, had found its way back into many lodge rooms. Much to the chagrin of older members, the emotional context that had once imparted meaning to the fraternal experience was being undone by members intent on having a good time.

For traditionalists the most disturbing trend was the emergence of recreational auxiliaries, such as the Masonic "Shriners" and the Pythian "Knights of Khorassan," which poked fun at the rituals of the parent body. Where the Masons and Pythians sought to make a man of the initiate, the Shriners and the Knights of Khorassan made him the butt of a joke. Such "horseplay," the Grand Chancellor–Elect of New York Pythians insisted in 1927, was an intolerable insult that devalued all initiations.[15]

Lynn Dumenil has proposed that the religious character of the rituals, which had demonstrated the order's accommodation to the values of Victorian America, became a hindrance as society itself became more secular in the twentieth century. The somber religious tone of its ceremonies placed Masonry "out of step with modern times."[16] But even in the nineteenth century the rituals were anachronistic, and consciously so. When men dressed up as High Priests, Roman Senators, or Medieval Knights and mouthed mysterious phrases from what they believed to be ancient sources, they did not merely reflect the values of the emerging urban-industrial order; they also evoked its antithesis.

Nor is it correct to assume that the modern world has proven inhospitable to religious and nonrational forms of expression; modernity and religiosity have cohabited quite comfortably. The age of Einstein also witnessed the rise of religious fundamentalism, and the institutionalization of Wagnerian mythology by the Nazis. The computer revolution has served Indian gurus and Rev. Sun Myung Moon alike, and the chemical and electronics industries have been indispensable in promoting the literal mindlessness of the drug culture and rock music. Fraternal ritual did not become obsolete because modern Americans chose to embrace rationality.

A clue to the decline of the orders is suggested by a shift in attendance patterns. In the nineteenth century the lodges were filled with young men, so much so that older members sometimes complained that they felt out of place. During the early twentieth century older men continued to attend faithfully, but more and more often young men who took the initiatory degree never set foot in the lodge again.[17] Saddened by their diminishing audiences of graybeards, orators wondered what had happened to the "great virile manhood" that had previously presented itself to the lodge.[18] The movement was dying of old age.

The absence of young members represented more than a threat to the lodge's mortgage or beneficiary funds. "When you've held all the offices and there's no new blood coming in," one member lamented, "there's just no point in keeping on going through the ritual."[19] All institutions depend on an empathic relationship between generations, but this was especially true of the fraternal movement. With good reason orators anguished over the younger generation: Would they, too, undertake the fraternal pilgrimage toward manhood, or would they discover their own paths to adulthood? On this depended the future of the orders and, more important, the emotional fate of the younger generation.

Strident assertions of masculinity speak less of men's strengths than their insecurities. The older members' assumption that the young lacked the virility to appreciate the masculine message of the rituals confirms the centrality of gender issues to the fraternal movement; it also suggests that during the early 1900s fewer young middle-class men were afflicted with their fathers' and grandfathers' gender anxieties. Although evidence on sex roles, child rearing, and childhood during the early twentieth century is nearly as thin as for the nineteenth century, there is reason to believe that the elderly members' grumblings that young men were different from themselves had some basis in social reality.

Changes in cultural patterns and social mores result from gradual accretions in behavior and thought patterns; the dating of any social or cultural phenomenon is problematical. Yet it is apparent that a reorientation in middle-class gender roles occurred in the early twentieth century. Historians have focused on women, who increasingly left the home to pursue careers or higher education, who bore fewer children, who drank and smoked, and who helped precipitate a revolution in morals and manners. Initially historians followed popular opinion in assuming the "new woman" first appeared in the 1920s.[20] More recently they have found that the "flapper" gyrating to the Charleston in the 1920s had an older sister who had danced the turkey trot before the war and had not hesitated to reject the moral authority of her parents, especially on matters concerning relations with men.[21] The enormous expansion of radio and film after the First World War simply gave new visibility to a preexisting social phenomenon. James R. McGovern concluded that the "great leap forward" in women's participation in the economy occurred during the first decade of the twentieth century. And John Higham argued that the "new woman," manly in appearance, assertive in social life, and "masculine" in her demand for political power, made her debut in the 1890s.[22]

The drive for education and financial independence was an effort to gain for women a measure of autonomy from parents. But this "woman's revolution" was the work of young people of both sexes, who together dismantled gender conventions. To a much greater extent than their mothers or grandmothers, women of this generation moved in the company of men. Improvements in birth control, particularly the development of the diaphragm after 1900, allowed a new measure of physical intimacy. Women now became "comrades in arms with male friends" in a revolt against the conventional sex roles their parents had accepted.[23]

Sharp distinctions in the appearance and behavior of the sexes began to fade. Women's cosmetics and clothing styles were no longer designed to emphasize maternal prowess. The "1914 Girl" was an altogether "boylike creature," one journalist noted, possessing "slim hips and boy-carriage."[24] In the 1920s women, their hair cropped close, became still more "manly." Young men, similarly, were abandoning the beards of their fathers and the individualistic and competitive norms that had prevailed during the nineteenth century.

Children began school at an earlier age, and more students attended college. Separated from parental supervision for long stretches of time, students looked more to each other to define acceptable values and behaviors. The young men and women who came of age in the 1920s were the first generation to fashion a "youth culture."[25]

Children, too, were no longer confronted with so rigid a division of gender models. Henry Seidel Canby observed that whereas parents in the decades prior to the twentieth century "put fatherhood and motherhood first," those coming immediately afterward were determined to lead their own lives. "There was more give and take between parents and children, more liberty, and more cheerfulness," Canby noted.[26] Parents indulged their children's efforts at self-expression because they placed such a high value on it for themselves.

Middle-class mothers in the late nineteenth and early twentieth centuries, influenced by new expectations of affectionate marriage, had begun to move "from the nursery to the bedroom."[27] They directed more of their emotional energies toward their husbands, and somewhat less toward children. G. Stanley Hall noted that children, formerly stifled by excessive maternal influence, began to receive a "longer tether."[28] Trumbell's *Hints on Child Training* reminded mothers that the child was "not a mere bit of child-material, to be worked up by the outside efforts and influences," but was already well formed. Long before John Watson's cranky indictment of mother love, women frequently were advised to avoid too close an identification with their children.[29]

The diminished role of mothers in child rearing corresponded to an increased involvement of fathers. A University of California survey of parent-child relationships over two generations—the first born around 1900, the second in 1927–28—concluded that fathers' involvement with their sons was increasing significantly.[30] Another study revealed that by the 1930s 75 percent of middle-class fathers regularly read articles on child care, and nearly as many fathers as mothers attended Parent-Teacher Association (PTA) meetings. (The National Congress of Mothers' Clubs had changed its name to the Parent-Teacher Association in 1924 because of a growing awareness that the raising of children involved both parents.)[31] The emotionally detached and distant fathers of the mid-nineteenth century were separated from the nurturing family men of the early twentieth by a cultural chasm.[32]

A redefinition of fatherhood was possible because the economic position of the middle-class family had become more secure. Small businesses were replaced by corporate bureaucracies, and solitary entrepreneurs by salaried employees. As organization men forced the robber barons into retirement, young men perceived that advancement resulted from amiability and cooperation rather than individualistic assertion. They ceased dreaming of spectacular rewards, and their evenings were bedeviled less frequently by nightmares of bankruptcy and family ruin. As work commanded fewer of their emotional energies, these men became, in the historian Margaret Marsh's apt phrase, "domestic husbands."[33]

Men born after 1900 were less likely to be plagued in their early twenties by the anxieties that had drawn their grandfathers at the same age to the lodge. Raised in a society that had come to question many of the assumptions about the separate spheres assigned to men and women, these young men came of age while in school, participants in a coeducational "youth culture." And they learned that the selfless and cooperative values formerly associated with feminine domesticity brought rewards in the workplace.

Still, at the encouragement or insistence of their fathers, fathers-in-law, or bosses, many of these young men agreed to join the lodge. They too walked past Jachin and Boaz, stared at the leonine portraits in the lobby, and fidgeted in the preparation room, trying to understand the muffled low voices beyond the door. But after their blindfolded procession, while the lodge official droned on about mystical symbols and secret meanings, their attention flagged. They thought about the picture show they had seen the night before or the dance planned for later in the week. And when the blindfolds were removed, they looked around the room, blinked at the lights and the skeletons, and gazed remotely at these mature men in Indian costumes and lambskin aprons.

Turner described how liminal ceremonies evoke a "weird domain" of masks, sacred icons, inverted relationships, and secrecy, which confer meaning by opposing the structural regularities of normal social life.[34] To the young men who visited the lodges in the 1920s and 1930s, the intentional strangeness of the liminal world of fraternal ritual had become incomprehensible. The symbolic inversions and oppositions that invested the lodge furniture with religious meanings and transformed the local insurance agent into an Old Testament patriarch struck them as nonsensical or, worse, as ludicrous. Many never returned, and they regaled friends with humorous accounts of what had transpired at the lodge. Within a few years the orders would be identified in the public mind with the televised antics of Ralph Kramden, a member of the Loyal Order of Raccoons. By mid-century few Americans took fraternal ritual seriously.

❖ MEANING AND METHOD ❖

Nearly all the orders have vanished. There is one important exception. Some of the remaining Blue Lodge Masons continue to put on moth-eaten costumes, to give tests to uncover "cowans and eavesdroppers," and to lead half-naked initiates on a pilgrimage through cavernous temples built a century ago.

Masons with whom I have spoken are moved by the experience. Conceivably these rituals, though greatly abbreviated, may still address psychological needs much like those of a hundred years ago but now a consequence, perhaps, of high rates of divorce and fatherless families or of a contemporary religious experience often devoid of faith. It is more likely, as the differences between the Victorian era and the present are greater than the similarities, that current members have rearranged the symbols and motifs of Freemasonry and conferred upon them new and different meanings.

The capacity to transform perceptions into symbols and to order them in ways that make sense is part of the endowment of the mind. Theorists who have examined this process have tended to view it apart from a historical context. Freud emphasized the mind's mediation between the demands of the body—a human constant—and the limitations imposed upon it in infancy by society. Durkheim replaced Freud's psychological determinism with a sociocentric model: Society itself stamped cultural patterns upon the homogeneous material of the brain. Claude Lévi-Strauss, rejecting both Freud and Durkheim, asserted that culture was essentially reducible to the "emanations of the intellect," that Freud was mistaken, for "impulses and emotions explain nothing." [35] Intellectual activity was not, as Durkheim maintained, a "reflection of the concrete organization of society," but a capacity that inhered in the species.[36]

Lévi-Strauss's insight that even the "savage" mind orders symbols and metaphors according to sophisticated correspondences and oppositions explains how fraternal ritualists could devise unconsciously the complex symmetries and structures that simultaneously subverted liberal theology, maternal nurture, and Victorian gender roles. But if this capacity to perform complex mental operations is a human constant, the impetus to create these particular structures and messages originated in the emotional needs of the ritualists themselves, which were shared to some extent by many middle-class men.

It is foolish to quarrel with Durkheim's view, shared by Lévi-Strauss, that emotions, "the most obscure side of man," are refractory to analysis.[37] But there can be no real understanding of man if, for reasons of analytical rigor, the emotional aspects of human nature are excluded from consideration.[38] This is especially true of understanding liminal phenomena, which turn normal social relations upside down and assert the primacy of emotions over reason and of intense experience over analysis. By separating emotions from intellect, and culture from those who create and live it, the social sciences potentially rob the mind of that which makes it human, and culture of all that matters to man.

The historian's task is to find out both what happened and why, to link behavior and motivation. He attempts by defective means to stitch the shreds of the past into something resembling the original. Social theory offers patterns, contradictory though they often may be, which can guide the historian's hand. But they must never lead it. Social scientists rightly maintain that, without a theoretical template, the historian will fail to find any order whatsoever in the tattered remnants of the record. Conversely, he may arrange them according to his own preconceptions, an ahistoricism all the more pernicious because of its mindlessness: He deceives himself in believing he can leap backward in time into the minds of others. But he has no choice, for all history is essentially a task of imaginative reconstruction.

The present study extends the study of cultural meaning to consider cultural origins, a subject about which little is known and one that belongs, almost by default, in the province of history. Turner, who perceived order in the seeming nonsense of liminal rituals, believed that liminality was itself subject to history: Formal rituals were disappearing in the modern world, their liminal functions replaced by leisure activities, art, and literature.[39] This insight challenges historians to study the origins of other phenomena that, like fraternal ritual, seem culturally marginal if not bizarre. The search for liminal cultural structures might well begin with young people, who feel the impingements of society with a special acuteness. For example, when the young attend rock concerts and surrender to explosions of light and color, to a drug-enhanced sense of otherness, and to the atavistic mindlessness of the music, they have entered a liminal realm in which the conventions of parents and society are repeatedly violated. Having expressed their liminal psychological needs in a predictably stylized and almost ritualistic manner, they are better able to cope with the hierarchies and structures of everyday life.

Once liminal environments have been located, how can we make sense of them? Social historians are often taken aback to find that novels written in the period they study provide more insight into the time than does even the most elegant analysis. Part of the explanation is that novelists, like fraternal ritualists, inhabit liminal worlds of fantasy and nonsense. The social scientist, detached and analytical, enters such worlds only reluctantly—and at considerable professional peril.

Fraternal ritual appealed particularly to the creative faculties of the mind. Joseph D. Weeks, a historian for the Knights of Pythias who worked during the day as a statistician for the Bureau of the Census, described his evenings at the lodge as a "mystic wonderland" where fantasy was incorporated into the "small prose domain of Sense."[40] The nature of this integration was the subject of this book, and the argument necessarily moved back and forth between the fantasy world of the ritual and the more tangible domains of work, gender, and family.

Explanation should go beyond analysis, and although the mystery of the lodge must be understood in light of Victorian society, it was nevertheless a world unto itself, protected from cowans and eavesdroppers by castles, armed guards—and secrecy. The vignettes that prefaced each chapter were attempts to move directly into the recesses of the fraternal imagination. Perhaps, as Weeks believed, this fantasy world necessarily had to exist apart from the well-defined and predictable structures of everyday life. Members were stripped of their clothing and identities before they could enter, for the "mystic wonderland" of the lodge would be destroyed if the outside world were allowed in. Social science, as the name implies, demands distance and scholarly detachment; it is difficult for analysis to cohabit with the wayward creative impulse. Yet for the study of imaginative phenomena, neither approach—alone—suffices.

Sources of Fraternal Rituals

The problems of analysis of fraternal ritual are compounded by the secrecy that enshrouded the affairs of the lodge. Most orders did not allow their rituals to be recorded or published. Fortunately, some orders—including the Knights of Pythias and the Knights of Labor—published versions of their ceremonies, written in simple codes. For example, a question in the cipher of the Knights of Pythias read: "Do y b in the ex of a S.B.?" which can be translated as "Do you believe in the existence of a Supreme Being?" (*The Secret Work of the Knights of Pythias: Ritual in Cipher*). Some publishers sold exposés to members who needed help in memorizing their parts or to the curious who wished to "fathom the wonderful secrets of Freemasonry" without paying for an initiation (*Richardson's Monitor*, p. iv). Sometimes enthusiasts published rituals after their organization had become defunct. After 1867 many exposés were published by the National Christian Association; although the organization rabidly opposed the orders, its exposés were accurate.

Not all published exposés were legitimate, however. I believe that some of the more preposterous examples were published by supporters of fraternal groups in order to discredit *all* exposés. The bogus versions bear little, if any, relation to the issues and symbols discussed in the official guidebooks. See, for example, [D. Wilson] *Scottish Rite Freemasonry* (1888?); James M. Madison [?], *Madison's Exposition of the Awful and Terrifying Ceremonies of the Odd Fellows* (New York: n.p., 1847); and M. E. Gustin, "Dr. J. Gustin's 'Experience, Confession and Burlesque on the Patrons of Husbandry' " in *Exposé, Experience and Confession of a Granger* (Dayton: Christian Publishing Association, 1875).

The best means of verifying the authenticity of exposés is to compare them to the guidebooks of the ritualists and scholars. The latter were remarkably inattentive to their order's secrecy provisions; occasionally their detailed explications included nearly verbatim accounts of portions of the rituals, although it was more usual for the guidebooks merely to allude to the themes. According to several exposés, the 1845 version of the Initiatory degree of Odd Fellowship included the following major motifs: The initiate (1) was blindfolded, placed in chains, and led around the lodge room; (2) was told that the darkness represented his ignorance; (3) was shown a skeleton and warned of the "vanity of all earthly things;" and (4) was again blindfolded and presented to officials who were made to resemble elderly men. Grosh's explanation of the ritual in *The Odd-Fellow's Improved Manual* did not reproduce the exact language of the ceremonies but did indicate the sequence of events in unmistakable terms. He wrote that man in his natural state was "surrounded by darkness" (blindfolded) and was "bound, by his ignorance and fears, in the indurating fetters of selfishness" (placed in chains). Later "the first ray of light will but increase the apparent gloom" (the blindfolds were removed and the initiate spied the skeleton). The ensuing scene will make the initiate cognizant of his "own mortality" (again, the skeleton). But the initiate, Grosh added, was still not ready to accept the "light" of fraternal truth: "Let him hear the voice of Antiquity" (the elderly patriarchs).

The exposés and coded rites are listed below in order of publication date.

AMERICAN FREEMASONRY

Allyn, Avery. *A Ritual of Freemasonry*. New York: William Gowan, 1828.

[Day, Benjamin Henry.] *Richardson's Monitor of Freemasonry*. Philadelphia: David McKay, 1861?

Bernard, David. *Light on Freemasonry: Revised Edition*. Dayton, Ohio: W. J. Shueys, 1874.

Lewis, A. *The Perfect Ceremonies of the Mark Master Mason and Royal Arch Degrees*. A. Lewis, 1876.

[Cook, Ezra A.] *Revised Knight Templarism Illustrated*. Chicago: Ezra A. Cook, 1879; and subsequent edition, 1904.

Blanchard, Jonathan. *Scotch Rite Masonry Illustrated*. Chicago: Ezra A. Cook, 1882; and subsequent editions, 1890, 1930.

Doesburg, Jacob O. *Freemasonry Illustrated*. Chicago: Ezra A. Cook, 1886.

More Light: A Ritual of the Three Symbolic Degrees. New York: Dick and Fitzgerald, 1896.

INDEPENDENT ORDER OF ODD FELLOWS

[Royer, J., comp.] *Lectures and Charges of the Degrees of the Independent Order of Odd Fellows*. Philadelphia: J. Royer, 1833.

[Willis, comp.] *Dr. Willis's Exposé of Odd Fellowship*. W. S. Damrell, 1846.

A True Key to Odd Fellowship. New York, 1847.

Kirk, John. *Kirk's Exposition of Odd-Fellowship*. New York: John Kirk, 1857.

[Cook, Ezra A.] *Odd Fellowship Illustrated*. Chicago: Ezra A. Cook, 1874.

Blanchard, Jonathan. *Revised Odd Fellowship Illustrated*. Chicago: Ezra A. Cook, 1881.

Blanchard, Jonathan. *Revised Encampment Degrees, I.O.O.F.: The Complete Ritual*. Chicago: Ezra A. Cook, 1911.

KNIGHTS OF PYTHIAS

[Cook, Ezra A.] *Knights of Pythias Illustrated*. Chicago: Ezra A. Cook, 1878.

The Secret Work of the Knights of Pythias: Ritual in Cipher. Chicago: W. S. Smith and Company, 1883.

[Roberts, Douglas, ed.] *Ritual for Subordinate Lodges of Knights of Pythias*. New York: Dick and Fitzgerald, 1894.

[Sanders, Harold, ed.] *Revised Ritual for Subordinate Lodges of Knights of Pythias of North America*. Danbury: Behrens Publishing Company, 1922.

IMPROVED ORDER OF RED MEN

[Ezra A. Cook.] *Red Men Illustrated: The Complete Illustrated Ritual of the Improved Order of Red Men*. Chicago: Ezra A. Cook, 1896. A student of the order, Thomas K. Donnalley, found a copy of the 1864 rituals while interviewing elderly members and published it. See Donalley, ed., *Handbook of Tribal Names of Pennsylvania* (Philadelphia: n.p., 1908), pp. 231–49.

GRAND ARMY OF THE REPUBLIC

[Cook, Ezra A.] *Ritual of the Grand Army of the Republic, adopted in General Convention at Philadelphia, Pennsylvania, January 17, 1868*. Chicago: Ezra A. Cook, 1875. More than a decade later a historian of the GAR, Robert B. Beath, included in his general work an account of the ritual nearly identical to that found in the Cook version. Beath noted that in 1871 an official of the GAR had carelessly lost the cipher and key, thereby allowing the secret work to become public. This was evidently a reference to the Cook exposé. See Beath, *History of the Grand Army of the Republic* (New York: Bryan, Taylor and Co., 1889), pp. 128, 232.

KNIGHTS OF LABOR

[Cook, Ezra A.] *Knights of Labor Illustrated: Adelphon Kruptos*. Chicago: Ezra A. Cook, 1886. John R. Commons published a coded manual, along with a key, which confirmed the accuracy of the Cook exposé. See Commons, *Documentary History of American Industrial Society* (Cleveland: A. H. Clark, 1910). See also Terence Powderly's Secret Circular purporting to be an "Explanation of the Signs and Symbols of the Order," in Commons, *Documentary History*, pp. 431–44.

BROTHERHOOD OF LOCOMOTIVE ENGINEERS

Pinkerton, Allan. "Ritual for Subordinate Lodges of the Brotherhood." In *Strikers, Communists, Tramps and Detectives*, pp. 90–130. New York: G. W. Carleton and Co., 1878.

KNIGHTS OF ST. CRISPIN

Ritual of the Order of Knights of St. Crispin. Boston: Weekly American Workman Office, 1869.

MACHINISTS AND BLACKSMITHS UNION

[Cook, Ezra A.] *Ritual of the Machinists and Blacksmiths Union.* Chicago: Ezra A. Cook, 1876.

KNIGHTS OF THE GOLDEN CIRCLE

Pomfrey, J. W. *A True Disclosure and Exposition of the Knights of the Golden Circle.* Cincinnati: By author, 1861.

ANCIENT ORDER OF GLEANERS

Ritual: Ancient Order of Gleaners. Cairo, Michigan: By the order, 1895.

PATRONS OF HUSBANDRY

Wells, John G. *The Grange Illustrated.* New York: Grange Publishing Co., 1874.

MODERN WOODMEN OF AMERICA

[Modern Woodmen of America.] *Official Ritual (Third Revision) of the Modern Woodmen of America.* M.W.A., 1909.
[Modern Woodmen of America.] *Official Ritual (Fourth Revision) of the Modern Woodmen of America.* M.W.A., 1915.

ANCIENT ORDER OF FORESTERS

First Supreme Executive Council of San Francisco, from the Revision of F.C. Hensley. *Ritual of the Ancient Order of Foresters.* N.p., 1890.

INDEPENDENT ORDER OF FORESTERS
(LATER, UNITED ORDER OF FORESTERS)

Ritual of the Independent Order of Foresters. Cleveland: Harper, 1892.

[Ezra A. Cook.] *The Foresters Illustrated: Complete Ritual of the United Order of Foresters Formerly Known as the Independent Order of Foresters*. Chicago: Ezra A. Cook, 1895.

The Ritual of the Independent Order of Foresters. N.p., 1898.

INDEPENDENT ORDER OF GOOD TEMPLARS

Right Worthy Grand Lodge of North America. *Ritual of the Independent Order of Good Templars*. Auburn, N.Y.: William J. Moses, 1855.

Right Worthy Grand Lodge of North America. *Ritual of the Independent Order of Good Templars*. Donnelley, Hamilton, 1858.

[Cook, Ezra A.] *Good Templarism Illustrated*. Chicago: Ezra A. Cook, 1879.

MISCELLANEOUS

Fultz, J. J. *Infancy, Youth and Manhood, or How to Work the K. of H. Ritual*. Mt. Vernon, Ohio: Knights of Honor, 1889.

[Butwell, Edward A.] *Ritual of the Order of the Knights of Cerberus*. Port Townsend, Washington: Job Office, 1895.

Powell, John B. *Ritual of the Dramatic Order Knights of Khorassan*. Milwaukee: Swain, Tate and Co., 1895.

[Aikman, Frederick Lewis.] *Ritual of the Knights of the Mystic Chain*. Lynchburg, Virginia, 1900.

Ritual of the Knights of Fidelity. N.p., 1901.

Committee, the Ancient Arabic Order Nobles of Mystic Shrine. *Ritual*. N.p., 1904.

"LADIES' DEGREES"

Order of the Eastern Star (Masonic)

Macoy, Robert. *Adoptive Rite Ritual*. New York: Macoy Publishing Co., 1868.

The Authorized Standard Ritual of the Order of the Eastern Star in the State of New York. New York: Grand Chapter O.E.S.N.Y., 1905.

[Bell, F. A.] *Order of the Eastern Star*. Chicago: Ezra A. Cook, 1923.

Degree of Rebekah (Odd Fellows)

Blanchard, Jonathan. *Revised Odd Fellowship Illustrated*. Chicago: Ezra A. Cook, 1881.

Ladies of the Maccabees of the World
Ritual of the Ladies of the Maccabees of the World. Port Huron, Mich.: Riverside
   Printing Co., 1896.

MILITARY AUXILIARIES

[Blanchard, Jonathan, comp.] *Patriarchs Militant Illustrated.* Chicago: Ezra A. Cook,
   1886.

Degree Sequences for Major Orders

FREEMASONRY

Ancient and Accepted Scottish Rite	*American Rite*

Blue Lodge	Blue Lodge
1st Entered Apprentice	Entered Apprentice
2nd Fellowcraft	Fellowcraft
3rd Master Mason	Master Mason
	(York Rite)
4th Secret Master	Mark Master [1]
5th Perfect Master	Past Master [1]
6th Intimate Secretary	Most Excellent Master [1]
7th Provost and Judge	Royal Arch Mason [1]
8th Intendant of the Building	Royal Master [2]
9th Elect of the IX	Select Master [2]
10th Elect of the XV	Super Excellent Master [2]
11th Sublime Knight Elect	Companion of the Red Cross [3]
12th Grand Master Architect	Knight Templar [3]
13th Knight of the 9th Arch	Knight of Malta [3]
14th Grand Elect Perfect and Sublime Mason	
15th Knight of the East or Sword	
16th Prince of Jerusalem	
17th Knight of the East and West	
18th Knight of the Rose Croix	
19th Grand Pontiff	
20th Master ad vitam	
21st Patriarch Noachite	
22nd Prince of Libanus	
23rd Chief of the Tabernacle	
24th Prince of the Tabernacle	
25th Knight of the Brazen Serpent	
26th Prince of Mercy	
27th Commander of the Temple	
28th Knight of the Sun	

29th   Knight of St. Andrew
30th   Grand Elect Knight Kadosh
31st   Grand Inspector, Inquisitor Commander
32nd   Sublime Prince of the Royal Secret
33rd   Sovereign Grand Inspector General
           (honorary degree)

[1] Conferred in Royal Arch Chapters
[2] Conferred in Councils of Royal and Select Masters
[3] Conferred in Commanderies of the Knights Templars

ODD FELLOWSHIP (1874 sequence)

Initiatory[4]
  1st   Friendship[4]
  2nd   Brotherly Love[4]
  3rd   Truth[4]
  4th   Remembrance[4]
Patriarchal[5]
Golden Rule[5]
Royal Purple[5]
Past Grand[6]
Past Vice Grand[6]
Past Secretary[6]

Martial degree
Patriarchs Militant

KNIGHTS OF PYTHIAS

Initiatory, or Page
Armorial, or Esquire
Chivalric, or Knight

Martial degree
Uniform Rank

IMPROVED ORDER OF RED MEN

Adoption
Hunter
Warrior
Chief

Martial degree
Chieftain's League

4 Lodge sequence
5 Encampment sequence
6 Honorary

❖ NOTES ❖

PROLOGUE

1. W. S. Harwood, "Secret Societies in America," *North American Review* 164 (May 1897), pp. 620–23. Harwood provided the following membership data (rounded to the nearest thousand) for 1896:

Odd Fellows	810,000
Freemasons	750,000
Knights of Pythias	475,000
Ancient Order of United Workmen	361,000
Knights of the Maccabees	244,000
Modern Woodmen of America	204,000
Royal Arcanum	189,000
United American Mechanics, Jr.	187,000
Improved Order of Red Men	165,000
Knights of Honor	118,000

Others argued for even higher figures. For example, Albert C. Stevens estimated that 40 percent of the adult male population belonged to a fraternal order in 1896. See Stevens, comp. and ed., *Cyclopaedia of Fraternities* (New York: E. B. Treat, 1907), p. xvi. He reprints membership figures, somewhat higher than Harwood's, first cited in the introduction to the 1897 edition.

2. Harwood, "Secret Societies in America," pp. 620–22.

3. Stevens, *Cyclopaedia of Fraternities*, p. xvi.

4. Alexis de Tocqueville, *Democracy in America*, vol. 2, trans. Henry Reeve (1840; reprint, New York: Schocken, 1961), p. 129.

5. Arthur M. Schlesinger, "Biography of a Nation of Joiners," *American Historical Review* 50 (October 1944), pp. 2, 15.

6. See, for example, Rowland Berthoff, *An Unsettled People: Social Order and Disorder in American History* (New York: Harper and Row, 1971), pp. 273–74; Sam Bass Warner, Jr., *The Private City: Philadelphia in Three Periods of Its Growth* (Philadelphia: University of Pennsylvania Press, 1968), pp. 61–62; and Don H. Doyle, "The Social Function of Voluntary Associations in a Nineteenth-Century American Town," *Social Science History* 1 (Spring 1977), pp. 338–43.

7. Lynn Dumenil, *Freemasonry and American Culture, 1880–1939* (Princeton, N.J.: Princeton University Press, 1984), pp. 32–42.

8. Dumenil, *Freemasonry and American Culture*, pp. 148–217.

9. Lynn Dumenil found that one-half to three-quarters of the members of Masonic lodges in Oakland, California, in 1880 were middle-class (*Freemasonry and American Culture, 1880–1939*, pp. 12–13, 226–29). John Gilkeson similarly concluded that approximately 60 percent of the Masons in Providence, Rhode Island,

in the 1870s were professionals or white-collar workers ("A City of Joiners: Voluntary Associations and the Formation of the Middle Class in Providence, 1830–1920" [Ph.D. diss., Brown University, 1981], p. 121). Earlier, Merle Curti had noted that with few exceptions the members of the three Masonic lodges in Trempeleau County, Wisconsin, in the late nineteenth century were prominent and well-to-do citizens (*The Making of an American Community: A Case Study of Democracy in a Frontier County* [Stanford, Calif.: Stanford University Press, 1959], p. 126). Don Harrison Doyle discovered that a high proportion of the leaders of fraternal orders in frontier Jacksonville, Illinois, were professionals or businessmen (*The Social Order of a Frontier Community: Jacksonville Illinois, 1825–1870* [Urbana, Ill.: University of Illinois Press, 1978], pp. 182–83, 269).

10. For example, 48 percent of the members of seventeen lodges of the Knights of Pythias in Buffalo in 1894 were employed in business, professional, or white-collar occupations. Similarly, 39 percent of the Knights of the Maccabee in Cleveland in 1900, and 29 percent of the Odd Fellows in Detroit in 1871 could be described as middle-class (Mary Ann Clawson, "Brotherhood, Class and Patriarchy: Fraternalism in Europe and America" [Ph.D. diss., University of New York at Stonybrook, 1980], pp. 393–99, 415). Brian Greenberg observed that membership in the Odd Fellows lodge in Albany typified and reflected Albany's diverse socioeconomic structure. See Greenberg, *Worker and Community: Response to Industrialization in a Nineteenth-Century American City, Albany, New York, 1850–1884* (Albany: State University of New York Press, 1985), pp. 92–93.

11. Theodore A. Ross, *Odd Fellowship: Its History and Manual* (New York: M. W. Hazen, 1888), p. 2.

12. The estimate of expenditures is taken from Harwood, "Secret Societies in America," pp. 617–23. The average annual wage for manufacturing workers in 1897 was $408; see the U.S. Bureau of the Census, *Historical Statistics of the United States*, vol. 1 (Washington, D.C.: 1975), Series D779–93, p. 168.

13. See Sigmund Diamond, *The Reputation of the American Businessman* (Cambridge, Mass.: Harvard University Press, 1955), pp. 8–9.

14. See Stevens, *Cyclopaedia of Fraternities*, p. 42–43, 52, 259.

15. Harwood found that over $650 million had been paid in fraternal insurance fees, this when the entire federal budget did not exceed half a billion dollars. The orders annually spent $42 million to rent lodge halls, a figure that did not include the ambitious construction programs of the major orders. The Masonic Temple in Philadelphia, by no means the nation's largest, was completed in 1875 at a cost of $1.6 million (*New England Freemason* [January 1875]). See also Stevens, *Cyclopaedia of Fraternities*, p. 260.

16. Stevens, *Cyclopaedia of Fraternities*, pp. xvi, 159; 190–91.

17. Grand Lodge of Massachusetts, "Action of the Grand Lodge of Massachusetts Against Spurious Rites and Degrees and Irregular Bodies Called Masonic" (Boston: Rockwell and Churchill, 1883), pp. 10–11.

18. "New Degrees," *Masonic Review* (April 1868). See also "Uniformity in Rituals," *Masonic Review* (May 1869).

19. Fewer than 70,000 men belonged to fraternities in 1883, a tiny figure compared to the millions in the orders; see *Baird's Manual of American College Fraternities* (New York: J. T. Brown, 1920), pp. 768–74. On the simple initiations, see Freeman H. Hart, *The History of Pi Kappa Alpha* ([Atlanta]: by the fraternity, 1934), pp. 177–93; and William F. Galpin, *Delta Upsilon, One Hundred Years, 1834–1934* (Camden, N.J.: Delta Upsilon, 1934), pp. 22, 115, 345. When Delta Upsilon enlarged its ritual in 1885 (pp. 347, 348–51), it still filled only four small pages, as opposed to the thirty- to fifty-page ceremonies for fraternal orders.

20. S. H. Goodwin, *Mormonism and Masonry* (Washington, D.C.: Masonic Service Association of the United States, 1924), pp. 35–38.

21. Fawn M. Brodie, *No Man Knows My History: The Life of Joseph Smith, the Mormon Prophet* (New York: Alfred A. Knopf, 1971), pp. 38ff.

22. Smith informed his followers that there was "a sort of divine Masonry among the angels who hold the priesthood, by which they can detect those who do not belong to their order. Those who cannot give the signs correctly are supposed to be imposters" (Cited in George B. Arbaugh, *Revelation in Mormonism: Its Character and Changing Forms* [Chicago: University of Chicago Press, 1950], p. 159). The best history of the Mormon church, written by Mormons, skirts this issue. The authors refer to Smith's "purported use of the Masonic ceremony in Mormon temple ordinances" and note that Mormons recognized that there were "similarities as well as differences" in the rituals; there is no further elaboration; see Leonard J. Arrington and David Bitton, *The Mormon Experience: A History of the Latter-Day Saints* (New York: Alfred A. Knopf, 1979), p. 55. See also Goodwin, *Mormonism and Masonry*; and John C. Reynolds, *History of the M. W. Grand Lodge of Illinois, Ancient, Free, and Accepted Masons* (Springfield: H. G. Reynolds, 1869), p. 166. Some of Smith's followers, most notably Brigham Young, were already familiar with Freemasonry. Young had belonged to a Masonic lodge in western New York in 1830; his biographer noted that "it is likely that Masonry held a stronger grip on his emotions than Methodism" (Ray B. West, Jr., *Kingdom of the Saints: The Story of Brigham Young and the Mormons* [New York: Viking Press, 1957], pp. 29–31). See also Kenneth W. Godfrey, "Joseph Smith and the Masons," *Journal of the Illinois State Historical Society* 64 (1971).

23. Mindful that many recruits had been Antimasons, the majority in the order decided against the elaborate and quasi-religious ceremonies of Freemasonry. Oaths would be brief and direct. Some founders thought these rituals "too simple," but voted for them anyway, assuming changes would be made later. See Samuel Ellis, *The History of the Order of the Sons of Temperance* (Boston: Stacy Richardson and Co., 1848), pp. 11–16. Ian R. Tyrrell notes that the founders designed the ceremonies to give temperance an "emotional appeal," in *Sobering Up: From Temperance to Prohibition in Antebellum America, 1800–1860* (Westport, Conn.: Greenwood Press, 1979), p. 212.

24. Stevens, *Cyclopaedia of Fraternities*, pp. 403–05, 411–12. Other temperance societies included the Independent Order of Good Samaritans and Daughters of Samaria (1847)—"a true descendent of the Sons of Temperance"—and the Royal Templars of Temperance (1870), whose founder, Cyrus K. Porter, had for many years

been "actively identified with the Freemasons, Odd-Fellows, and Sons of Temperance, and so acquired the experience necessary to frame a ritual for an organization which should be educational and uplifting in its character" (Stevens, *Cyclopaedia of Fraternities*, p. 408). See also I. Newton Pierce, *The History of the Independent Order of Good Templars* (Philadelphia: Daughaday and Becker, 1869), pp. 42–47, 64.

25. Stevens, *Cyclopaedia of Fraternities*, p. 313–15, 318–19, 319n, 320.

26. Louis Dow Scisco, *Political Nativism in New York State* (New York: AMS Press, 1968) pp. 68–71; Ray Allen Billington, *The Protestant Crusade, 1800–1860: A Study of the Origins of American Nativism* (New York: Macmillan, 1938), pp. 336–37.

27. Billington, *Protestant Crusade*, pp. 380–85, 389–92; Leon Cyprian Soule, *The Know-Nothing Party in New Orleans* (New Orleans: Louisiana Historical Association, 1961); Peyton Hurt, "The Rise and Fall of the 'Know-Nothings' in California," *California Historical Society Quarterly* 9 (1930), pp. 38, 111, 118.

28. See Ollinger Crenshaw, "The Knights of the Golden Circle: The Career of George Bickley," *American Historical Review* 47 (October 1941), pp. 23–25. Compare the Knight's oath for the third degree to the Master Mason oath. See J. W. Pomfrey, *A True Disclosure and Exposition of the Knights of the Golden Circle* (Cincinnati: by author, 1861), p. 37; and [Benjamin Henry Day], *Richardson's Monitor of Freemasonry* (Philadelphia: David McKay [1872?]) p. 29.

29. Crenshaw, "Knights of the Golden Circle," pp. 34–36; Mayo Fesler, "Secret Political Societies in the North," *Indiana Magazine of History* 14 (1918), pp. 197–98, 234; Felix G. Stidger, ed., *Treason History of the Order of the Sons of Liberty, formerly . . . Circle of Honor Succeeded by Knights of the Golden Circle Afterward Order of American Knights*, pp. 182–84; and Stevens, *Cyclopaedia of Fraternities*, p. 419–20.

30. The man most responsible for the growth of the order in the north, Phineas Wright, "revelled in the mysterious and meaningless phrases of secret societies," as one biographer put it. Wright completely revised Bickley's rituals and created five elaborate degrees. Religious phrases soon echoed throughout the Knights' temples, which were now furnished with Bibles and altars. See Fesler, "Secret Political Societies," pp. 225, 285–86. For the Wright rituals, see Stidger, *Treason History*, pp. 188–218.

31. During the Indiana treason trials in 1864, in which four Knights were convicted and three of them sentenced to death, prosecutors focused on the secret rituals (Fesler, "Secret Political Societies," p. 278).

32. Fesler, "Secret Political Societies," pp. 281, 285–86.

33. Stanley F. Horn believed that the Ku Klux Klan borrowed its rituals from college fraternities, but Albert Stevens traced them to the Sons of Malta and other orders. See Horn, *Invisible Empire: The Story of the Ku Klux Klan, 1866–1871* (Cos Cob, Conn.: John E. Edwards, 1969), p. 14, and Stevens, *Cyclopaedia of Fraternities*, pp. 416–17.

34. Horn, *Invisible Empire*, p. 14. See also Wyn Craig Wade, *The Fiery Cross: The Ku Klux Klan in America* (New York: Simon and Schuster, 1987), pp. 34–35.

35. On the early history of the Grange, see Oliver H. Kelley, *Origin and Progress of the Order of the Patrons of Husbandry in the United States: A History from 1866 to 1873*

(Philadelphia: J. A. Wagenseller, 1875), pp. 13–15; see Kelley's letter to Anson Bartlett: "I see nothing that will be lasting, unless [the Patrons] combines the advantages which an order similar to our Masonic fraternity will provide," p. 22; also pp. 18–20.

36. The success of the Grange owed more to the rate practices of the western railroads than to its ceremonies; nevertheless, nearly all members went through the four basic initiatory degrees; and the greater portion of meetings were occupied with initiation. After the political and economic programs of the Patrons failed, the order lost members; yet for the remainder of the century hundreds of thousands of members kept it alive, attracted by its social features and, perhaps, by its rituals; see Charles W. Pierson, "The Rise of the Granger Movement," *Popular Science Monthly* 32 (1887), p. 199.

37. Stevens, *Cyclopaedia of Fraternities*, pp. 385–87. See the Ancient Order of Gleaners, *Ritual* (Cahiro, Michigan, 1895), pp. 5–15.

38. M. W. Sackett, *Early History of Fraternal Beneficiary Societies in America: Origin and Growth, 1868–1880* (Meadville, Pa.: Tribune Publishing Co., 1914), pp. 27, 34. No mention of benefit features appeared in the original constitution of the AOUW; see Sackett, pp. 15–16, and J. J. Upchurch, *The Life, Labors, and Travels of Father J. J. Upchurch, Founder of the A.O.U.W.*, ed. Samuel Booth (San Francisco: A. T. Dewey, 1887).

39. Stevens, *Cyclopaedia of Fraternities*, pp. 128–29.

40. "New York State Insurance Department Report, 1898," cited in Georges Tricoche, "Sociétés Secrètes et Assurances Fraternelles aux Etats-Unis," *Journal des Economistes*, March 15, 1901, p. 12. On the 1898 revenues, see Stevens, *Cyclopaedia of Fraternities*, p. 113.

41. The Knights of the Maccabees, for example, stagnated until 1882, when new leaders, including some Freemasons, changed its ritual; by the end of the century it had more than 200,000 members. See also information on the Order of the Heptasophs and the Tribe of Ben-Hur in Stevens, *Cyclopaedia of Fraternities*, pp. 151–54, 176–80, 190–91.

42. Other examples include the Brotherhood of Locomotive Engineers (1863), the Sons of Vulcan (puddlers and boilers; 1876), the Knights of St. Crispin (shoemakers; 1869), the Machinists' and Blacksmiths' Union (1867), the Order of Railway Conductors of America (1868), the American Flint Glass Workers' Union (1878), the Brotherhood of Railway Train Trainmen (1883), the International Association of Machinists (1880), and the Brotherhood of Railway Carmen of America (1890). See Norman J. Ware, *The Labor Movement in the United States, 1860–1895* (Gloucester, Mass.: Peter Smith, 1959), p. 155n. For decades prospective engineers were blindfolded, conducted slowly around a meeting room, brought before an altar, and made to swear allegiance to the Brotherhood upon penalty of having their eyes "torn from their sockets" (George L. Stevenson, "The Brotherhood of Locomotive Engineers and Its Leaders, 1865–1920 [Ph.D. diss., Vanderbilt University, 1954), pp. 29–33]). See also Stevens, *Cyclopaedia of Fraternities*, p. 380–83; and Allan Pinkerton, *Strikers, Communists, Tramps, and Detectives* (New York: G. W. Carleton and Co., 1878), pp. 122–23.

43. Ware, *Labor Movement*, p. 27.

44. Carroll D. Wright, "An Historical Sketch of the Knights of Labor," *Quarterly Journal of Economics* (January 1887).

45. Gregory S. Kealey and Bryan D. Palmer, *Dreaming of What Might Be: The Knights of Labor in Ontario, 1880–1900* (Cambridge: Cambridge University Press, 1982), citation from p. 287.

46. See Pierce, History of Good Templars, p. 325; the discussion of ritual inadequacies begins on p. 151. For the importance of solemn ritual to the Good Templars, see also S. B. Chase, *The Good of the Order, and History of the Independent Order of Good Templars* (Mauston, Wis.: Grand Lodge, Independent Order of Good Templars, 1888), pp. 77–79; and R. Alder Temple, *A Brief History of the Order of the Sons of Temperance* (New York: National Temperance Society and Publishing House, [1886?]).

47. John Van Valkenburg, *Knights of Pythias Complete Manual and Text-book* (Canton, Ohio: Knights of Pythias, 1887), p. 446.

48. Oliver M. Wilson, *The Grand Army of the Republic Under Its First Constitution and Ritual* (Kansas City, Mo.: Hudson Publishing Co., 1905), p. 204. See also pp. 151–207.

49. General Assembly of the Knights of Labor, *Proceedings* (1887), p. 1516, cited in Ware, *Labor Movement*, p. 95.

50. Rather than meet the issue of initiatory ritual head-on, Powderly drafted a "Secret Circular" during the General Assembly of 1884. It was a long disquisition on the mystical meanings of the symbols of the Stephens ritual. He later recalled that he had duped the proritualists into believing that Stephens had tutored him on the secret arcana of the order, in Terence V. Powderly, *The Path I Trod* (New York: Columbia University Press, 1940) p. 65. The secret circular appears as an appendix on pp. 431–43. On the emotional importance of the initiation, see *Journal of United Labor*, July 15, 1880. When the ritualist-socialist faction drove Powderly from office in 1893, his successor returned to the religious ritualism of Stephens (Stevens, *Cyclopaedia of Fraternities*, p. 394).

51. Pinkerton, *Strikers, Communists, Tramps, and Detectives*, pp. 89–90.

52. Tricoche, "Sociétés Secrètes," p. 12. The New York State Insurance Department reported that life insurance companies had 2,166,274 policies in force, while fraternal beneficiary societies had 2.6 million insured members (p. 7).

53. Tricoche, "Sociétés Secrètes," pp. 6–7, 13–14, 22–23, 38–39.

54. Eric Hobsbawm, *Primitive Rebels: Studies in Archaic Forms of Social Movement in the 19th and 20th Centuries* (New York: Frederick A. Praeger, 1963), pp. 152–54.

55. Jonathan Blanchard, *Scotch Rite Masonry Illustrated* (Chicago: Ezra A. Cook, 1882), 2:438.

56. See especially Theodore Reik, *Ritual: Four Psycho-Analytic Studies* trans. Douglas Bryan (New York: Farrar, Strauss, 1946), pp. 91–166.

57. Bruno Bettelheim, *Symbolic Wounds: Puberty Rites and the Envious Male* (Glencoe, Ill.: Free Press, 1954).

58. For a summary of objections to the use of psychoanalytical models in these

and similar contexts, see David Stannard, *Shrinking History: On Freud and the Failure of Psychohistory* (New York: Oxford University Press, 1980).

59. See especially S. F. Nadel, *Foundations of Social Anthropology* (London: Cohen and West, 1951), pp. 64, 71; *Nupe Religion* (London: Routledge and Kegan Paul, 1954), p. 108; and Monica Wilson, *Rituals of Kinship among the Nyakyusa* (London: Oxford University Press, 1957), p. 6.

60. See especially Victor Turner, *The Forest of Symbols: Aspects of Ndembu Ritual* (Ithaca, N.Y.: Cornell University Press, 1967). Turner seized upon Carl Jung's distinction between signs and symbols to justify a deeper exploration of ritual meanings. Jung held that a sign is an abbreviation or condensation of something that is known; a symbol, on the other hand, is the best possible expression of something which includes aspects of the unknown. To examine ritual symbols without considering their unstated meanings was nonsensical (Turner, *Forest of Symbols*, pp. 26–27; Carl Jung, *Psychological Types* [London: Routledge and Kegan Paul, 1949], p. 601).

61. Emile Durkheim and Marcel Mauss, *Primitive Classification*, trans. Rodney Needham (Chicago: University of Chicago Press, 1963), p. 88.

CHAPTER I. MASKS

1. Some information on the emotional states of initiates came from interviews with current members of the order. "Wilmot's book" refers to A. B. Grosh's *The Odd-Fellow's Improved Manual* (Philadelphia: T. Bliss, 1871). See chapter 4, "Application and Admission." On the ritual itself, see [Willis, comp.], *Dr. Willis's Exposé of Odd Fellowship* (W. S. Darmrell, 1846). The information on the Past Noble Grands is taken from E. M. Ruttenber and L. H. Clark, comps., *History of Orange County* (Philadelphia: Everts and Peck, 1881). The lodge referred to was the Ustayantha Lodge, No. 143, I.O.O.F., Port Jervis, pp. 731–32. Biographical information on the Past Noble Grands was found throughout the section on Deerpark, pp. 698–753. The account of Colfax's appearance in Poughkeepsie in 1873 and his remarks on Odd Fellowship is based on O. J. Hollister, *Life of Schuyler Colfax* (New York: Funk and Wagnalls, 1886), pp. 446–47.

2. *Willis's Exposé of Odd Fellowship*, p. 23.

3. Joseph D. Weeks, *History of the Knights of Pythias* (Pittsburgh: Joseph D. Weeks and Co., 1874).

4. Charles H. Litchman, *Official History of the Improved Order of Red Men* (Boston: Fraternity Publishing Co., 1893), pp. 243, 320. Thus the year 1492 A.D. became GSD year 1 (Great Sun of the year of Discovery); the order was established in 1834.

5. John G. Wells, *The Grange Illustrated* (New York: Grange Publishing Co., 1874), p. 19.

6. Albert Mackey, *An Encyclopaedia of Freemasonry* (Philadelphia: L. H. Everts and Co., 1884), p. 71. Each subdivision of American Masonry had its own system of dating time. The Scottish Rite Masons commenced with 3760 B.C., *Anno Mundi* (In the Year of the World); the Knights Templar with *Anno Ordinis* (In the Year of the

Order, 1118 A.D.); the Royal Arch Masons dated from 530 B.C., *Anno Inventionis* (In the Year of the Discovery); and Royal and Select Master Masons from 1000 B.C., *Anno Depositionis* (In the Year of the Deposit).

7. Note also the orders which expressed in their names a special relationship to antiquity: the Ancient Order of United Workmen, the Supreme Tribe of Ben-Hur, the Ancient Order of Druids, the Ancient Essenic Order, the Ancient Order of Foresters, the Ancient Order of the Knights of Malta, the Ancient Arabic Order of the Nobles of the Mystic Shrine, as well as the scores of fraternal orders whose names included some reference to knights and knighthood.

8. Dorothy Ann Lipson, *Freemasonry in Federalist Connecticut, 1789–1835* (Princeton, N.J.: Princeton University Press, 1977), pp. 16–33; Steven C. Bullock, "The Ancient and Honorable Society: Freemasonry in America, 1730–1830" (Ph.D. diss., Brown University, 1986), pp. 57, 84.

9. Bullock, "Ancient and Honorable Society," pp. 91–101. Bullock argued that for members in the mid-eighteenth century, the fraternity "never became central to their identities" (p. 101).

10. Bullock, "Ancient and Honorable Society," pp. 232–33; Peter Ross, *A Standard History of Freemasonry in the State of New York* (New York and Chicago: Lewis Publishing Co., 1899), 1:213–14.

11. Bullock, "Ancient and Honorable Society," pp. 103–43; Lipson, *Freemasonry in Federalist Connecticut*, pp. 69–71, 147. At the turn of the century the total number of Masons in the nation approached 3,000; by the mid-1820s approximately 50,000 men belonged to Masonic lodges, most of them located in Massachusetts, Connecticut, and New York. See G. L. Gibbs, *Proceedings of the Grand Lodge of Massachusetts* (Cambridge, Mass.: Caustic-Claflen Co., 1918), pp. 500ff.

12. Toivo H. Nekton, *Morton Lodge #63 of Free and Accepted Masons: Its History, 1797–1947* (Hempstead, New York: Morton Lodge, 1949), p. 35. See also Columbia Lodge of Boston, *Centenary of the Columbia Lodge* (Boston: Columbia Lodge, 1895), p. 90.

13. See especially Lipson, *Freemasonry in Federalist Connecticut*, pp. 8, 73–74, 259–66.

14. See the address by Roscoe Pound to the Grand Lodge of Massachusetts, "The Cause of Divergence in Ritual," in *Proceedings of the Council of Deliberation, State of New York, Ancient and Accepted Scottish Rite, 1917*, pp. 182–85; and Committee of the Grand Council, Royal and Select Masters of Illinois, *Fifty Years of Cryptic Masonry in Illinois* (Chicago: Grand Council of the Royal and Select Masters, 1902), pp. 2–3.

15. Bullock, "Ancient and Honorable Society," pp. 55, 232–33, 231–37. See also Ross, *Standard History*, pp. 214–15.

16. Stevens pointed out that the crucial story concerning Hiram Abiff in the Master Mason degree was introduced into Masonic ritual in 1825. The Past Master degree, similarly, was "of American origin and . . . did not appear until the second decade of the [nineteenth] century." See Albert C. Stevens, ed. and comp., *Cyclopaedia of Fraternities* (New York: E. B. Treat, 1907) pp. 22, 34. The Most Excellent Master degree was also of American origin, although it may have been somewhat

older. See A. T. C. Pierson, *Traditions of Freemasonry and Its Coincidences with the Ancient Mysteries* (New York: Macoy and Sickels and Pierson, 1865), pp. 300–301; and Bullock, "Ancient and Honorable Society," pp. 239–40.

17. In the most thorough study of Masonic membership during the Federalist period, Dorothy Lipson compared the occupations of Masons and non-Masons in the Town of Woodstock, Connecticut, for which records were quite complete. In 1822, 22.7 percent of all Masons worked in commerce or the professions while only 1.5 percent of the entire population held those occupations (*Freemasonry in Federalist Connecticut*, appendix 4, table 7, p. 354). Kathleen Kutolowski found that "four-fifths of the [Genesee County] Masons were engaged in the professions and business at a time when some ninety-three percent of Genesee County's work force made its living on farms" (Kathleen S. Kutolowski, "Freemasonry and Community in the Early Republic: The Case for Antimasonic Anxieties," *American Quarterly* 34 [Winter 1982], p. 553).

18. Ross, *Standard History*, p. 179. Lipson reports that in 1815 one lodge banished strong liquor and voted that only wine should be drunk during meetings (*Freemasonry in Federalist Connecticut*, pp. 261–62). On the emotional character of the new rituals, see Bullock, "Ancient and Honorable Society," pp. 197, 260–62.

19. Rev. C. G. Finney, *The Character, Claims, and Practical Workings of Freemasonry* (Cincinnati: Western Tract and Book Society, 1869), p. 49.

20. Lipson, *Freemasonry in Federalist Connecticut*, pp. 80–111.

21. Ronald Formisano and Kathleen S. Kutolowski, "Antimasonry and Masonry: The Genesis of Protests—1826–1827," *American Quarterly* 29 (Summer 1977), pp. 140–64.

22. See, for example, William Preston Vaughn, *The Antimasonic Party in the United States, 1826–1843* (Lexington, Ky.: University Press of Kentucky, 1983), pp. 184–86. Only a quarter of the Masons in Connecticut signed the Declaration of Freemasons in 1832, a document defending the institution from the charges of the Anti-Masons (Lipson, *Freemasonry in Federalist Connecticut*, pp. 9, 325–26). Not a single new Mason was initiated in Rhode Island from 1829 to 1840 (John Gilkeson, "A City of Joiners: Voluntary Associations and the Formation of the Middle Class in Providence, 1830–1920," Ph.D. diss., Brown University, 1981], p. 118). In the state of New York membership declined from approximately 20,000 in 1825 to 1,500 in 1832 (Ossian Lang, *History of Freemasonry in the State of New York* (New York: Grand Lodge of New York, 1922), p. 209. On Antimasonry see also Michael Holt, "Antimasonic and Know-Nothing Parties," in *History of U.S. Political Parties*, 4 vols., ed. Arthur M. Schlesinger, Jr. (New York: Chelsea House, 1973), pp. 592, 619; and Alphonse Cerza, *Anti-Masonry* (Fulton, Mo.: Ovid Bell Press, 1962), p. 39.

23. Ross, *Standard History*, p. 179; Nekton, *Morton Lodge #63*, pp. 36–37; Columbia Lodge of Boston, *Centenary of the Columbia Lodge*, p. 90; Henry W. Rugg, *History of Freemasonry in Rhode Island* (Providence: E. L. Freeman and Son, 1895), p. 460.

24. For a fascinating study of the origins of Masonic law, see Roscoe Pound, "Lectures on Masonic Jurisprudence," (originally published in *The Builder*, 1916) in *Masonic Addresses and Writings of Roscoe Pound* (Richmond: Macoy Publishing Co.,

1953). On the new forms of discipline, see "Masonry and Temperance," *Ashlar* (December 1859); "Lodges in Taverns," *American Freemason* (September 1859); and "Weed Them Out," *Voice of Masonry* (February 1877).

25. James L. Ridgely, *History of American Odd Fellowship: The First Decade* (Baltimore: Grand Lodge, I.O.O.F., 1878), p. 7; see also p. 32.

26. "Such was the condition in every lodge in 1823," Ridgely wrote (ibid., pp. 42–43). The minutes of a lodge in Philadelphia in 1824 confirmed this appraisal, as rounds of toasts constituted the chief activity of the meeting. Rev. A. B. Grosh recorded some of the early Odd Fellows' songs, which emphasized the order's convivial purpose. See, for example, a "long-standing favorite" (Odd Fellow's Improved Manual), p. 23n.:

> "Oh what pleasure for to meet
> With friends so blithe and jolly,
> Who all delight for to dispel
> The gloom of melancholy!
> Then let us throw all care aside
> Let's merry be and mellow . . .

27. Ridgely, *American Odd Fellowship*, pp. 149–50.

28. Ridgely, *American Odd Fellowship*, pp. 7, 32, 142–43; Stevens, *Cyclopaedia of Fraternities*, p. 258; D. W. Bristol, *The Odd Fellows' Amulet* (Auburn, New York: Derby, Miller and Co., 1848), pp. 127–30.

29. Grosh, *Odd-Fellow's Improved Manual*, p. 49.

30. In the *Odd-Fellow's Improved Manual*, Grosh maintained that the Investigating Committee was the order's most important body. He advised the committee, which screened applicants, to "write abroad" to ascertain the character of candidates who were not "old residents," adding, "reflect that our Lodge is our family, and that admission into *it*, frequently almost necessarily, admits into our domestic circles also." In a catalogue of middle-class values, Grosh advised the committee to reject "the man of lax morals or loose principles," the "despiser of public opinion in matters of reputation," the "slanderer and contemner of female virtue," and "the mean in conduct" (pp. 205–09). On the justification for the benefits measures, see pp. 63–68. For a description of procedures to expel miscreants, see pp. 213–15.

31. Ridgely, *American Odd Fellowship*, pp. 204, 234–35.

32. See Grosh, *Odd-Fellow's Improved Manual*, pp. 30–31. See also Henry L. Stillson, ed., *The Official History and Literature of Odd Fellowship* (Boston: Fraternity Publishing Co., 1898), p. 520; and Elvin J. Curry, *The Red Blood of Odd Fellowship* (Baltimore: Fleet-McGinley Co., 1903), pp. 217–19.

33. Ridgely, *American Odd Fellowship*, p. 319.

34. Ridgely, *American Odd Fellowship*, pp. 244–45, 319–25. See also Curry, *Red Blood of Odd Fellowship*: "It is established beyond question that the early English lodges had quite simple ceremonies" (p. 211), and "the ritualistic element connected with the work of the lodge was considered of little importance" in the early 1800s (p. 217).

35. Grosh, *Odd-Fellow's Improved Manual*, p. 39.

36. Independent Order of Odd Fellows, *Journal of Proceedings* (Baltimore: Sovereign Grand Lodge, 1841) pp. 376–77.

37. Ridgely, *American Odd Fellowship*, p. 319. See also Grosh, *Odd-Fellow's Improved Manual*, pp. 39–40.

38. "Uniformity of Working," *Masonic Review* (January 1870). See also "Uniformity in Rituals," *Masonic Review* (May 1869). W. R. Singleton noted that the American ritual was "altered many times" after 1840. See "Ancient York Masonry," *Voice of Masonry* (September 1876).

39. A. T. C. Pierson, "The Capitular Degrees," *American Quarterly Review of Freemasonry* (April 1859). The editor of the *Masonic Review* called for a "return to the rites and rituals which [the framers of the Royal Arch] laid down for our guidance, which we seem unfortunately to have lost." He advised, ironically, further revision ("H.R.A. Degree," *Masonic Review* [June 1868]). See also "New Degrees," *Masonic Monthly* (July 1865); "Additional Degrees," *Masonic Review* (March 1868); "Templar Masonry," *Masonic Review* (February 1868); [Hiram Abiff (pseud.)], "The Modern Origin of the Higher Degrees," *Masonic Monthly* (September 1865); and "Preservation of the Rituals," *Masonic Review* (January 1865).

40. The "mere shell" quotation appears in "Innovations in Masonry," *Voice of Masonry* (November 1867). The editor of the journal further defied any Mason who had belonged to the order for the past twenty years to "deny the fact that, within that short period of time, innovations after innovations have been added to the ritualistic work of Freemasonry." The "murderously perverted" reference appears in "The True Ritual," *Ashlar* (October 1858). The editor of *Ashlar* discovered, to his "mortification and horror," that after the Morgan debacle nearly every Grand Lodge had established its own ceremonies, "each peculiar to its own jurisdiction, and all differing from each other." The "too progressive" quotation appears in *Masonic Review* (March 1855). See also "Extracts from the Annual Official Address of Brother A. G. Mackey, Grand Secretary of the Grand Lodge of South Carolina," *Ashlar* (May 1859).

41. See, for instance, M. Rhigellini, "The Egyptian Origin of Masonry," *American Quarterly Review of Freemasonry* (July 1858); Albert Mackey, "The Ancient Mysteries and Modern Freemasonry: Their Analogies Considered," *Voice of Masonry* (November 1876); and Homer Bartlett, "History of Initiation: As Practiced by the Ancient Rites and Perpetuated by Freemasonry," *Voice of Masonry* (May 1877).

42. John Sheville and James L. Gould, *Guide to the Royal Arch Chapter: A Complete Monitor for Royal Arch Masonry* (New York: Macoy, 1867), p. 43.

43. "Tinkering Degrees," *Voice of Masonry* (February 1879). See also Grand Lodge of Massachusetts, "Action of the Grand Lodge of Massachusetts Against Spurious Rites and Degrees and Irregular Bodies Called Masonic" (Boston: Rockwell and Churchill, 1883), pp. 17, 44, 51; and William Homan, *The Scottish Rite of the Supreme Council of the Northern Masonic Jurisdiction* (New York, 1905), pp. 125, 134–35.

44. William Rounseville, "Masonic Mutation," *Voice of Masonry* (January 1876); and *Masonic Review* (March 1855).

45. Ridgely, *American Odd Fellowship*, p. 320.

46. Stevens, *Cyclopaedia of Fraternities*, pp. 257–59; and Noel Gist, "Secret Societies in the United States," *University of Missouri Studies* 15 (October 1940), p. 42.

47. "Masonic Female Institute," *Masonic Signet and Mirror* (May 1851).

48. Mark Twain's *A Connecticut Yankee in King Arthur's Court* was written in part as a reaction against the fraternal movement's romantic recreation of the past. Its hero, Henry Morgan, also journeyed into the past and surmounted numerous challenges. Unlike the fraternal members, Morgan employed modern technology and shattered romantic illusions.

49. [Ezra Cook, comp.] *Good Templarism Illustrated: A Full Illustrated Exposition of the Ceremonies of the Three Degrees of the Lodge and Temple* (Chicago: Ezra A. Cook, 1879), pp. 96–97.

50. Albert Mackey, *Encyclopaedia of Freemasonry*, s. v. "Secret Vault" (Philadelphia: L. H. Everts, 1886), p. 823.

51. Mircea Eliade, *Rites and Symbols of Initiation* (New York: Harper and Row, 1958), pp. ix–xiii.

52. *Voice of Masonry* (August 1870).

53. Grosh, *Odd-Fellow's Improved Manual*, p. 41; Ridgely, *American Odd Fellowship*, p. 10.

54. Albert Mackey, *The Symbolism of Freemasonry: Illustrating and Explaining Its Science and Philosophy, Its Legends, Myths, and Symbols* (New York: Clark and Maynard, 1869), p. 311.

55. See especially Louis Hartz, *The Liberal Tradition in America: An Interpretation of American Political Thought Since the Revolution* (New York: Harcourt, Brace, 1955), pp. 51–52.

56. This discussion is informed by Stuart Blumin's astute analysis in "The Hypothesis of Middle-Class Formation in Nineteenth-Century America: A Critique and Some Proposals," *American Historical Review* 90 (April 1985), pp. 299–338. See Bledstein, *The Culture of Professionalism: The Middle Class and the Development of Higher Education in America* (New York: W. W. Norton, 1976); Paul E. Johnson, *A Shopkeeper's Millennium: Society and Revivals in Rochester, New York, 1815–1837* (New York: Hill and Wang, 1978); Paul Boyer, *Urban Masses and Moral Order in America: 1820–1920* (Cambridge, Mass., Harvard University Press, 1978); and Mary P. Ryan, *Cradle of the Middle Class: The Family in Oneida County, New York, 1790–1865* (Cambridge: Cambridge University Press, 1981).

57. Johnson, *Shopkeeper's Millennium*, p. 8; also Anthony F. C. Wallace, *Rockdale: The Growth of an American Village in the Early Industrial Revolution* (New York: Alfred A. Knopf, 1978).

58. Brian Greenberg, *Worker and Community: Response to Industrialization in a Nineteenth-Century American City, Albany, New York, 1850–1884* (Albany: State University of New York Press, 1985), pp. 89–101; Mary Ann Clawson, "Brotherhood, Class and Patriarchy: Fraternalism in Europe and America" (Ph.D. diss., University of New York at Stonybrook, 1980), pp. 136, 245–46, 415.

59. Wallace, *Rockdale*, pp. 345–47.

60. See chapter 3. Grosh, for instance, who conceived of Odd Fellowship as an agency to promote industriousness and sobriety and to "improve and elevate the character of man," emerges in Ryan's Utica as editor of a magazine, the *Evangelical Magazine and Gospel Advocate*, that opposed the revivals (Ryan, *Cradle of the Middle Class*, p. 123).

61. Johnson, *Shopkeeper's Millennium*, pp. 10, 138.

62. [Ezra A. Cook] *Red Men Illustrated: The Complete Illustrated Ritual* (Chicago: Ezra A. Cook, 1896), p. 30.

63. Victor Turner, *The Ritual Process: Structure and Anti-Structure* (Ithaca: Cornell University Press, 1969), pp. 94–130.

64. Victor Turner, *Process, Performance, and Pilgrimage* (New Delhi: Concept, 1979), p. 129.

65. Lipson, *Freemasonry in Federalist Connecticut*, pp. 11–12.

66. Grosh, *Odd-Fellow's Improved Manual*, pp. 184–85.

67. See Mary Douglas, "Jokes," in Douglas, *Implicit Meanings* (London: Routledge and Kegan Paul, 1975), pp. 90–114.

68. Grosh, *Odd-Fellow's Improved Manual*, p. 185.

69. Rounseville, "The Impression of the Candidate," *Voice of Masonry* (January 1877); also see reminiscences of Salem Town in Temple R. Hollcroft, "Salem Town: Partial Autobiography and Masonic Biography" *American Lodge of Research Transactions* 5 (1949–1951), pp. 240–66.

70. Albert Pike [comp.], *Morals and Dogma of the Ancient and Accepted Rite of Freemasonry* (Charleston: Southern Jurisdiction, A.A.S.R., 1872) p. 22.

71. Weeks, *History of the Knights of Pythias*, pp. 281–82.

72. Charles J. Creller, *The Golden Shield of Pythian Knighthood* (San Francisco: Rosemont Press, 1928), p. 85.

73. Ibid.

74. [Benjamin Henry Day], *Richardson's Monitor of Free-Masonry* (Philadelphia: David McKay, [1872?]), pp. 25–26.

75. Pike, *Morals and Dogma*, pp. 104–05, 246, and 819.

76. Jonathan Blanchard, *Scotch Rite Masonry Illustrated* (Chicago: Ezra A. Cook, 1882).

77. Weeks, *History of the Knights of Pythias*, p. 283.

CHAPTER II. WORDS

1. All of the quotations are from speeches at the memorial ceremony for Dr. John Brown held on November 7, 1884, as reported in Charles H. Halstead, *History of Hudson River Lodge, #607, Free and Accepted Masons* (Newburgh, N.Y.: Hudson River Lodge, 1896), pp. 129–52. (Spelling and punctuation have been modernized.) Also appearing there are Estabrook's reflections on Brown (pp. 151–52) and references to Halstead's talk two days before the memorial service entitled "Symbolism of Masonry" (p. 132). Halstead later contributed to the lodge several books which touched

on the Egyptian origins of Freemasonry (pp. 386–87); whether he actually mentioned that subject in 1884 is conjecture. On the theology and character of Bishop John Hobart, see John McVickar, *The Early Years of the Late Bishop Hobart* (New York: Protestant Episcopal Press, 1834), and *The Professional Years of the Rev. John Henry Hobart* (New York: Protestant Episcopal Press, 1836). Brown's manuscript sermons are in the possession of St. George's Church, Newburgh, New York. The description of the temple's architecture is based on the existing Masonic temple in Newburgh.

2. Halstead, *History of the Hudson River Lodge #607*, pp. 140–43.

3. David Bernard, *Light on Masonry* (1874; reprint, Utica: W. Williams, 1929). Brown did make some excisions, which will be considered later. Most of the prayer was taken from the High Priest's second prayer in the Royal Arch initiation; the remaining portion came from an alternative prayer reprinted in many sources, including John Sheville and James L. Gould, *Guide to the Royal Arch Chapter: A Complete Monitor for Royal Arch Masonry* (New York: Macoy, 1867) p. 143.

4. On the difference between English and American interpretations of the degree, see Albert Mackey, *Encyclopaedia of Freemasonry* (Philadelphia: L. H. Everts, 1886), pp. 803–04.

5. Ibid., pp. 784, 800, 804.

6. Jacob O. Doesburg, *Freemasonry Illustrated* (Chicago: Ezra A. Cook, 1886) p. 547.

7. Ibid., p. 508.

8. Bernard, *Light on Masonry*, p. 143.

9. The seeming heresy of the ritual was further sustained by the opening ceremony, in which God's temple was symbolically raised by men in the form of a "living arch". The "ineffable" word came not as a gift from God, in the way that Moses had received it, but from the mouths of Royal Arch officials, who had taken it upon themselves to give voice to God's "unspeakable" perfections.

10. Charles Lloyd Cohen, *God's Caress: The Psychology of Puritan Religious Experience* (New York: Oxford University Press, 1986) pp. 180–81.

11. John Bunyan, *Solomon's Temple Spiritualized* (London: Larkin, 1688); quoted in Dorothy Ann Lipson, *Freemasonry in Federalist Connecticut, 1789–1835* (Princeton, N.J.: Princeton University Press; 1977), pp. 122–23.

12. Bernard, *Light on Masonry*, p. 136.

13. Bernard, *Light on Masonry*, p. 144.

14. See the "Charge to the Candidates" cited in Sheville and Gould, *Guide to the Royal Arch Chapter*, p. 206.

15. "Under his hand the lodge became a schoolroom; the Master, the teacher; the candidate, the pupil," writes H. L. Haywood in *The Great Teachings of Masonry* (New York: George H. Doran Co., 1923), p. 141. By the early 1800s several American editions of Preston's *Illustrations of Freemasonry* (1788) had been widely circulated.

16. William Preston, *Illustrations of Freemasonry* (London: 1796 edition), cited in Lipson, *Freemasonry in Federalist Connecticut*, p. 37n.

17. Roscoe Pound, "The Cause of Divergence in Ritual," *Proceedings of the Council of Deliberation, State of New York* (New York: 1917), pp. 182–83.

18. Thomas Smith Webb, *The Freemason's Monitor* (Albany, N.Y.: Spencer and Webb, 1797); Sheville and Gould doubt that Webb himself wrote the revised versions but offer no suggestion as to who was their author (*Guide to the Royal Arch Chapter*, p. 42).

19. See Webb, *Freemason's Monitor*, pp. 40ff. The quote appears on p. 26. "Webb's lectures," Sheville and Gould wrote, "were only a revision of the Prestonian system" (*Guide to the Royal Arch Chapter*, p. 22).

20. Quotations are from Webb, *Freemason's Monitor*, pp. 155, 26, 39. On the relation between Deism and Freemasonry, see Lipson, *Freemasonry in Federalist Connecticut*, pp. 123–24.

21. Salem Town, *A System of Speculative Masonry* (Salem, New York: Dodd and Co., 1822), cited in Sheville and Gould, *Guide to the Royal Arch Chapter*, p. 44.

22. Sheville and Gould, *Guide to the Royal Arch Chapter*, pp. 45–46.

23. On Pike and Mackey's affiliation, see Committee of the Grand Council, Royal and Select Masters of Illinois, *Fifty Years of Cryptic Masonry in Illinois* (Chicago: Grand Council, 1902), pp. 2–3.

24. *Lectures and Charges of the Degrees of the Independent Order of Odd Fellows in the United States* (Philadelphia: J. Royer, 1833), pp. 5–9.

25. A. B. Grosh, *The Odd-Fellow's Improved Manual* (Philadelphia: T. Bliss and Co., 1871), pp. 27–29.

26. William Ellery Channing, "A Sermon Delivered at the Ordination of the Rev. Jared Sparks to the Pastoral Care of the First Independent Church of Baltimore, May 5, 1819" (Baltimore: J. Robinson, 1819).

27. On the significance of the speech, see Sidney E. Ahlstrom, *A Religious History of the American People* (New Haven and London: Yale University Press, 1977), p. 395; also *Dictionary of American Biography*, s.v. "Jared Sparks" and "William Ellery Channing."

28. See Channing, "A Sermon at the Ordination of the Rev. Jared Sparks," pp. 4, 5–13, 26–27, 29, 30, 32–36.

29. James Ridgely, *History of American Odd-Fellowship: The First Decade* (Baltimore: J. L. Ridgely, 1878), p. 322–24.

30. On the inadequacies of the White degree, see J. Fletcher Williams, "The Encampment Branch of the Order," in Henry L. Stillson, ed., *The Official History and Literature of Odd Fellowship* (Boston: Fraternity Publishing Co., 1897), p. 427. The Initiatory degree did not refer to Adam by name, but the references were unmistakable.

31. According to Genesis 3:19, God punished Adam for his sin by forcing him to work "till thou return unto the ground; for out of it wast thou taken: for dust thou art, and unto dust shalt thou return"; unceasing toil was a prelude to mortality.

32. These and other passages from the 1845 ritual are taken from [Willis, comp.] *Dr. Willis's Exposé of Odd Fellowship* (Boston: W. S. Damrell, 1846), pp. 18–25. Willis's exposé is substantially the same as that found in John Kirk, *Kirk's Exposition of Odd-Fellowship* (New York: by author, 1857).

33. Grosh, *Odd-Fellow's Improved Manual*, p. 95.

34. *Willis's Exposé of Odd Fellowship*, pp. 9–10, 23–24.

35. Mackey, *Encyclopaedia of Freemasonry*, s. v. "Knight of the Sun," pp. 213–19.

36. [Benjamin Henry Day], *Richardson's Monitor of Freemasonry* (Philadelphia: David McKay [1872?]), pp. 160–66.

37. Jonathan Blanchard, *Scotch Rite Masonry Illustrated* (Chicago: Ezra A. Cook, 1882), p. 217.

38. [Ezra A. Cook], *Knights of Pythias Illustrated*, (Chicago: Ezra A. Cook, 1878), pp. 69–71.

39. The Pythians' allusion to the Adam of Genesis required some ingenuity, insofar as the ritual took place in a hell ruled by the Roman god of the dead. But, as in the hell of the Bible, Pluto's domain was filled with snakes, and Pluto stated that he had "tempted" Eve to entrap Adam. See Joseph D. Weeks, *History of the Knights of Pythias* (Pittsburgh, Pa: Joseph D. Weeks and Co., 1874), pp. 17–18.

40. See discussion of the rank of Esquire of the Knights of Pythias in *Knights of Pythias Illustrated*, pp. 33–44.

41. See the Neophyte degree of the Knights of the Golden Circle in Felix G. Stidger, ed., *Treason History: Sons of Liberty* (Chicago: By the author, 1903), pp. 189–226.

42. Jonathan Blanchard, *Scotch Rite Masonry Illustrated* (Chicago: Ezra A. Cook, 1882), p. 217.

43. Cited in David E. Stannard, *The Puritan Way of Death: A Study in Religion, Culture, and Social Change* (New York: Oxford University Press, 1977), p. 185.

44. Henry Ward Beecher, *Notes from Plymouth Pulpit: A Collection of Memorable Passages from the Discourses of Henry Ward Beecher*, ed. Augusta Moore (New York: Derby and Jackson, 1859), pp. 194–95; cited in James J. Farrell, *Inventing the American Way of Death, 1830–1920* (Philadelphia: Temple University Press, 1980), p. 80.

45. Beecher, *Royal Truths* (Boston: Ticknor and Fields, 1866), cited in Farrell, *American Way of Death*, p. 80.

46. E. L. Youmans, "Concerning the Belief in Hell," *Popular Science Monthly* 12 (March 1878), pp. 627–30; cited in Farrell, *American Way of Death*, p. 82.

47. Masonic burial practices were well established by the 1840s; the burial services of most other orders dated from the 1870s. See *The Funeral Book of the Freemasons* (Chicago: J. C. W. Bailey, 1868); E. M. L. Ehlers, comp., *Burial of the Dead* (New York, 1891); [George Wingate Chase, comp.], *Burial Services for the Ancient and Honorable Fraternity of Free and Accepted Masons* (Boston: A. W. Pollard and Co., 1865); "Funeral Procession and Service, As Ordered by G.L.U.S. [Grand Lodge of the United States] at Its Session in 1866," in Grosh, *Odd-Fellow's Improved Manual*, pp. 377–82; Sovereign Grand Lodge, Independent Order of Odd-Fellows, *Funeral Ceremony to be Observed at the Burial of Members of the Independent Order of Odd-Fellows* ([Baltimore]: Sovereign Grand Lodge, I.O.O.F., 1880); [Supreme Lodge, Knights of Pythias], *Form of Funeral Service* (Columbus, Ohio: Supreme Lodge, Knights of Pythias, 1877).

48. If other lodges chose to perform graveside services, Masons were told to pro-

ceed "as though no other persons (save the mourners) were present," *The Funeral Book of the Freemasons*, p. 47.

49. *Funeral Book of the Freemasons*, pp. 38–47. See also Albert Mackey, *Symbolism of Freemasonry* (New York: Clark and Maynard, 1869): "It is only beyond the grave, and when released from the earthly burden of life, that man is capable of fully receiving and appreciating the revelation [of divine Truth]," p. 308.

50. Mackey, *Symbolism of Freemasonry*, p. 308.

51. Ibid., p. 853.

52. Ibid., p. 309.

53. Mackey, *Encyclopaedia of Freemasonry*, p. 112; and Robert Macoy, ed., *A Cyclopedia of Freemasonry* (New York: Masonic Publishing and Manufacturing Co., 1867), p. 30.

54. Mackey, *Encyclopaedia of Freemasonry*, pp. 112, 327.

55. Weeks, *History of the Knights of Pythias*, p. 40.

56. Stidger, *Treason History*, p. 191; and J. W. Pomfrey, *A True Disclosure and Exposition of the Knights of the Golden Circle* (Cincinnati: by author, 1861).

57. Weeks, *History of the Knights of Pythias*, pp. 17–19.

58. [Ezra A. Cook], *Red Men Illustrated: The Complete Illustrated Ritual of the Improved Order of Red Men* (Chicago: Ezra A. Cook, 1896), p. 84.

59. The fire triangle was opposed to the water triangle, point downward, which denoted a "kind, good, gracious, and merciful God" (Macoy, *Encyclopedia of Freemasonry*, pp. 618–19). Significantly, the water triangle rarely appeared in Masonic rituals.

60. Sovereign Grand Lodge, Independent Order of Odd Fellows, *Funeral Ceremony to be Observed at the Burial of Members*, p. 23.

61. Compare Pike's pantheistic rendering of the Deity as the "centre of Light whose rays or emanations pervade the Universe" to Jonathan Edwards's reference to God as "an effulgence or emanation of light from a luminary," the "abundant, extensive emanation and communication of the fulness of the sun" (Albert Pike, *Morals and Dogma of the Ancient and Accepted Rite of Freemasonry* (Charleston, S.C.: Southern Jurisdiction of the A.A.S.R., 1878), p. 252; Jonathan Edwards, "The Nature of True Virtue," *Works* (Andover: Allen, Morrill and Wardwell, 1842) 2:261–62.

62. He recommended attention to *Pilgrim's Progress*, "as there may be somebody at work writing up a new set of Rituals of the Scotch Rite, a thing which each member has the same right to do that Brother Pike had" ("The Pilgrim's Progress as a Masonic Allegory," *Voice of Masonry* [May 1867]).

63. [Blanchard], "Knights of the Sun," in *Scotch Rite Masonry*, p. 213.

64. Ibid., p. 219.

65. Among the major orders, only the Knights Templars and the Good Templars referred to Christ in their rituals.

66. Oliver wrote some fifteen major books on this subject. The most important were *Theocratic Philosophy of Freemasonry* (London: Hamilton, Adams and Co., 1840), *The History of Initiation* (London: R. Spencer, 1841), *Star in the East* (London,

R. Spencer, 1842), and *Signs and Symbols of Freemasonry* (New York: J. W. Leonard and Co., 1856).

67. Albert Mackey, *The Masonic Ritualist* (New York: Clark, Maynard, 1877), pp. 23–24.

68. Donald M. Scott, *From Office to Profession* (Philadelphia: University of Pennsylvania Press, 1978), pp. 138–39.

69. Catharine Beecher, ed., *The Biographical Remains of Rev. George Beecher* (New York: Leavitt, Trow and Co., 1844), pp. 150–51; cited in Scott, *From Office to Profession*, p. 139.

70. Dumenil, *Freemasonry and American Culture*, p. 54.

71. Nowhere was this disjunction between secret ritual and public pronouncements more jarring than in the work of Albert Pike. In the "Knights of the Sun" ritual, he described God as "the awful being" (Blanchard, *Scotch Rite Masonry*, p. 210). Yet in *Morals and Dogma of Freemasonry*, he concluded that "there is no Savage, Revengeful, and Evil God: but there is an Infinite God, seen everywhere as Perfect Cause, everywhere as Perfect Providence, transcending all, yet in-dwelling everywhere, with perfect power, wisdom, justice, holiness, and love" (p. 716).

72. See Grosh, *Odd-Fellow's Improved Manual*, pp. 40–41; *Dictionary of American Biography*, s.v. "John McCabe"; and Sumner Ellis, *Life of Edwin H. Chapin, D.D.* (Boston: Universalist Publishing House, 1882), pp. 282–84.

73. Cited in Ellis, *Life of Chapin*, pp. 87–89.

74. The amplified third degree of the Knights of Pythias, featuring a journey through Hades, was written in 1872 by the Right Reverend Bishop William Ussher of the Reformed Episcopalian Church, which was organized in the following year to halt the ritualism of the General Convention of the Episcopalian church. On Ussher, see Annie D. Price, *A History of the Formation and Growth of the Reformed Episcopalian Church, 1873–1902* (Philadelphia: J. M. Armstrong, 1902), p. 185. See James R. Carnahan, *Pythian Knighthood: Its History and Literature* (Cincinnati: The Pettibone Manufacturing Co., 1888), p. 262; and Ahlstrom, *Religious History*, p. 631. Other important fraternal ritualists included A. B. Grosh (*Odd-Fellow's Improved Manual*) a Universalist minister and ritualist for the Patrons of Husbandry, and Joseph D. Weeks (*History of the Knights of Pythias*), who prepared for the Methodist ministry.

75. Carnahan, *Pythian Knighthood*, p. 268. Rev. D. W. Bristol, D.D., who had gained a reputation as a theorist on the ritualism of the Odd Fellows, was given the task of revising the three degrees of the Independent Order of Good Templars in 1853. See I. Newton Peirce, *The History of the Independent Order of Good Templars* (Philadelphia: Daughaday and Becker, 1869) pp. 41, 61–62; and D. W. Bristol, *The Odd fellows' Amulet, or, The Principles of Odd Fellowship Defined* (Auburn, New York: Derby, Miller and Co., 1848). Another example is Rev. Thomas Beharrell, author of the *Odd Fellows Monitor and Guide* (Indianapolis Ind.: Brotherhood Publishing Co., 1877).

76. Vincent J. Falzone, *Terence V. Powderly: Middle Class Reformer* (Washington, D.C.: University Press of America, 1978), pp. 15–16.

77. Ministerial Affiliation with Freemasonry, New York, 1890

Denomination	Number of Ministers Belonging to Masons	Total Number of Ministers (estimated)	Percentage Belonging to Masons
Baptists	112	755	15%
Congregational	21	358	6
Episcopalian	146	665	22
Lutheran	11	183	13
Methodist	288	1635	18
Presbyterian	59	838	7
Universalist	31	118	26

Source: On the denominational division of clergyman-Masons in New York in 1891, see Albert C. Stevens, comp. and ed., *Cyclopaedia of Fraternities* (New York: E. B. Treat, 1907), p. 12n. The 1890 *Federal Census of Religious Bodies* (available on microfilm) does not include a denominational breakdown of ministries by state. It does include data on the number of church edifices by denomination and by state (table 2), and it gives national statistics on the number of ministers and church edifices (table 9). For each denomination a ratio was derived of church edifices to ministers. None of the denominations varied more than .3 from the ratio of one minister per edifice; predictably, the Methodists and Baptists, who often relied on itinerant ministers, had the lowest ratio of ministers to churches (.7 to 1); the well-to-do Unitarian and Congregationalist churches had the highest (1.2 to 1 and 1.1 to 1 respectively). The minister-to-edifice proportion for each denomination was then multiplied by the number of church edifices for that denomination in New York to provide and approximation of the number of ministers in the denomination.

See also Lipson, *Freemasonry in Federalist Connecticut*, pp. 127–29.

78. Ahlstrom, *Religious History*, p. 775.

79. Albert Pike, "Gnosticism, the Kabbala, and the Mysteries as Connected with and Illustrating Masonry," *American Quarterly Review of Freemasonry*, July 1858.

80. Victor Turner, *Process, Performance and Pilgrimage* (New Delhi: Concept, 1979), pp. 14–15. An alternative view is that of C. J. Jung, who held that the meaning of some symbols lies deep in the roots of the human psyche (*Psyche and Symbol: A Selection from the Writings of C. G. Jung*, ed. Violet S. de Laszlo [New York: Doubleday, 1958]).

81. See John W. Dadmun, *The Masonic Choir: A Collection of Hymns and Tunes for the Use of the Fraternity* (Boston: G. D. Russell and Company, 1864), p. 4.

82. See, for example, the testimony of one renouncing Mason, in Charles G. Finney, *The Character, Claims and Practical Workings of Freemasonry* (Cincinnati: Western Tract and Book Society, 1869) pp. 109–11.

83. Critics of secret societies noted the inherent contradictions in fraternal rituals. "Truth and error," one wrote, "have been artfully commingled." See Jonathan Sarver, "Sermon on Odd-Fellowship and Other Secret Societies" (Chicago: Ezra A. Cook, 1876) p. 4.

84. Pike, *Morals and Dogma*, p. 291; Macoy, *Encyclopedia of Freemasonry*, p. 139.

85. Pike, *Morals and Dogma*, pp. 504–05. So pervasive was the fraternal use of the cross symbol that one Pythian scholar was surprised that his order did not develop its symbolism more elegantly: "Pythianism has its cross although one seldom hears of it. For some cause this primitive symbolical religious ornament has been over-looked" (Charles J. Creller, *The Golden Shield of Pythian Knighthood* [San Francisco: The Rosemont Pr., 1928], p. 92).

86. Turner, *The Forest of Symbols: Aspects of Ndembu Ritual* (Ithaca, N.Y.: Cornell University Press, 1977), p. 50.

87. Audrey Richards, *Chisungu: A Girl's Initiation Ceremony Among the Bemba of Northern Rhodesia* (London: Faber, 1956), pp. 164–65.

88. Turner, *The Forest of Symbols*, p. 44.

89. Ibid., pp. 22–23.

90. Pike, *Morals and Dogma*. "More than one meaning" appears on page 148; "under symbols" appears on page 246.

91. The frightening 1845 Initiatory degree of the Odd Fellows was said to be designed to "please the initiate." Similarly, Bishop Ussher's version of a passage through the "howling wastelands of hell" was reported to have "grown into very great favor." See Henry L. Stillson, ed., *The Official History and Literature of Odd Fellowship* (Boston: Fraternity Publishing Co., 1897), p. 552; Elvin J. Curry, *Red Blood of Odd Fellowship* (Baltimore: by the author, 1903), p. 212; and William D. Kennedy, *Pythian History* (Chicago: Pythian History Publishing Co., 1904), p. 262.

92. The phrase "summit of complacency" is used in the title of chapter 2, Henry F. May, *Protestant Churches and Industrial America* (New York: Harper and Row, 1949), and "the golden age of liberal theology" in the title of chapter 46, Sydney E. Ahlstrom, *A Religious History of the American People* (New Haven: Yale University Press, 1972).

CHAPTER III. DARKNESS

1. Charles Grandison Finney, *Memoirs of Charles G. Finney* (New York: A. S. Barnes and Co., 1876), pp. 13–23.

2. See William McLoughlin's introduction to Charles G. Finney, *Lectures on Revivals of Religion*, ed. William McLoughlin (Cambridge, Mass.: Harvard University, Belknap Press, 1960), p. xxxviii. As one contemporary critic of Finney noted, there was "a close and logical connexion" between Finney's theology and his strategy to precipitate conversion. See [Albert Dod], "Review of *Lectures on Revivals of Religion* and *Sermons on Various Subjects*," *Biblical Repertory and Theological Review* 7 (July and October 1835), p. 484, cited in Keith J. Hardman, *Charles Grandison Finney, 1792–1875* (Syracuse, New York: Syracuse University Press), p. 290.

3. Keith Hardman asserted "God's love for humans, and our response in love, played a very small part in Finney's appeal to audiences, as a broad reading of his sermons and lectures will demonstrate. Indeed, one can read in his writings for

dozens of pages, and the prominent biblical term 'love' will never appear" (*Charles Grandison Finney*, p. 100).

4. Finney, *Lectures on Revivals*, p. 14.

5. See "What a Revival of Religion Is," in Finney, *Lectures on Revivals*, pp. 9–12. Whether man or God was responsible for man's excitability was an issue on which Finney was unclear. See McLoughlin's introduction to *Lectures on Revivals*, pp. xxvi–xxviii.

6. Cited in Hardman, *Charles Grandison Finney*, pp. 99–100.

7. Charles Grandison Finney, *The Character, Claims and Practical Workings of Freemasonry* (Cincinnati: Western Tract and Book Society, 1869), pp. v–vi.

8. Finney, *Memoirs*, p. 7.

9. The early evangelical opposition to fraternal ritualism included Jabaz Swan, who brought Finneyite techniques to Baptist revivalism. He indicted the Odd Fellows in the 1850s; see William McLoughlin, *Modern Revivalism: Charles Grandison Finney to Billy Graham* (New York: Ronald Press Co.), p. 139.

10. Clyde S. Kilby, *Minority of One: The Biography of Jonathan Blanchard* (Grand Rapids, Mich.: Eerdmans, 1959), p. 171; Charles G. Finney, *Character, Claims, and Practical Workings*, p. 21. See also Rev. Richard Horton, *The Image of the Beast, A Secret Empire; or, Free-Masonry A Subject of Prophecy* (Summerfield, Ohio: W. A. Wallace, 1871), pp. 104–05.

11. The NCA endorsed various reforms, especially prohibition, and again the influence of Finneyite evangelism was substantial. Blanchard spearheaded temperance drives, and in 1884 former U.S. Senator Samuel C. Pomeroy, an NCA official, was nominated by the American Prohibition national convention to run for president. The NCA also favored free trade, direct vote for the election of the President, and the use of the Bible in educational institutions. For the individuals mentioned, see the *Dictionary of American Biography*. Also see *Brief History of the National Christian Association* (Chicago: Ezra Cook, 1875), pp. 10–12; [hereafter, *Brief History of the NCA*] and Richard S. Taylor, "Seeking the Kingdom: A Study in the Career of Jonathan Blanchard, 1811–1892" (Ph.D. diss., Northern Illinois University, 1977), pp. 43, 520.

12. Timothy L. Smith, "The Cross Demands, the Spirit Enables," *Christianity Today*, February 16, 1979, p. 24; cited in Hardman, *Charles Grandison Finney*, p. 294.

13. Keith Hardman concluded that Finney's greatest contribution to the antislavery movement was his ability to fire the consciences of young men (*Charles Grandison Finney*, pp. 185, 270–73, 368–69). This point is also developed by Gilbert Barnes in *The Antislavery Impulse, 1830–1844* (New York: Harcourt, Brace and World, 1933).

14. Kilby, *Minority of One*, pp. 171, 176. Finney was Oberlin's president from 1851 to 1866; James H. Fairchild, an NCA official, from 1866 to 1889. Their association with the institution dated from the 1830s. See entries for each in the *Dictionary of American Biography*. The theological diversity of the group is reflected in the fact that Blanchard, an orthodox Congregationalist, nevertheless in the pages of the *Christian Cynosure* praised Gerrit Smith, who espoused a rationalistic religion and wrote an

essay titled "A Religion of Reason" (1864). Blanchard forgave him his theological "errors." See Kilby, *Minority of One*, p. 176. On the NCA and abolitionism, see *History of the NCA*, pp. 10–12, 22, 26; and Taylor, "Seeking the Kingdom," pp. 518–20.

15. *Minutes of the Christian Convention at Aurora, Illinois* (Chicago: Dean and Ottaway, 1867), pp. 45, 2, 9.

16. *Minutes of the Christian Convention* (1867), p. 22. As early as 1852 one minister had complained that fraternal orders were "eating out the vitals of religion." See John Lawrence, *Plain Thoughts on Secret Societies* (Circleville, Ohio, 1852), p. 183; see also the Rev. Joseph T. Cooper, *Odd-Fellowship Examined in the Light of Scripture and Reason* (Philadelphia: William S. Young, 1853), pp. 30–31.

17. Quoted in the *Christian Cynosure*, November 26, 1891. See also *Brief History of the NCA*, p. 22; and I. J. Rosenberger, *Secret Societies Incompatible with Christianity*, (Elgin, Ill.: Brethren's General Mission Board, [189–?]), p. 12.

18. J. H. Brockmann, *Odd-Fellowship, Its Doctrine and Practice Examined in the Light of God's Word, and Judged by its Own Utterances* (Milwaukee: Brockmann, 1874), p. 30.

19. *Minutes of the Christian Convention* (1867), p. 50.

20. *Christian Cynosure*, January 4, 1891.

21. Rosenberger, *Secret Societies Incompatible*, p. 14.

22. The Catholic Church also took note of the advance of fraternal orders among Protestant clergy. Because "Christianity is dying among Protestant men," a theologian in Omaha concluded, the Catholic church must lead the assault against fraternal ritualism (Charles Coppens, S.J., "Is Freemasonry Anti-Christian?" *American Ecclesiastical Review* 21 [1899], p. 593).

23. The Reverend John Levington, *Key to Masonry and Kindred Secret Combinations* (Dayton, Ohio: United Brethren Publishing House, 1871), pp. 393, 397–98. See also the *Daily Christian Advocate*, 1876, cited in *Christian Cynosure*, January 14, 1892.

24. The Wesleyan Methodists, German Baptists, and Lutheran Evangelical Synod, with combined communicants of under half a million, had such prohibitions. See *History of the NCA*, pp. 24–28.

25. *Minutes of the Christian Convention* (1867), p. 45.

26. Quoted in Jonathan Blanchard, *Scotch Rite Masonry Illustrated* (Chicago: Ezra Cook, 1882) 1:130, 440.

27. Jonathan Blanchard, *Revised Odd-Fellowship Illustrated* (Chicago: Ezra Cook, 1881), p. 99.

28. Cited in Robert Wayne Smith, "A Study of the Speaking in the Anti-Secrecy Movement: 1868–1882, with Special Reference to the National Christian Association" (Ph.D. diss., University of Iowa, 1956), p. 206.

29. *Minutes of the Christian Convention* (1867), pp. 22–23.

30. Rev. Richard Horton, *The Image of the Beast*, p. 97. Still others located the satanic pedigree even further back in time. John Levington, a Methodist minister, cited the reports of missionaries in Africa about "savage" initiation ceremonies that

engaged in "devil-worship" and, like Freemasonry, excluded women. See Levington, *Key to Masonry*, pp. 382–84.

31. When the Great Fire destroyed the *Cynosure's* offices in Chicago in 1871, the circulation was near 6,000. See *Brief History of the NCA*, pp. 8, 18.

32. Speech by E. Honeywell, *Proceedings of the Sixth Anniversary of the National Christian Association* (Chicago: Cook, 1874), pp. 116–17 [hereafter, "*Proceedings of the NCA*, 1874"].

33. Albert Pike [comp.], *Morals and Dogma of the Ancient and Accepted Scottish Rite of Freemasonry* (Charleston: Southern Jurisdiction, A.A.S.R., 1872), p. 161; Albert Mackey, *Encyclopaedia of Freemasonry* (Philadelphia: L. H. Everts, 1886), 639ff. Pythian historian Joseph D. Weeks wrote in 1874 that "the highest and holiest principles of true religion receive their most perfect exemplification in the Secret societies." He thought the "Church of today"—rent by acrimonious theological disputes and petty squabbles—"should hang its head in shame" (*A History of the Knights of Pythias* [Pittsburgh: Joseph Weeks and Co., 1874], p. 15).

34. Significantly, this speech was included in L. S. Myler, ed., *Jewels of Masonic Oratory* (New York: M. W. Hazen, 1898), pp. 274–75.

35. Robert Ramsay, "The Masonic Church," *Voice of Masonry*, October 1878.

36. William Rounseville, "How Cynosurism Destroyed a Church," *Voice of Masonry*, November 1877.

37. Pike, *Morals and Dogma*, pp. 213–14.

38. Rev. F. H. Johnson, *Masonry, Past, Present and Future: Proved by Tradition, History and Revelation, Including 275 Evidences that Masonry and Religion Are the Same* (Buffalo, 1871), pp. 241–42.

39. See "Prof. Blanchard's Tilt Against Freemasonry," *Voice of Masonry* (March 1871).

40. *Chicago Tribune*, August 20–25, 1880, cited in John McClaughry, "John Wolcott Phelps: The Civil War General Who Became a Forgotten Presidential Candidate in 1880," *Vermont History* 38 (Autumn 1970), p. 287.

41. See Rev. Richard Horton, *Image of the Beast*, pp. 19–31, 105; and the Hon. Pliny Merrick, *Renunciation of Free-Masonry* (Worcester, Mass.: C. A. Blanchard [1871]), p. 6.

42. *Seventh Anniversary of the National Christian Association, Held at Pittsburgh* (Chicago: Ezra Cook, 1875), p. 68) [hereafter, *Seventh Anniversary of NCA*]. Finney's decision to speak against Freemasonry after the Civil War had been prompted by a flood of letters from women who complained that the orders had harmed their marriages and had discouraged husbands and sons from converting to Christ; see Leonard I. Sweet, *The Minister's Wife: Her Role in 19th-Century American Evangelicalism* (Philadelphia: Temple University Press, 1983), p. 214.

43. Warren C. Hubbard, "Sermon to Members of Aurora Grata Lodges" (New York: Nathan Lane's Sons, 1888), pp. 6–8, 18–21.

44. "Women in the Pulpit," *Voice of Masonry*, March 1872.

45. *Seventh Anniversary of NCA*, p. 10.

46. A study of religious and fraternal affiliation in nineteenth-century San Francisco found that the Masonic lodge was "composed overwhelmingly of non-church and non-synagogue members," although Masons were slightly more likely to belong to Protestant churches than were adult males in general. The author concluded that Masonry "served widely as a substitute for church and synagogue membership, virtually as a denomination in its own right." See Tony Fels, "Religious Assimilation in a Fraternal Organization: Jews and Freemasonry in Gilded-Age San Francisco," *American Jewish History* 74 (June 1985).

47. Edward Anderson, "Church and Lodge," a paper read before the State Association of Congregational Churches at Princeton, Illinois, May 28, 1879; cited in the *Congregationalist*, June 1879.

48. Martha T. Blauvelt, "Women and Revivalism," in *Women and Religion in America: The Nineteenth Century*, 2 vols., ed. Rosemary Ruether and Rosemary Keller (San Francisco: Harper and Row, 1981), 1:5. By 1830 in Baltimore over 70 percent of the church members were female; from 1800 to 1835, 69 percent of the communicants of the Congregational churches in New England were women. See Terry David Bilhartz, "Urban Religion and the Second Great Awakening: A Religious History of Baltimore, Maryland 1790–1830" (Ph.D. diss., George Washington University, 1979), pp. 62–63; and Richard D. Shiels, "The Feminization of American Congregationalism, 1730–1835," *American Quarterly* 33 (Spring 1981) p. 48. Mary P. Ryan found that the proportion of female converts in various denominations and churches ranged from 52 percent to 72 percent in Oneida County, New York (*Cradle of the Middle Class: The Family in Oneida County, New York, 1790–1865* [Cambridge: Cambridge University Press, 1981], pp. 79–81.) Ryan notes, further, that statistical indicators may understate women's influence, since women "disproportionately" preceded their male relations into the church, which suggested that women may have "cajoled" or "manipulated" their husbands and sons into joining. Most converts affirmed the faith of their mothers rather than of their fathers (pp. 81, 93). On women's predominant role in revivals in Rochester, see Paul Johnson, *A Shopkeeper's Millennium: Society and Revivals in Rochester, New York, 1815–1837* (New York: Hill and Wang, 1978), p. 108. Frances Trollope observed, some thirty years before Anderson's remarks, that she had never heard of a country "where religion had so strong a hold upon the women, or a slighter hold upon the men" (Frances Trollope, *Domestic Manners of the Americans*, ed. Donald Smalley [New York: Viking, 1949], p. 75). Whitney Cross observed that women "should dominate a history of enthusiastic movements, for their influence was paramount." See *The Burned Over District; The Social and Intellectual History of Enthusiastic Religion in Western New York, 1800–1850* (Ithaca: Cornell University Press, 1950), p. 84.

49. The Oneida Female Missionary Society in 1824 allocated $192 to support Finney; see Ryan, *Cradle of the Middle Class*, pp. 60–61; 83–96.

50. In his *Memoirs* Finney neglected to mention that Lydia Andrews, his future wife, had taken it upon herself to convert him in 1820. The Finneys were married in October 1824. After being left at home for the first six months of her marriage, Lydia Finney joined her husband's revivals, organizing maternal associations and meeting

with women's church and reform groups. According to one recent historian, her activist conception of the minister's wife inspired evangelical women and encouraged them to venture beyond the tightly circumscribed world of Victorian domesticity. See Leonard I. Sweet, *The Minister's Wife: Her Role in Nineteenth-Century American Evangelicalism* (Philadelphia: Temple University Press, 1983), pp. 76–106, 112–13, 107–08.

51. Ann Douglas, *The Feminization of American Culture* (New York: Alfred A. Knopf, 1977) pp. 17–93; Barbara Welter, "The Feminization of American Religion: 1800–1860," in Mary Hartman and Lois W. Banner, ed., *Clio's Consciousness Raised* (New York: Harper and Row, 1974); Nancy F. Cott, *The Bonds of Womanhood* (New Haven: Yale University Press, 1977), pp. 126–58; D. Shiels, "Feminization of Congregationalism." On the shift in women's roles in the economy see Alice Morse Earle, *Home Life in Colonial Days* (New York: Macmillan Co., 1898); Julia C. Spruill, *Women's Life and Work in the Southern Colonies* (New York: W. W. Norton, 1972).

52. Donald M. Scott, *From Office to Profession: The New England Ministry, 1750–1850* (Philadelphia: University of Pennsylvania Press, 1978) pp. 112–32; also Douglas, *Feminization of American Culture*, pp. 114–34.

53. Ministers were indispensable to the revivals, but less for their organizational talents than for their ability to enthrall their largely female audiences through powerful and, undeniably, "masculine" forms of preaching. Ann Douglas noted that Perry Miller described Finney "in terms which come close to equating religious and sexual prowess" (*Feminization of American Culture*, p. 18). On the relation between revivalist ministers and women, see Sweet, *Minister's Wife*, p. 249 n69; Cross, *Burned-Over District*, p. 84; and Barbara Leslie Epstein, *The Politics of Domesticity: Women, Evangelism and Temperance in Nineteenth-Century America* (Middletown, Conn.: Wesleyan University Press, 1981).

54. Sandra S. Sizer, *Gospel Hymns and Social Religion: The Rhetoric of Nineteenth-Century Revivalism* (Philadelphia: Temple University Press, 1978), p. 113.

55. J. D. Fulton, *The True Woman: A Series of Discourses by Rev. J. D. Fulton, (Tremont Temple, Boston) to Which Is Added Woman Vs. Ballot!* (Boston: Lee and Shepard, 1869), pp. 71–72; cited in Sweet, *Minister's Wife*, p. 181. See *Dictionary of American Biography*, s.v. "Justin Dewey Fulton."

56. See Douglas, *Feminization of American Culture*, pp. 143–96.

57. William McLoughlin has written that by the mid-nineteenth century Arminian evangelism had become the "national religion" of America. Liberal factions now dominated most of the branches of the major Protestant denominations. See William McLoughlin, *Modern Revivalism*, pp. 65–66. See also Robert T. Handy, *A History of the Churches in the United States and Canada* (Oxford: Oxford University Press, 1977), p. 289. Despite differences in organizational structure and style, both liberal and evangelical Protestantism shared an Arminian theology, and both were profoundly influenced by women. Finney's attack upon Calvinism was not evident from the outset, for he cited Jonathan Edwards and evoked the horrors of hell with appropriately unnerving detail. Only later did orthodox ministers realize that, despite appearances, Finney's theology emphasized man's capacity to influence his prospects of salvation.

There were important theological differences between the Arminianism of Finney and that of Channing, but they agreed that men could, by their actions, influence their chances for salvation. Finney's defense of women's participation in the worship service was anticipated by Channing, who wrote that his hopes for the "regeneration of the future" depended on "the exalting influence of woman." (cited in Welter, "Feminization of American Religion," p. 156 n42.

58. *Liberal Advocate*, September 29, 1832, cited in Johnson, *Shopkeeper's Millennium*, p. 108. See also Sweet, *Minister's Wife*, pp. 42–43.

59. Dorothy Ann Lipson, *Freemasonry in Federalist Connecticut* (Princeton, N.J.: Princeton University Press, 1977), pp. 329–38. See also William Preston Vaughn, *The Antimasonic Party in the United States, 1826–1843* (Lexington, Ky.: University Press of Kentucky, 1983), pp. 18–19.

60. "Early Impressions of Masonry," *Mystic Star*, April 1873; "Anti-Masonry," *Masonic Review*, March 1869; "Women and Masonry," *Voice of Masonry*, January 1882; Lawrence, *Plain Thoughts on Secret Societies*, p. 76; "Protest Against the Installation of Hon. Reuben H. Walworth as Grand Master of the Grand Lodge of Free and Accepted Masonry of State of New York" (New York: Jenkins, 1853), pp. 5–6. D. W. Bristol wrote that not all women were opposed to his order; many just didn't understand it (*The Odd fellows' Amulet* [Auburn, N.Y.: Derby, Miller, 1848], pp. 238–39.

61. *Freemasonry in the Family* (National Christian Association, 1880?), p. 4.

62. *Proceedings of the NCA*, 1874, p. 126. Gage helped organize the National Woman's Suffrage Association and composed, with Elizabeth Cady Stanton and Susan B. Anthony, the *Woman's Declaration of Rights* (1876).

63. Hardman, *Charles Grandison Finney*. The general tenor of the New Lebanon Convention was amicable until Justin Edwards proposed a resolution forbidding women from praying in mixed religious groups (p. 136). The issue was never resolved (pp. 137–38). Finney also had close ties to the New York Female Moral Reform Society, which was organized in his Chatham Street Chapel in 1834; see Carroll Smith-Rosenberg, *Religion and the Rise of the American City: The New York City Missionary Movement: 1812–1870* (Ithaca, New York: Cornell University Press, 1971).

64. Taylor, "Seeking the Kingdom," p. 176.

65. *Proceedings of the NCA*, 1874, pp. 40–41, 123, 129, 135.

66. Kilby, *Minority of One*, pp. 190, 199.

67. Smith, "Speaking in the Anti-Secrecy Movement," p. 99. When Jonathan Blanchard's son, Charles (C. A.), an anti–secret society lecturer, visited Utica, New York, in 1874 he reported that his audience was largely composed of women. Another NCA speaker noted that his lecture was attended by "over one hundred of the best ladies" in Wenona, Illinois.

68. The change appeared on January 1870, *Masonic Review* (January 1870); see also the *American Freemason*, which added a "Family Department" in the summer of 1859.

69. "Ladies at Our Banquets," *Masonic Review* (December 1869).

70. "Letter from a Lady," *Masonic Review* (April 1866); see also *Masonic Review* (December 1855).

71. "Too Late at the Lodge," *Masonic Review* (January 1868).

72. "Eastern Star," *Voice of Masonry* (April 1870).

73. *Masonic Review* (December 1855). See also "Experience of a Mason's Wife," *Masonic Review* (July 1861), in which a woman said that if more men had been Masons, there would have been no Civil War. Editors often drew the analogy between fraternal members and ministers, but occasionally they contrasted the caring members with unfeeling and uncharitable ministers. In "Why Mrs. Herbert Loved Masonry," a story published in *Freemason's Repository* (October 1876), a young wife, traveling alone by train, is robbed and left penniless in a strange town. Mrs. Herbert goes to the local minister, who stares at her with "cold grey eyes" and turns her away. She then wanders past the Masonic lodge, where a member comes to her aid and takes her to his home.

74. "Masonic Poetic Caution. By the Wife of a Master Mason;" and "Mrs. Grumbler's Grumbling. The Age of Truth, Justice and Equality," in *Voice of Masonry* (April 1870).

75. One orator insisted that "the purity of womanhood" and the "exaltation of childhood" were the "cardinal doctrines" of every lodge (*Proceedings of the Grand Lodge of Free and Accepted Masons of the State of New York*, [New York: J. J. Little and Co., 1898], p. 29).

76. "Women in the Pulpit," *Voice of Masonry* (March 1872).

77. Augustus C. L. Arnold, *The Signet of King Solomon; Or, The Freemason's Daughter* (New York: Masonic Publishing and Manufacturing Co., 1866). The prevalence of the theme of knighthood in fraternal rituals and ideology was a means of idealizing womanhood and circumscribing the woman's role; see also "Perilous Adventure of a Mason's Wife," *Masonic Review* (October 1863).

78. Rev. Richard S. Martin, *Sunshine in Shadowed Lives; or, The Royal Secret of Morg. Bayne* (Chicago: W. B. Conkey and Co., 1892).

79. Arnold, *Signet of King Solomon*, pp. 43–45.

80. Ibid., p. 133.

81. Robert Morris, *Life in the Triangle; or, Freemasonry at the Present Time* (Louisville: Printed by J. F. Brennan and Co., 1854), pp. 28–29.

82. Quotes are from A. B. Grosh, *The Odd-Fellow's Improved Manual* (Philadelphia: T. Bliss and Co., 1871), 169–70; and Rev. Thomas G. Beharrell, *Odd-Fellows Monitor and Guide* (Indianapolis: Robert Douglas, 1882), p. 14.

83. From Edward S. Ellis, *Low Twelve* (New York: F. R. Niglutsch, 1907), a collection of stories on Freemasonry, p. vi.

84. Charles H. Halstead, *History of Hudson River Lodge, #607* (Newburgh, New York: Masonic Lodge #607, 1896), p. 232.

85. See "Ladies and Masonry," *Masonic Monthly* (January 1870).

86. "Woman and Masonry," *Voice of Masonry* (July 1877). See also "Adoptive Masonry," *Freemason's Repository* (September 1857); *Masonic Review* (February 1856); "Make Haste Slowly," *Freemason's Repository* (April 1878); "Androgynous Masonry,"

Masonic Review (February 1869); and "More Humbuggery," *New England Freemason* (March 1875).

87. Quoted in Paschal Donaldson, *The Odd-fellows' Pocket Textbook*, revised ed. (Philadelphia: Moss and Co., 1867), p. 41.

88. The Reverend Mr. Beharrell, in his revised *Odd-Fellows Monitor and Guide*, counseled members to "convert" their wives to the Odd Fellows by getting them to join the auxiliary; otherwise, he said, they would "sooner or later outwit you" (p. 22). The Vice Grand's remarks appear in the ritual as cited in Jonathan Blanchard, *Odd-Fellowship Illustrated* (Chicago: Ezra A. Cook, 1881), p. 244.

89. Individual Freemasons established the Order of the Eastern Star in 1869. See Jean McKee Kenaston [comp.], *History of the Order of the Eastern Star* (Cedar Rapids, Iowa: Torch Press, 1917), p. 22. The Grand Lodge of the Independent Order of Odd-Fellows created the Degree of Rebekah in 1851 by a vote of forty-seven to thirty-seven and narrowly defeated a movement to abolish the degree in 1867; see Beharrell, *Odd-Fellows Monitor and Guide*, pp. 16–19; and John W. Stebbins, *The Half-Century History of Rebekah Odd-Fellowship* (Rochester? New York: by author, 1901). In the 1880s members of the Knights of Pythias created the Rathbone Sisters and the Pythian Sisterhood, which the Grand Lodge did not formally acknowledge. The Improved Order of Red Men established the Daughters of Pocahontas auxiliary in 1887, thirty-five years after it was first proposed. In 1890 the Knights of the Maccabees granted approval to the Ladies of the Maccabees.

90. "Androgynous Masonry."

91. "More Humbuggery." See also "Adoptive Masonry" and *Masonic Review* (February, 1857).

92. *Record of Institution of the Great Council: Degree of Pocahontas, New York State* (1896), p. 15; Grosh, *Odd-Fellow's Improved Manual*, p. 165.

93. "Response to Letter to Editor," *Voice of Masonry* (February 1876).

94. Sarah J. Fairman, Grand Matron of the Order of the Eastern Star in Vermont, reported that when she searched for an explanation of the decree "No initiation into this Woman's Order can take place unless [a man] is present," she could find no answer (New York Grand Council, Order of the Eastern Star, *Proceedings of 1891*, "Report on Vermont Proceedings," pp. 69–70).

95. Cited in Blanchard, *Odd-Fellowship Illustrated*, p. 250. See also "The Great Mission of Woman," which asserted that woman's task was "not to make laws, not to lead armies, not to govern empires; but to *form* those by whom laws are made, armies led, and empires governed" (*Voice of Masonry* [January 1872]).

96. The sociologist Noel Gist observed that the "dramatic ordeals so common to the male organizations" were "conspicuous by their absence in women's societies," although he offered no explanation for the phenomenon. See Noel Gist, "Secret Societies in the United States," *University of Missouri Studies* 15 (October 1940), p. 85.

97. William Rounseville, "Order of the Eastern Star," *Voice of Masonry* (December 1877).

98. [Robert Macoy], *Adoptive Rite Ritual* (1868; reprint, New York: Macoy Publishing Co., 1923), pp. 58–62.

99. B. Kenaston, *Order of Eastern Star*, p. 506. See also [Macoy], *Adoptive Rite Ritual*, p. 73.

100. Mackey, *Encyclopaedia of Freemasonry*, p. 428.

101. Donaldson, *Donaldson's Pocket Textbook*, p. 290.

102. "A Chapter on Adoptive Masonry," *Masonic Review* (March 1861).

103. "Are the Ladies Interested in Masonry[?]" *Masonic Review* (May 1861).

104. *Masonic Review* (January 1857).

105. A common joke concerned the woman who, intent on proving that she could keep secrets, proceeded to divulge them to a casual listener. See "A Chapter on Adoptive Masonry," and "Are the Ladies Interested in Masonry[?]."

106. Stevens, *Cyclopaedia of Fraternities*, pp. 98, 246, 259, 279–80. That women found their own sources of satisfaction from the auxiliaries is suggested by the inclusion of statistics on membership in volume 4 of Elizabeth Cady Stanton's *History of Woman Suffrage* (Indianapolis, 1902). She reported total membership of more than half a million women in 1900. The four largest orders reported as follows: Order of the Eastern Star, 218,000; Daughters of Rebekah, 201,000; Supreme Hive of the Ladies of the Maccabees of the World, 85,000; Supreme Temple Rathbone Sisters of the World, 71,000 (4:1067–73).

107. In *The Bonds of Womanhood*, Nancy Cott has argued that in the early nineteenth century women were able to shape some institutions, especially church organizations, to provide for their collective needs. The female auxiliaries of the fraternal orders may have become part of the affective network binding women later in the century; see Mary Ann Clawson, "Brotherhood, Class and Patriarchy: Fraternalism in Europe and America" (Ph.D. diss. University of New York at Stonybrook, 1980).

108. *Proceedings of the NCA*, 1874, p. 34.

109. In the *Brief History of the NCA* (1875), the *Christian Cynosure* was reported to have 4,650 subscribers. The December 24, 1891, issue of the magazine claimed there were 2,714 subscribers (p. 81).

110. *Christian Cynosure*, November 13, 1890.

111. *Christian Cynosure*, October 22, 1891. The NCA, already moribund by 1890, faded rapidly after the death of Jonathan Blanchard in 1892.

112. John McClaughry has called Phelps's performance arguably the worst ever of any national candidate for the Presidency. See "John Wolcott Phelps: The Civil War General Who Became A Forgotten Presidential Candidate in 1880," *Vermont History* 38 (1970), p. 264.

113. Fergus MacDonald, *The Catholic Church and the Secret Societies in the United States*, ed. Thomas J. McMahon, United States Catholic Historical Society Monograph Series, no. 22 (New York: United States Catholic Historical Society, 1946), p. 100.

114. *Christian Cynosure*, October 1, 1891.

115. *Christian Cynosure*, November 5, 1891.

116. Lynn Dumenil, *Freemasonry and American Culture, 1880–1939* (Princeton, N.J.: Princeton University Press, 1984) pp. 70, 72–111.

117. Finney, *Character, Claims and Practical Workings*, pp. 248, 250–51, 241, 245, 250. See also Lawrence, *Plain Thoughts on Secret Societies*, pp. 131–32.

118. Albert Mackey, *Symbolism of Freemasonry: Illustrating and Explaining its Science and Philosophy, its Legends, Myths, and Symbols* (New York: Clark and Maynard, 1869), pp. 154–58. One motto of Freemasonry was *Lux e tenebris* ("Light out of darkness").

CHAPTER IV. FATHERS

1. This vignette is largely based on the Manuscript Journals of Lewis Henry Morgan (hereafter, LHM Manuscripts), which are located in the Rush Rhees Library at the University of Rochester. The main sources are vol. 1, no. 15 (hereafter, 1/15), "Notes of an Expedition to Tonawanda, Genesee County, New York, to attend a Great Council of the Six Nations which was Held on the 1, 2, and 3 days of October, 1845," pp. 281–98; and 1/18, "Notes of an Expedition to Tonawanda, Genesee County, New York, to attend a great Council of the Six Nations of Indians which was held on the 1, 2, and 3 days of October, 1845," pp. 335–72. Morgan's account is supplemented with details from George Riley and Isaac N. Hurd, who attended the ceremony with Morgan; see "Description of an Indian Council at Tonawanda, October 1, 2, and 3, 1845" by George Riley (1/12); and "A Sketch Embracing the Doings at the Grand Council of the Iroquois Held October 1, 2, and 3, 1845" by Isaac N. Hurd, box 21/29. These are also found in the Morgan Archives at the Rush Rhees Library.

The speech of Jimmy Johnson, the grandson of Handsome Lake, Prophet of the New Revelation of the Iroquois, is presented verbatim in Arthur C. Parker, *The Life of General Ely S. Parker* (Buffalo: Buffalo Historical Society, 1919), pp. 253–61.

2. Cited in Carl Resek, *Lewis Henry Morgan, American Scholar* (Chicago: University of Chicago Press, 1960), p. 20.

3. "An Address by Schenandoah Delivered on the Second Anniversary of the We-yo Hao-de-za-da-na Ho-de-naw-saw-nee," LHM Manuscripts, box 21/6. See also Elisabeth Tooker, "Lewis Henry Morgan Writings" (to be published).

4. Lewis H. Morgan, "Address to the Order," August 9, 1843. Cited in Tooker, "Writings" 1:6.

5. "Address by Schenandoah," LHM Manuscripts, box 21/6.

6. The ritual as recorded, though not in Morgan's handwriting, bore the unmistakable imprint of his style and ideas; see "Form of Inindianation adopted, Aurora, Aug. 9, 1844," LHM Manuscripts, box 21/10. Subsequent drafts of the ritual appear in Morgan's handwriting and are attributed to him by his biographer, Bernard J. Stern, in Stern, *Lewis Henry Morgan, Social Evolutionist* (Chicago: University of Chicago Press, 1931), p. 10.

7. "Special Form of Initiation, [March] 1845," LHM Manuscripts, box 21/19.

8. Stern, *Lewis Henry Morgan*, p. 10.

9. Freemasons, Scipio Lodge, No. 110 (Aurora, N.Y.), *A Short History of Sciopio Lodge No. 110* (Ann Arbor, 1940).

10. William H. Armstrong, *Warrior in Two Camps: Ely S. Parker, Union General and Seneca Chief* (Syracuse: Syracuse University Press, 1978), p. 37.

11. Resek, *Lewis Henry Morgan*, p. 4.

12. Morgan to Eben Horsford, February 16, 1875, LHM Manuscripts, box 7.

13. Stern, *Lewis Henry Morgan*, p. 20.

14. Resek, *Lewis Henry Morgan*, p. 13.

15. Stone is described as a "high Mason" in the *Dictionary of American Biography*. The list also included Washington Irving, George Bancroft, William Cullen Bryant, John Quincy Adams, and Governor Lewis Cass of Michigan (Resek, *Lewis Henry Morgan*, p. 25).

16. Cited in Armstrong, *Warrior in Two Camps*, p. 12.

17. Morgan, *League of the Ho-de-no-sau-nee, or Iroquois* (Rochester: Sage and Brother, 1851), p. 60. This will be cited hereafter as *League of the Iroquois*. See also his *Systems of Consanguinity and Affinity of the Human Family* (Washington: Smithsonian Institution, 1870).

18. Stern, *Lewis Henry Morgan*, p. 18.

19. Resek, *Lewis Henry Morgan*, pp. 23–24.

20. Stern, *Lewis Henry Morgan*, p. 16.

21. Morgan, *Ancient Society; or, Researches in the Lines of Human Progress from Savagery, through Barbarism to Civilization* (Chicago: Kerr, 1877), p. 5.

22. Charles H. Litchman, *Official History of the Improved Order of Red Men* (Boston: Fraternity Publishing Co., 1893) pp. 212–49.

23. Litchman, *History of Red Men*, pp. 252–55, 292.

24. Albert C. Stevens, comp. and ed., *Cyclopaedia of Fraternities* (New York: E. B. Treat, 1907), p. 244; also Litchman, *History of Red Men*, pp. 294–96.

25. On the struggle to find a satisfactory ritual, see Thomas K. Donnalley, ed., *Handbook of Tribal Names of Pennsylvania* (Philadelphia: n.p., 1908), pp. 231–49.

26. Nearly forty years later, in 1908, elderly Red Men recalled that the "whole desire" of members of the order had been to perform the Adoption ceremony (Donnalley, *Handbook*, p. 231).

27. *Record of the Great Council of New York: Improved Order of Red Men* (Elmira: Gazette Co., 1890), p. 315. This can be found in the annex of the New York Public Library.

28. Stevens, *Cyclopaedia of Fraternities*, p. 246. See also Noel Gist, "Secret Societies in the United States," *University of Missouri Studies* 15 (October 1940), p. 42.

29. As membership in the Improved Order of Red Men approached 200,000 in the 1890s, the NCA published its exposé, from which the account of the Adoption degree in these pages is taken.

30. See Donnalley, *Handbook*, pp. 231–40.

31. Quotations in the text are from [Ezra A. Cook], *Red Men Illustrated: The Complete Illustrated Ritual of the Improved Order of Red Men* (Chicago: Ezra A. Cook, 1896), pp. 13–61.

32. Arnold van Gennep, *Les rites du passage: etude systematique des rites* (Paris: E. Nourry, 1909).

33. The ritual even included a stage direction to remind the Sachem to use an "angry tone" with the initiate.

34. In his official history of the order, Litchman did not outline the process by which the Committee on Ritual settled on these ceremonies, but he cited several pages of Morgan's "admirable" *League of the Iroquois* verbatim and noted that the rituals had been "prepared" from his theory of Iroquois life (Litchman, *History of Red Men*, pp. 606–09).

35. Roscoe Pound, *Masonic Addresses and Writings* (New York and Richmond, Va.: Macoy Publishing and Masonic Supply Co., 1953), pp. 99–100. This idea has been updated by Lionel Tiger, who views initiation as part of an innate "male bonding" process among men. See his *Men in Groups* (New York: Random House, 1969).

36. Psychogenic models presume that rituals help preserve social structures by alleviating an individual's psychological stress; sociogenic theories presume that although the essential function of rituals is related to social structure, participants may invest them with emotional meanings. For an explanation of male initiation ceremonies that incorporates both models, see Klaus-Friedrich Koch, "Sociogenic and Psychogenic Models in Anthropology: The Functions of Male Initiation," *Man* 9, no. 3 (September 1974).

37. Fredrik Barth, *Cosmologies in the Making: A Generative Approach to Cultural Variation in Inner New Guinea* (Cambridge: Cambridge University Press, 1987), pp. 7–9.

38. See Johan Huizinga, "Historical Conceptualization," in Fritz Stern, ed., *Varieties of History: From Voltaire to the Present* (New York: Meridian Books, 1960), pp. 292–93.

39. A. R. Radcliffe-Brown, *Structure and Function in Primitive Society: Essays and Addresses* (London: Cohen and West, 1952), p. 3; Edward Evans-Pritchard, *Theories of Primitive Religion* (Oxford: Clarendon Press, 1969), p. 101.

40. Fredrik Barth, *Process and Form in Social Life* (London: Routledge and Kegan Paul, 1981), pp. 105–18; and Gilbert H. Herdt, ed., *Rituals of Manhood: Male Initiation in Papua New Guinea* (Berkeley: University of California Press, 1982), p. xvii.

41. Robert Murphy, "Social Structure and Sex Antagonism," *Southwestern Journal of Anthropology* 15 (1959), pp. 97–98.

42. Murphy, "Social Structure and Sex Antagonism," p. 96.

43. Another difficulty with psychoanalytical models, examined in the Prologue, is that they are often contradictory. See, for example, the opposed explanations of Theodore Reik, *Ritual: Four Psycho-Analytic Studies* trans. Douglas Bryan (New York: Farrar, Strauss, 1946), pp. 91–166; and Bruno Bettelheim, *Symbolic Wounds: Puberty Rites and the Envious Male* (Glencoe, Ill.: Free Press, 1954).

44. Robert V. Burton and J. M. W. Whiting, "The Absent Father and Cross-Sex Identity," *Merrill-Palmer Quarterly* 7 (1961), pp. 87–90. This article superseded an earlier interpretation by Whiting, Richard Kluckhohn, and Albert Anthony found in "The Function of Male Initiation Ceremonies at Puberty," in Eleanor E. Maccoby,

T. M. Newcomb, and E. L. Hartley, eds., *Readings in Social Psychology* (New York: Henry Holt and Company, 1958). Technical criticisms of Whiting's second argument are found in Edward Norbeck, D. E. Walker, and Mimi Cohen, "The Interpretation of Data: Puberty Rites," *American Anthropologist* 64, no. 3, 1962.

45. See Frank W. Young, "The Function of Male Initiation Ceremonies: A Cross-Cultural Test of an Alternative Hypothesis," *American Journal of Sociology* 68 (January 1962), pp. 381–86.

46. For example, by suggesting that primitive and contemporary adolescents had similar emotional needs, Whiting, whose research had been undertaken primarily among primitive peoples, felt justified in prescribing a solution to juvenile delinquency. The antisocial behavior of adolescents, he suggested, could be "countered" by decreasing the exclusiveness of early mother-child relationships, by increasing the role of the father, or by "instituting a formal means of coping with adolescent boys functionally equivalent" to primitive initiation ceremonies. Service in the Civilian Conservation Corps or military conscription might serve as institutional surrogates for puberty rites (Whiting, Kluckhohn, and Anthony, "Function of Male Initiation Ceremonies," pp. 359, 369–70).

47. Elizabeth C. Stanton, Susan B. Anthony, and Matilda J. Gage, *History of Woman Suffrage*, 6 vols. (New York, 1881–1922). See also Barbara Welter, "The Cult of True Womanhood, 1820–1860," *American Quarterly* 18 (1966), pp. 151–74.

48. Kathryn Kish Sklar, *Catharine Beecher: A Study in American Domesticity* (New Haven: Yale University Press, 1973); Carroll Smith-Rosenberg, "The Female World of Love and Ritual," *Signs: A Journal of Women in Culture and Society* 1 (1975), pp. 1–29.

49. For an early and important synthesis of the subject, see John Demos, "The Changing Faces of Fatherhood," in Demos, *Past, Present, and Personal* (New York: Oxford University Press, 1986), pp. 41–67.

50. Edmund S. Morgan, *The Puritan Family: Religion and Domestic Relations in Seventeenth-Century New England* (New York: Harper and Row, 1966) pp. 98, p. 136.

51. Ruth H. Bloch, "American Feminine Ideals in Transition: The Rise of the Moral Mother, 1785–1815," *Feminist Studies* 4 (June 1978) p. 113; idem., "Untangling the Roots of Modern Sex Roles: A Survey of Four Centuries of Change," *Signs* 4 (Winter 1978), p. 251; Carl N. Degler, *At Odds: Women and the Family in America from the Revolution to the Present* (New York: Oxford University Press, 1980), p. 73; Demos, *Past, Present, and Personal*, pp. 43–48.

52. This transference was underscored at the age of five or six by a shift in clothing: The gowns worn by young children of both sexes were set aside, and boys were given breeches, shirts, and doublets—an outfit which closely resembled the clothing of their fathers; see John Demos, *A Little Commonwealth: Family Life in Plymouth Colony* (New York: Oxford University Press, 1970), pp. 57–58, 122. See also Michael Zuckerman, *Peaceable Kingdoms: New England Towns in the Eighteenth Century* (New York: Vintage, 1970), pp. 73–75; W. J. Rorabaugh, *The Craft Apprentice: From Franklin to the Machine Age in America* (New York: Oxford University Press, 1986), pp. 10–11; and Morgan, *Puritan Family*, p. 75.

53. Daniel Scott Smith, "Parental Power and Marriage Patterns: An Analysis of Historical Trends in Hingham, Massachusetts," *Journal of Marriage and the Family* 35 (August 1973), pp. 426–27; Philip G. Greven, *Four Generations: Population, Land, and Family in Colonial Andover, Massachusetts* (Ithaca, N.Y.: Cornell University Press, 1970), pp. 83–84, 133, 143–44; Morgan, *Puritan Family*, pp. 84–85; Ellen K. Rothman, *Hands and Hearts: A History of Courtship in America* (New York: Basic Books, 1984), pp. 26–30.

54. For example, Timothy Pickering wrote in 1796 that his "greatest happiness" with his children resulted from his "familiarity, and their consequent affection, freedom, and confidence." Yet Pickering acknowledged that his affectionate behavior was exceptional: "When we see so many parents unsociable and stern, can we wonder that others uninfluenced by allurements of affection should be distant?" The quotation appears in E. Anthony Rotundo, "Manhood in America: The Northern Middle Class, 1770–1920," Ph.D. diss., Brandeis University, 1982, p. 90. Rotundo's analysis of letters and diaries indicates that fathers felt "deep affection for their sons" (p. 85), but sons' expressions of filial affection were "rare and guarded" (pp. 91–92). Most of Rotundo's evidence on the eighteenth century dates from the 1770s and the 1780s, after father-son relations had undergone a major transformation.

Similarly, the widespread practice of early apprenticeship can be attributed to either parental closeness or distance. Carl Degler regarded the custom as "surely a sign of parents' detachment from their children" (Degler, *At Odds*, p. 69), while Edmund Morgan believed it an effort by loving parents to avoid spoiling children who might thus fail to apprehend God's will. "By allowing a strange master to take over the disciplinary function," Morgan added, "the parent could meet the child upon a plane of affection and friendliness" (Morgan, *Puritan Family*, pp. 77–78).

55. Philip Greven has offered a differing assessment. Of his three paradigmatic styles of childrearing, the "ideal evangelical" would be closest to the seventeenth- and early eighteenth-century child rearing paradigm here. Greven contends that many such Puritans were not self-assured in their masculine identification, but were "selfless and feminine." They denied their own sexuality, and their masculinity, partly because they "identified with and felt intense hostility toward women, and their own mothers in particular" (Philip Greven, *Protestant Temperament: Patterns of Child-rearing, Religious Experience and the Self in Early America* [New York: Alfred A. Knopf, 1977], pp. 124–32). I agree with the assessment of Richard Bushman, who located the "key to the Puritan character" in the "responses of individuals to the series of stern fathers who stood over them in the homes of their childhood, in the church, in society, and in the state." Deference did not imply meekness, for "the dominion of stern fathers also injected strength into all who lived under their sway. The firm hand of authority, structuring all of life, framed steady and resolute personalities, sure of the world in which they lived and as stern in exercising authority as their fathers" (Richard Bushman, *From Puritan to Yankee: Character and the Social Order in Connecticut, 1690–1765* [New York: W. W. Norton, 1970], pp. 18–20).

56. Demos, *A Little Commonwealth*, pp. 147–48.

57. Demos, *A Little Commonwealth*, p. 150. Ross W. Beales, Jr., observed that

despite their dependence, sons were given a "moratorium, a freedom from adult responsibilities, during which the elements of a youthful 'culture' might emerge." See Beales, "In Search of the Historical Child: Miniature Adulthood and Youth in Colonial America," in *American Quarterly* 27 (October 1975), pp. 22–23.

58. Greven, *Protestant Temperament*, pp. 275, 277, 323–31.

59. Greven, *Four Generations*, pp. 229–30, 241–42, 272. Daniel Scott Smith's study of Hingham, Massachusetts, provides evidence of "an erosion and collapse of traditional family patterns in the middle and late 18th century" ("Parental Power and Marriage Patterns," p. 246).

60. Daniel Scott Smith and Michael S. Hindus, "Premarital Pregnancy in America, 1640–1971: An Overview and Interpretation," *Journal of Interdisciplinary History* 4 (Spring 1975), pp. 537–70.

61. Joseph Kett argues that the period from 1790 to 1840 was a critical one in the history of child rearing in America. See his seminal study *Rites of Passage: Adolescence in America, 1790 to the Present* (New York: Basic Books, 1977), p. 5. Degler found a dramatic change in child rearing attitudes "around the turn from the 18th to the 19th century" (*At Odds*, p. 66).

62. Kenneth T. Jackson, "Urban Deconcentration in the Nineteenth Century: A Statistical Inquiry," in Leo Schnore, ed., *The New Urban History: Quantitative Explorations by American Historians* (Princeton, N.J.: Princeton University Press, 1975), pp. 110–42. On the middle-class character of the commuters and the increasing distance of their journey to work, see Theodore Hershberg, Dale Light, Jr., Harold E. Cox, and Richard R. Greenfield, "The 'Journey-to-Work': An Empirical Investigation of Work, Residence and Transportation, Philadelphia, 1850 and 1880," in Theodore Hershberg, ed., *Philadelphia: Work, Space, Family, and Group Experience in the 19th Century: Essays Toward an Interdisciplinary History of the City* (New York: Oxford University Press, 1981), pp. 128–73.

63. On the psychological pressures engendered by the mid-nineteenth century economy, see Margaret Marsh, "Suburban Men and Masculine Domesticity," *American Quarterly* 40 (June 1988). Statistical studies of mobility of even prosperous communities reveal that the precariousness of the economy led to widespread despair and disillusionment among the middle classes. See Peter R. Decker, *Fortunes and Failures: White Collar Mobility in 19th-Century San Francisco* (Cambridge, Mass.: Harvard University Press, 1978), pp. 252–53.

64. Rev. John S. C. Abbott, "Paternal Neglect," *Parent's Magazine*, 2 (March 1842) p. 148, cited in Anne Louise Kuhn, *The Mother's Role in Childhood Education: New England Concepts, 1830–1860* (New Haven, Conn.: Yale University Press, 1947), p. 4. See also Bernard W. Wishy, *The Child and the Republic: The Dawn of Modern American Child Nurture* (Philadelphia: University of Pennsylvania Press, 1968) pp. 26–29; and Joe L. Dubbert, *A Man's Place: Masculinity in Transition* (Englewood Cliffs, N.J.: Prentice-Hall, 1979), p. 27.

65. Alexis de Tocqueville, *Democracy in America*, ed. Phillips Bradley (reprint; New York, 1948) 2:192–95; cited in Degler, *At Odds*, p. 75.

66. Mary Ryan found that from 1840 to 1860 the proportion of family partner-

ships in Utica, New York, was reduced to one-fourth its former size. Of 331 of the businesses listed in the city directory from 1860 to 1865, apparently only 10 were run by the sons of proprietors; *Cradle of the Middle Class: The Family in Oneida County, New York, 1790–1865* (Cambridge: Cambridge University Press, 1981) p. 152.

67. Richard Sennett argues that by the 1870s many middle-class men who themselves had failed to achieve career goals had become ineffective and passive fathers; see *Families Against the City: Middle-Class Homes of Industrial Chicago, 1872–1890* (Cambridge, Mass.: Harvard University Press, 1970), pp. 154, 179, 187–90; also Burton J. Bledstein, *The Culture of Professionalism: The Middle Class and the Development of Higher Education in America* (New York: W. W. Norton, 1976) pp. 162–69.

68. Ryan, *Cradle of the Middle Class*, chap. 4; William E. Bridges, "Warm Hearth, Cold World: Social Perspectives on the Household Poets," *American Quarterly* 21 (Winter 1969), p. 767; Daniel Scott Smith, "Family Limitation, Sexual Control, and Domestic Feminism in Victorian America," in Mary S. Hartman and Lois W. Banner, eds., *Clio's Consciousness Raised* (New York: Harper Colophon, 1974); Linda K. Kerber, *Women of the Republic: Intellect and Ideology in Revolutionary America* (Chapel Hill: University of North Carolina Press, 1980), chap. 7; Wishy, *Child and Republic*, p. 29.

69. Robert L. Griswold, *Family and Divorce in California, 1850–1890: Victorian Illusions and Everyday Realities* (Albany: State University of New York Press, 1982), pp. 153–55.

70. George Combe, *A System of Phrenology*, 2d ed. (Edinburgh: J. Anderson, 1825), p. 76; also his *Moral Philosophy; or, The Duties of a Man* (New York: Colyer, 1844).

71. Ryan, *Cradle of the Middle Class*, p. 232. Demos similarly perceives a trend during the nineteenth century toward "limited fatherhood," in "Changing Faces," p. 57. Joe Dubbert, with less evidence but more passion, calls the alienation of fathers from Victorian home life "one of the most diabolical features" of the modern family, in *A Man's Place*, p. 21. This analysis of the psychological dynamics of boyhood in Victorian America clearly relates to a debate concerning the timing of the emergence of the "companionate" marriage, which was characterized by close and mutually dependent emotional relationships.

Carl Degler and Robert Griswold have provided the most forceful arguments that the companionate family in America emerged during the mid-nineteenth century. Degler's argument is based chiefly on letters from long-separated lovers and spouses; Griswold's, on the testimony of divorce cases. Both arguments, however, were at least partly preconditioned by the nature of the evidence. It is unlikely that distant spouses would choose to vent their anger through letters or that witnesses and judges in divorce proceedings would acknowledge an emotionally detached marital standard. See Degler, *At Odds*, and Griswold, *Family and Divorce in California*.

I agree with historian Margaret Marsh, who concludes that the companionate marriage did not emerge until about the turn of the twentieth century. See "Suburban Men and Masculine Domesticity, 1870–1915," *American Quarterly* 40 (June 1988). See also Suzanne Lebsock, *The Free Women of Petersburg: Status and Culture in a Southern Town, 1784–1860*, pp. 30–33, 52.

72. J. S. C. Abbott, *The Mother at Home* (1834; reprint, New York: Arno Press, 1972) p. 61.

73. Nancy Schrom Dye and Daniel Blake Smith, "Mother Love and Infant Death, 1750–1920," *Journal of American History* 73 (September 1986), p. 338; and Kirk Jeffrey, "The Family as a Utopian Retreat from the City: The Nineteenth-Century Contribution," *Soundings* 55 (1972).

74. Wilson H. Grahill, Clyde V. Kiser, and Pascal K. Whelpton, *The Fertility of American Women* (New York, 1958), pp. 14–15. Carl Degler has described this drop in fertility as "certainly the single most important fact about women and the family in American history" in Degler, *At Odds*, p. 181.

75. Ryan, *Cradle of the Middle Class*, p. 106.

76. See Sklar, *Catharine Beecher*, p. 235.

77. Horace Mann, Massachusetts Board of Education, *Tenth Annual Report, 1845–1846*, cited in Redding S. Sugg, *Motherteacher: The Feminization of American Education* (Charlottesville: University Press of Virginia, 1978), p. 62; see also p. 74.

78. *Report of the U.S. Commissioner of Education, 1891–1892*, cited in Sugg, *Mother-teacher*, pp. 112–16. Of the 3,300 teachers in Chicago in 1892, for example, nearly 3,100 were female. See also Carl F. Kaestle, *Pillars of the Republic: Common Schools and American Society, 1780–1860* (New York: Hill and Wang, 1983). As early as 1860, more than three-quarters of the teachers in Massachusetts were female (p. 123). See also Ryan, *Cradle of the Middle Class*, p. 163.

79. See, for example, Cott, *Bonds of Womanhood*, p. 33.

80. Mark C. Carnes, "The 'Making of the Self-Made Man': The Emotional Experience of Boyhood in Victorian America," paper presented at the annual meeting of the Organization of American Historians, Minneapolis, April 1984.

81. Of the more than three million boys aged fifteen to nineteen in 1891, only 85,219 were enrolled in public high schools; approximately 50 percent more girls were enrolled (Kett, *Rites of Passage*, pp. 292n, 129–30).

82. See Karen Halttunen, *Confidence Men and Painted Women: A Study of Middle-Class Culture in America, 1830–1870* (New Haven, Conn.: Yale University Press, 1982), chap. 2.

83. See "The Two Clerks," in *Ladies' Repository* (January 1857).

84. Ryan found that only 29.7 percent of native-born youths in Utica boarded in 1855, and only 11.1 percent a decade later (*Cradle of the Middle Class*, p. 168). See also Michael B. Katz, *The People of Hamilton, Canada West: Family and Class in a Mid-Nineteenth-Century City* (Cambridge, Mass.: Harvard University Press, 1975), p. 274; and Mark Peel, "On the Margins: Lodgers and Boarders in Boston, 1860–1900," *Journal of American History* 72 (March 1986), pp. 813–34.

85. Richard Sennett reported that in middle-class Union Park, Chicago during the 1870s, of males aged 20 to 24, 71.9% remained at home under the protection of the family head, as did 55.4% of males aged 25 to 29; only 9.5% of those aged 15 to 19 lived alone (*Families Against the City*, pp. 102–05). Also see Katz, *People of Hamilton*, pp. 274–76; and Ryan, *Cradle of the Middle Class*, p. 168. In Newark, New Jersey, the proportion of sons aged 15 through 19 staying home in 1850 was

40%; by 1860 that percentage had increased to 71%; see Susan E. Hirsch, *Roots of the American Working Class: The Industrialization of Crafts in Newark, 1800–1860* (Philadelphia: University of Pennsylvania Press, 1978), pp. 41–71. The median age nationwide for a male's first marriage in 1890 was 26.9; in Philadelphia in 1880 it was 26.8 (Modell, Furstenberg, and Hershberg, "Social Change and Transitions to Adulthood in Historical Perspective," in Hershberg, *Philadelphia*, pp. 320–21).

86. Kett refers to this chaotic stage as "semi-dependency" in "Growing Up in Rural New England," in Tamara K. Hareven, ed., *Anonymous Americans: Explorations in Nineteenth-Century Social History* (Englewood Cliffs, N.J.: Prentice-Hall, 1971), pp. 1–10. Michael Katz describes an analogous stage—he uses the term "semi-autonomy"—to describe the transition in an urban setting (*People of Hamilton*, pp. 256–57).

87. See G. R. Bach, "Father-fantasies and father-typing in father-separated children," *Child Development* 17 (1946) pp. 63–80; David B. Lynn, "A Note on Sex Differences in the Development of Masculine and Feminine Identification," *Psychological Review* 66 (1959), pp. 126–35; R. R. Sears, M. H. Pintler, and P. S. Sears, "Effect of Father Separation on Pre-School Children's Doll Play Aggression," *Child Development* 17 (1946), pp. 219–43; M. M. Leichty, "The Effect of Father-Absence during Early Childhood upon the Oedipal Situation as Reflected in Young Adults," *Merrill-Palmer Quarterly* 6 (1960), pp. 212–17. Talcott Parsons believed that when fathers largely were absent during child rearing, sons would be deprived of essential connections to society; conversely, excessive maternal emotion would discourage sons from embarking into the instrumental world inhabited by men. See Talcott Parsons and R. F. Bales, *Family, Socialization and Interaction Process* (Glencoe, Ill.: 1955).

88. For a forceful exposition of this argument, see Joseph H. Pleck, *The Myth of Masculinity* (Cambridge, Mass.: MIT Press, 1984).

89. Some learning theorists insist that children identify with nurturing and affectionate parents rather than those who are perceived as powerful; see Albert Bandura and Althea C. Huston, "Identification as a Process of Incidental Learning," *Journal of Abnormal and Social Psychology* 63 (1961), pp. 311–18; E. M. Hetherington and G. Frankie, "Effects of Parental Dominance, Warmth, and Conflict on Imitation in Children," *Journal of Personality and Social Psychology*, 6 (1967), pp. 119–25; and P. H. Mussen and L. Distler, "Masculinity, Identification, and Father-Son Relationships," *Journal of Abnormal and Social Psychology* 59 (1959), pp. 350–56.

90. See E. Anthony Rotundo, "Boy Culture: The World of Middle-Class Boys in Nineteenth-Century America," in Mark C. Carnes and Clyde Griffen, eds., *Meanings for Manhood: Constructions of Masculinity in Victorian America* (Chicago, Ill.: University of Chicago Press, 1990); and Carnes, "Making of the 'Self-Made Man.'"

91. Burton and Whiting, "Absent Father and Cross-Sex Identity," pp. 93–94.

92. Bloch, "American Feminine Ideals in Transition;" pp. 115–16.

93. Peter Gregg Slater, *Children in the New England Mind: In Death and in Life*

(Hamden, Conn.: Archon Books, 1977), pp. 74–90, 112–50; and Sklar, *Catharine Beecher*, chap. 11. On the Romantic style of childrearing, see Kuhn, *Mother's Role*; and Daniel Calhoun, *The Intelligence of a People* (Princeton, N.J.: Princeton University Press 1973), pp. 139–55.

94. Horace Bushnell, *Christian Nurture*, with an introduction by Luther A. Weigle (New Haven, Conn.: Yale University Press, 1947), p. 202, also pp. 12–14.

95. Mary Ryan, who documented the close relationship between revivalism and women in Oneida County, New York, found ministers who proposed an "affectionate, maternal and gradual method of courting children's souls" as early as 1815. In 1824 a local pastor anticipated Bushnell: "Behold our beloved teachers—whose care for us is like a mother's for her infant child—whose kind instructions drop like honey from her lips," Ryan, *Cradle of the Middle Class*, pp. 99–100.

96. On the decline in corporal punishment, see Wishy, *Child and Republic*, pp. 42–49; Sugg, *Motherteacher*, pp. 90–105; Bledstein, *Culture of Professionalism*, pp. 214–16; and Slater, *Children in the New England Mind*, pp. 112–14.

97. Catharine E. Beecher, *The Evils Suffered by American Women and American Children: The Causes and the Remedy* (New York: Harper and Brothers, 1847), pp. 3, 5; also W. Mischel, "A Social-Learning View of Sex Differences in Behavior," in Eleanor E. Maccoby, ed., *The Development of Sex Differences* (Stanford, Calif.: Stanford University Press, 1966).

98. Almira H. Phelps, "Remarks on the Education of Girls," *Godey's Lady's Book* 18 (June 1839), p. 253; cited in Kuhn, *Mother's Role*, p. 57.

99. Horace Mann, *The Powers and Duties of Women*, cited in Kaestle, *Pillars of the Republic*, p. 86.

100. The story is summarized in Jeffrey, "Family as Retreat," p. 31.

101. "The Worth of Money," *Ladies Magazine* 3 (February 1830) p. 53; cited in Kuhn, *The Mother's Role*, pp. 94, 128.

102. Rev. William Thayer, *Life at the Fireside* (Boston, 1857), p. 259; cited in Kuhn, *Mother's Role*, p. 95. Wishy makes much the same point: "The inner conflict in young Americans between the will for righteousness and will for success must have been extraordinary and without recognizing its strong sources in American home life, we probably cannot fully understand the complex play of moralism and materialism in American culture well into this century" (*Child and Republic*, p. 20).

103. "Ancient Initiations," *Voice of Masonry* (April 1867).

104. Degler, *At Odds*, pp. 253–78.

105. Here and elsewhere, Degler ascribes to men motivations that I suspect were probably more common to women. The concept of "passionlessness," as Nancy Cott observed, more likely originated among women, who could use it to assert moral supremacy and enhance their position within the home; see Cott, "Passionlessness: An Interpretation of Victorian Sexual Ideology, 1790–1850," *Signs* 4 (Winter 1978), pp. 219–36.

106. *Masonic Review* (August 1869); see also R. S. Dement, "The Silent Influence of Masonry," *Voice of Masonry* (July 1876).

107. "Surpassing the Love of Woman," *Masonic Review* (September 1869); also "A Mother's Memories," *American Odd Fellow* (June 1870); and "St. Leon's Toast—'My Mother,'" *Masonic Review* (December 1869).

108. "My Mother's Grave," *Masonic Review* (January 1865).

109. "A Mother's Refrain," *Masonic Review* (August 1869); see also "A Mother's Influence," *Voice of Masonry* (December 1871).

110. *Voice of Masonry* (October 1877).

111. *Masonic Review* (April 1869).

112. "Early Impressions of Masonry," *Mystic Star* (April 1873).

113. *Mystic Star* (May 1873).

114. "Address Delivered by J. A. M'Dougall Before the Grand Lodge of Illinois at Its Second Grand Annual Communication, at Jacksonville" (1841), in L. S. Myler, ed., *Jewels of Masonic Oratory* (New York: M. W. Hazen, 1898), p. 296.

115. "Silent Influence of Masonry."

116. James R. Carnahan, *Pythian Knighthood: Its History and Literature* (Cincinnati: Pettibone Mfr. Co., 1890), pp. 222–23; J. J. Fultz, Grand Dictator, *Infancy, Youth and Manhood; or How to Work the "K of H" Ritual* (Mt. Vernon, Ohio: Knights of Honor, 1889).

117. Grosh, *Odd-Fellow's Improved Manual*, p. 285. H. L. Haywood described the candidate as a "child"—needing a guide and "patient guardians"—who eventually "sees the light" and can stand "on his own two feet" as a result of initiation, in *The Great Teachings of Freemasonry* (New York: George H. Doran Co., 1923), p. 137. The last reference appears in the High Priest's final lecture to the initiate during the summation of the Royal Purple degree.

118. *Lectures and Charges of the Degrees of the Independent Order of Odd Fellows in the United States* (Philadelphia: J. Royer, 1833), p. 7.

119. A fuller exposition of the first part of this ritual appears at the beginning of chapter 1.

120. J. Fletcher Williams, "The Encampment Branch of the Order," in Henry L. Stillson, ed., *The Official History and Literature of Odd Fellowship* (Boston: Fraternity Publishing, 1898), p. 418; also see p. 552. The revisions were so successful that the Grand Lodge of the subordinate branch of the Odd Fellows feared an exodus of members to the Encampment. The Grand Lodge therefore proposed "mergement" with the Encampment so that the subordinate lodges could confer the revenue-producing Patriarchal degrees.

121. Cited in Williams, "Encampment Branch," pp. 426, 427. Also see Stillson, *History of Odd Fellowship*, pp. 548–49.

122. I could not locate an account of the 1845 Patriarchal degree; the version cited here is based on the 1875 NCA exposé, *Odd-Fellows Illustrated* (Chicago: Ezra Cook, 1875). Stillson noted that from 1845 until 1880 there was only one revision (1873) of the ritual and that it offered no important modifications (*History of Odd Fellowship*, p. 552).

123. An almost identical addition was made in the Royal Arch degree in the 1880s. A new section challenged the identity of those who returned from the Babylonian

Captivity. The initiates affirmed their bonds of family: "We are of your own brethren and kin, children of the captivity, true descendants of those noble families of Giblemites who wrought so hard at the building of the first temple. . . . We were also present at the destruction of the temple by Nebuzaradan, by whom we were carried away captive to the king of Babylon." See Jacob O. Doesburg, *Freemasonry Illustrated* (Chicago: Ezra A. Cook, 1886) pp. 524–25.

124. John Cawelti, after noting the usual dangers of a Freudian interpretation of literary works, asserts that the Alger formula "cries out for this kind of treatment": "Consider the following brief summary, which can apply with variations to almost any of the Alger books: an adolescent boy, the support of a gentle, loving and admiring mother, is threatened by a male figure of authority and discipline. Through personal heroism he succeeds in subverting the authority of this figure and in finding a new male supporter who makes no threats to his relationship with the mother and does not seek to circumscribe his independence. The pattern is too obvious to require extended comment." Cawelti characterizes the mid-nineteenth century as an era of strict paternal discipline and concludes that the Alger books may have been appreciated as "phantasies of father-elimination." See John G. Cawelti, *Apostles of the Self-Made Man* (Chicago: University of Chicago Press, 1965), pp. 122–23.

The Oedipal interpretation is interesting, but in one respect it fails: The boys' relationship to their mothers is seldom of much importance, and it becomes less so as the plot progresses. It appears that the boys are trying not to preserve Oedipal ties, but to free themselves from them.

125. H. L. Haywood compared the initiatory experience to the "crisis of adolescence when a boy finds himself passing through a mysterious change that throws his whole being into turmoil." Like the man who has experienced a religious conversion, the fraternal initiate understands that "he can never become what he was"; see *Great Teachings of Freemasonry*, pp. 30–31.

CHAPTER V. SECRETS

1. The phrases of the ritual are from Jonathan Blanchard, *Scotch Rite Masonry Illustrated* (Chicago: Ezra A. Cook, 1882), pp. 415–16. For general biographical details, see Frederick Allsopp, *Albert Pike* (Little Rock: Parke-Harper Company, 1928); Walter Brown, "Albert Pike," (Ph.D. diss., University of Texas, 1955); and Robert L. Duncan, *Reluctant General: The Life and Times of Albert Pike* (E. P. Dutton and Co., New York: 1961); and *Dictionary of American Biography*, s.v. "Albert Pike."

2. For a standard description of the various interpretations, see Albert C. Stevens, comp. and ed., *Cyclopaedia of Fraternities* (New York: E. B. Treat, 1907), pp. 43–53; also Brown, "Albert Pike," pp. 719–22. Pike believed that the rituals of the Scottish Rite originated in England in the early 1700s and were then copied in France; the English reading of the Scottish Rite was ruined in the early 1800s, and the defective variant was transmitted to America shortly thereafter. Pike claimed that his version of the Scottish Rite was akin to the original English rituals; see Pike, "A Comparison of Rites," *Masonic Review* (June 1858).

3. Albert Pike, *Morals and Dogma of the Ancient and Accepted Scottish Rite of Freemasonry* (Charleston, S.C.: Supreme Council of the A.A.S.R., 1871?). "The Scotch Rite: The Quarrel as It Stands," *Voice of Masonry* (February 1867) credited Pike as the initiator of the great interest in the Scottish Rite and described him as its "Second Creator." The reference to Pike as the "Moses" of the rite is found in James D. Richardson, "Centennial Address" (Washington, D.C.: Pearson Printing Office, 1901), p. 26. Richardson added that prior to Pike's reconstruction, the Scottish Rite was in a "perishing and almost famished condition." Pike "smote the rock of chaos and darkness, and brought forth a system of morality more nearly perfect than was ever before builded by human hands." In 1891 J. D. Buck doubted whether "any man for the past century and a half" had done as much to restore Masonry to its "birthright" as Pike (*Mystic Masonry, or the Symbols of Freemasonry* [Cincinnati: Robert Clarke Co., 1891], pp. 262–63). See also Joseph Newton, "Address on Albert Pike, 33rd degree: The Master Genius of Masonry," in Cedar Rapids, Ia.: Torch Press, 1909), p. 3; and Brown, "Albert Pike," p. 728.

4. On Pike's multiple affiliations with various Masonic and other fraternal organizations, see Allsopp, *Albert Pike*, p. 240; and William L. Boyden, "Masonic Record of Albert Pike," *New Age Magazine* 28, pp. 34–37.

5. Ancient and Accepted Scottish Rite, "Ancient and Accepted Scottish Rite," *Official Bulletin* (1878). Pike is quoted in Arnold Whitaker Oxford, *The Origin and Progress of the Supreme Council 33rd Degree of the Ancient And Accepted Scottish Rite* (London: Humphrey Milford, 1933), pp. 60–61. (See Charles Sumner Lobingier, *The A.A.S.R. of Freemasonry* (Louisville, 1932). Lobingier wrote that Pike's rituals for the nineteenth through thirty-second degrees were new: "The only one [of the pre-Pike rituals] which contained more than a description, Lodge, title and dress, together with the obligation and signs of recognition, is the 27 degree." Prior to Pike, for example, the thirty-second degree filled four pages in [Benjamin Henry Day], *Richardson's Monitor of Freemasonry* (Philadelphia: David McKay, 1861?). Pike's recension filled nearly 100 pages in Blanchard, *Scotch Rite Masonry Illustrated*.

6. *Official Bulletin* 8, p. 532; Supreme Council, *Transactions, 1857–1866*, cited in Brown, "Albert Pike," p. 90.

7. On the eventual approval of the rite, see Allsopp, *Albert Pike*, p. 243.

8. "Ancient and Accepted Rite," *Masonic Review* (April 1865).

9. Stevens, *Cyclopaedia of Fraternities*, p. 52.

10. "The Scotch Rite: A Synopsis," *Voice of Masonry* (June 1867). See also *Voice of Masonry* (December 1867).

11. Duncan, *Reluctant General*, pp. 14–21.

12. Pike, "Taos," *Nugae* (Philadelphia: G. Sherman, 1854) p. 258. His "Hymns to the Gods" appeared in the prestigious *Blackwood's Edinburgh Magazine*. Its editor, John Wilson, proclaimed Pike one of America's finest poets.

13. Cited in Duncan, *Reluctant General*, pp. 227–28.

14. Pike's translations include: "Irano-Aryan Theosophy and Doctrine as Contained in the Zend Avesta," a manuscript of 2344 pages in three volumes, 1874;

Lectures of the Arya (1873; reprint, Louisville, Ky.: 1930), 8 vols. (1,499 pages); "Indo-Aryan Deities and Worship as Contained in the Rig-Veda," a manuscript of 650 pages, 1872; "Translations of the Rig-Veda: The Maruts," a manuscript of 2,641 pages in four volumes, 187–?; "Translations from the Rig-Veda: Friends of Indra: Svadha: The Purusha: Skuta: Savitri: Names of Rishis," a manuscript of 562 pages, 187–?; and "Translations of the Rig-Veda: Consecutive," a manuscript of 6,939 pages in ten volumes, 1872–86.

15. Pike, *Morals and Dogma*, p. 853.

16. As an adult Pike weighed nearly three hundred pounds. Ethnographers of the Ozarks have recorded legends concerning his equally expansive sexual appetites. See Duncan, *Reluctant General*, pp. 146–47.

17. Albert Pike, "Monotone," *Nugae*, pp. 277–78. See also "Taos" (1832), and "To Ambition" (1836), *Nugae*, pp. 253–58, 238–40.

18. Duncan, *Reluctant General*, p. 14.

19. *Richardson's Monitor of Freemasonry*, pp. 183–87.

20. Of the many ancient ceremonies, moreover, the Eleusinian rites were among the few that initiated women as well as men; see Harold R. Willoughby, *Pagan Regeneration: A Study of Mystery Initiations in the Graeco-Roman World* (Chicago: University of Chicago Press, 1929), p. 38.

21. On the popularity of the Royal Purple, see Elvin J. Curry, *Red Blood of Odd Fellowship* (Baltimore: By author, 1903), p. 247.

22. This account is from the 1881 version of the ritual, in Jonathan Blanchard, "Revised Odd Fellowship Illustrated" (Chicago: Ezra A. Cook, 1881), pp. 203–22.

23. "Oration, by W. M. James Laird, Grand Orator, at the Annual Session of the Grand Lodge of Nebraska" (1876), in L. S. Myler, ed., *Jewels of Masonic Oratory* (New York: M. W. Hazen, 1898), pp. 137, 149.

24. James R. Carnahan, *Pythian Knighthood: Its History and Literature* (Cincinnati: Pettibone Mfr. Co., 1890), p. 539.

25. Henry L. Stillson, ed., *The Official History and Literature of Odd Fellowship* (Boston: Fraternity Publishing Co., 1897), pp. 147, 667–68.

26. Stillson, *History of Odd Fellowship*, p. 677, also pp. 676–86, 692–94, 701–02. The Pythians already had established the Uniform Rank in 1877. The Red Men created the Chieftain's League in 1885, the Ancient Order of Foresters established the Uniformed Branch in 1887, and the Knights of the Maccabees formed the Uniform Rank in 1890.

27. [Jonathan Blanchard comp.], *Patriarchs Militant Illustrated* (Chicago: Ezra Cook, 1886), pp. 302–27.

28. "Freemasonry and Odd Fellowship," *Voice of Masonry* (April 1874).

29. *Masonic Mirror and Keystone*, February 10, 1858.

30. See "Physical Qualifications," *Masonic Review* (March 1870); "Physical Perfection," *Masonic Review* (January 1869).

31. "Maimed Candidates," *Voice of Masonry* (January 1878); "No Maim," *Voice of Masonry* (April 1878).

32. "Want of an Arm," *Mystic Star* (July 1872).

33. "Physical Qualifications," *Masonic Review* (March 1870). See also "Physical Perfection," *Masonic Review* (January 1869).

34. "Physical Perfection," *Masonic Review* (January 1869). See also "Want of an Arm," *Mystic Star* (July 1872).

35. John Higham, "The Reorientation of American Culture in the 1890's," in *The Origins of Modern Consciousness* ed. John Weiss (Detroit: Wayne State University Press, 1965), pp. 25–48.

36. E. W. H. Ellis, "Song for the Lodge Room," *Masonic Review* (July 1865), p. 284. See also the first song in George B. Chase, *The Masonic Harp* (Boston: Oliver Ditson and Co., 1858), p. 1.

37. *Ritual of the Grand Army of the Republic, adopted in General Convention at Philadelphia, Pennsylvania, January 17, 1868* (Chicago: Ezra A. Cook, 1875).

38. *Official Ritual (Third Revision) of the Modern Woodmen of America* (Modern Woodmen of America, 1909), pp. 24–35.

39. See Talcott Parsons, "The Kinship System of the Contemporary United States," *American Anthropologist* 45 (1943), pp. 22–38; and id., "The Social Structure of the Family," in *The Family: Its Function and Destiny*, ed. Ruth Nanda Anshen (New York, 1959).

40. See Eleanor E. Maccoby and Carol N. Jacklin, *The Psychology of Sex Differences* (Stanford, Calif.: Stanford University Press, 1974), pp. 343, 363–64.

41. Louisa May Alcott, *Little Women* (1868; reprint, New York, Bantam, 1983), p. 10.

42. William D. Kennedy, *Pythian History* (Chicago: Pythian History Publishing Co., 1904) pp. 27–36.

43. Gary Scharnhorst and Jack Bales, *The Lost Life of Horatio Alger, Jr.* (Bloomington, Ind.: Indiana University Press, 1985) p. xix.

44. Duncan, *Reluctant General*, pp. 253–72.

45. Richard Sennett, *Families Against the City: Middle Class Homes of Industrial Chicago, 1872–1890* (New York: Vintage, 1974), pp. 187, 215, 225.

46. See Perry Duis review of *Families Against the City* in *American Journal of Sociology* 76 (March 1971).

47. Blanchard, *Scotch Rite Masonry Illustrated* 2:397–98.

48. Ibid., 2:438.

49. Pike, *Morals and Dogma*, pp. 849–51.

50. Pike, *Morals and Dogma*, pp. 789–90, 861; see also Mackey, *Symbolism of Freemasonry*, pp. 184–95.

51. Pike, *Morals and Dogma*, pp. 697–99, 800; see also Mackey, *Symbolism of Freemasonry*, pp. 111–16.

52. Pike, *Morals and Dogma*, p. 861. The emphasis on the two opposing principles in man is also discussed in Carnahan, *Pythian Knighthood*, p. 593.

53. Pike discusses phallic worship at several places in *Morals and Dogma*. The secret was also disclosed in Mackey's *Symbolism of Freemasonry*, in Masonic maga-

zines, and by Masonic lecturers. See, for example, Homer Bartlett, "History of Initiation: As Practiced by the Ancient Rites and Perpetuated by Freemasonry," *Voice of Masonry* (May 1877); and Robert W. Hill, "Dissertation: The Name of God [1896]" in L. S. Myler, ed., *Jewels of Masonic Oratory*, pp. 341–46.

EPILOGUE

1. Data on fraternal membership are taken from *Statistics on Fraternal Societies* (Rochester, N.Y.: Fraternal Monitor) an annual compendium of information on orders that offered insurance benefits. From 1926 to 1935 *Statistics on Fraternal Societies* reported a decline in adult male membership of nearly four million.

2. James West noted that "a few years back nearly every formally approved male joined one or more of the well-known lodges," but now the lodges were "all dying in function"; see "Plainville, U.S.A.," in *The Psychological Frontiers of Society* (New York: Columbia University Press, 1945), pp. 382–83. W. Lloyd Warner similarly observed that a generation earlier "every important man" was a Mason, an Odd Fellow, or a Woodman, but prominent men no longer joined the lodges; see Warner, *Democracy in Jonesville; A Study in Quality and Inequality* (New York: Harper and Brothers, 1949), pp. 118–19.

3. *Proceedings of the Grand Lodge of Free and Accepted Masons of New York State* (New York: Lent and Graff, 1920); pp. 36–37; see also the *Proceedings of the Ninth Annual Convention of the Grand Lodge of the Knights of Pythias of New York, 1927*, particularly the speech by the Grand Chancellor entitled "The Tuberculosis of Fraternalism," p. 356.

The proceedings listed in these notes of the various state grand lodges and conventions are available at the New York Public Library Annex.

4. Robert and Helen M. Lynd, *Middletown* (New York: Harcourt Brace, 1929), p. 306.

5. *Proceedings of the Grand Lodge of Free and Accepted Masons of the State of California* (By the Lodge, 1920), p. 79; cited in Lynn Dumenil, *Freemasonry and American Culture, 1880–1939* (Princeton, N.J.: Princeton University Press, 1977), p. 188.

6. In *Freemasonry and American Culture*, Dumenil provides the best synthesis of these factors. On the problems of the 1920s, see pp. 180–82; on the increase in blue-collar members, see pp. 151, 230–31; on the changing recruitment policies, see pp. 151–54.

7. Ernest L. West, *The Masonic World* 7 (January 1926), p. 5; cited in Dumenil, *Freemasonry and American Culture*, p. 185. See Dumenil, ibid., pp. 185–217.

8. Cited in Francis J. Scully, *History of the Grand Encampment Knights Templars of the U.S.A.* (Greenfield, Ind.: W. M. Mitchell, 1952), p. 173.

9. *Illinois Freemason* 36 (August 20, 1921); cited in Dumenil, *Freemasonry and American Culture*, p. 188.

10. Dumenil, *Freemasonry and American Culture*, pp. 185–217.

11. The orders that managed to survive, some scholars argue, "secularized their behavior to a great degree, minimizing the lodge ritual and its dependent features including the use of passwords, the wearing of lodge regalia, and the performance of the secret ritual" (Warner, *Democracy in Jonesville*, pp. 119–20).

12. *Proceedings of the Grand Lodge . . . of New York State*, 1933, pp. 34–35.

13. *Proceedings of the Improved Order of Odd-Fellows, Grand Lodge of Connecticut, 1924*, p. 126.

14. "Report on Correspondence," *Proceedings of the Grand Lodge . . . of New York State*, 1931, p. 16.

15. *Ninth Annual Convention of Pythians*, 1927, p. 241.

16. Dumenil, *Freemasonry and American Culture*, p. 163.

17. Members in the nineteenth century had noted that the "*regular, habitual* [their emphasis]" attenders were "almost universally" the young men, with a sprinkling of elderly regulars; see "Visit to My Old Lodge—Too Few Attend—Why?" *Voice of Masonry* (April 1867); "I am Too Old," *Masonic Review* (October 1866); and "Uniformity in Rituals," *Masonic Review* (May 1869). By contrast, in 1949 Warner reported that the sons of prominent men "have not joined and express no interest in doing so" (*Democracy in Jonesville*, p. 119); West, in 1945, had observed: "Young men are no longer anxious to join; the rituals are carried on mainly by the old" (*Psychological Frontiers*, p. 283). See also *Ninth Annual Convention of Pythians*, 1927, p. 356; and *Proceedings of the Independent Order of Odd-Fellows, Maine*, 1923, pp. 413–14.

18. "Address of the Most Worshipful Robert H. Robinson," *Proceedings of the Grand Lodge . . . of New York State*, 1921, p. 35.

19. Cited in Warner, *Democracy in Jonesville*, p. 119.

20. See Frederick Lewis Allen, *Only Yesterday: An Informal History of the Nineteen-Twenties* (New York: 1931), pp. 88–122; and William E. Leuchtenburg, *The Perils of Prosperity: 1914–1932* (Chicago: University of Chicago Press 1958); pp. 158–77. More recently, Peter Filene has argued that World War I killed "Victorian concepts of manliness and womanliness" and that the 1920s marked the beginning of a new era in sex roles; see Filene, *Him / Her / Self: Sex Roles in Modern America* (Baltimore: Johns Hopkins University Press, 1986), p. 115.

21. Lewis A. Erenberg, "Everybody's Doin' It: The Pre–World War I Dance Craze, the Castles, and the Modern American Girl," *Feminist Studies* 3 (1975).

22. James R. McGovern, "The American Woman's Pre–World War I Freedom in Manners and Morals," *Journal of American History* Vol. 55 (1968); John Higham, "The Reorientation of American Culture in the 1890s," in John Weiss, ed., *The Origins of Modern Consciousness* (Detroit: Wayne State University Press, 1965), pp. 30–31. See also John C. Burnham, "The Progressive Era Revolution in American Attitudes Toward Sex," *Journal of American History* 59 (1973).

23. James Reed, *From Private Vice to Public Virtue: The Birth Control Movement and American Society since 1830* (New York: Basic Books, 1978), p. 61.

24. Cited in McGovern, "American Woman's Pre–World I Freedom," pp. 324–25.

25. Kenneth Keniston, "Social Change and Youth in America," *Daedalus* (Winter

1961), pp. 145–71. The peer culture received intellectual support from G. Stanley Hall, who suggested that adolescence be extended to ensure that students could experience the full measure of emotional growth; see G. Stanley Hall, *Adolescence* (New York: D. Appleton and Co., 1904), 2:61–70.

26. Henry Seidel Canby, *The Age of Confidence: Life in the Nineties* (New York: Farrar and Rinehart, 1934), pp. 50–51, 71.

27. The phrase is the title of chapter 5 (p. 218) in Sheila Rothman, *Woman's Proper Place: A History of Changing Ideals and Practices, 1870 to the Present* (New York: Basic Books, 1978).

28. Cited in Rothman, *Woman's Proper Place*, p. 98.

29. See also "Maternal Instinct Run Riot," *Good Housekeeping* (June 1911). A pamphlet entitled "Child Management," from the Children's Bureau, gave this advice: "The very love of a mother for her child may be the 'stumbling block'. . . . This love is invariably associated with excessive worry, anxiety, and, at times, definite fear which prevent the most intelligent approach to many problems of childhood"; cited in Rothman, *Woman's Proper Place*, p. 211. Ernest and Gladys H. Groves, in *Wholesome Childhood* (Boston: Houghton Mifflin, 1924) added that mothers in the past erred by holding their children emotionally captive. Emma Marwedal's child rearing manual, *Conscious Motherhood* (Boston: D. C. Heath, 1889) insisted that a solely feminine influence would limit a child's potential; see Davis, *Childhood and History in America* (New York: Psychohistory Press, 1976), p. 99. Henry Clay Trumbell, *Hints on Child Training* (Philadelphia: J. D. Wattles, 1890).

30. Wanda C. Bronson, Edith S. Katten, and Norma Livson, "Patterns of Authority and Affection in Two Generations," *Journal of Abnormal and Social Psychology* 58 (1959), pp. 143–52.

31. White House Conference on Child Health and Protection, *The Young Child in the Home, A Survey of 3,000 American Families* (New York, 1936); these and related materials are summarized in Paula Fass, *The Damned and the Beautiful: American Youth in the 1920's* (New York: Oxford University Press, 1977), pp. 53–118.

32. Margaret Marsh, "Suburban Men and Masculine Domesticity, 1870–1915," *American Quarterly* 40 (June 1988).

33. Ibid.

34. Victor Turner, *Process, Performance and Pilgrimage* (New Delhi-Concept, 1979), p. 38.

35. Claude Lévi-Strauss, *Totemism* (Boston: Beacon Press, 1963), trans. Rodney Needham, pp. 69, 71.

36. Ibid., p. 96; see also id., *The Savage Mind* (Chicago: University of Chicago Press, 1962).

37. Both Durkheim and Lévi-Strauss use the term *refractory*. See Emile Durkheim and Marcel Mauss, *Primitive Classification*, trans. Rodney Needham (Chicago: University of Chicago Press, 1963) p. 88; and Lévi-Strauss, *Totemism*, p. 69. "The most obscure side of man" is Lévi-Strauss's description.

38. Durkheim's work, for example, is oddly inconsistent insofar as he dismissed

explanations rooted in human emotions, yet conceived of society itself as the product of emotions, the articulation of the "collective conscience."

39. Turner, *Process, Performance and Pilgrimage*, p. 37.

40. Joseph D. Weeks, *History of the Knights of Pythias* (Pittsburgh: Joseph Weeks and Co., 1874) p. 284.

Schlesinger, Arthur M., Sr., 2, 4
Schoolcraft, Henry Rowe, 97
Schools: on women's increasing role in, 112
Scotch Rite Freemasonry: origins of, 12, 22, 134–35; described, 52, 55–56, 64–65, 135, 137–39, 146–47. *See also* Mackey, Albert; Pike, Albert
Sennett, Richard, 145–46
Sexuality, women's: denial of, 117
Shriners, 152
Signet of King Solomon, The (Arnold), 82–83
Sizer, Sandra, 78
Sklar, Kathryn Kish, 107
Smith, Gerrit, 73
Smith, Joseph, 6, 72
Smith-Rosenberg, Carroll, 107
Social learning theory, 115
Solomon's Temple (Bunyan), 46–47
Sons of Honor, 7
Sons of Liberty, 22
Sons of Malta, 8
Sons of Temperance, 7, 173*n*23
Sparks, Jared, 50
Stephens, Uriah S., 9, 10, 61
Stevens, Thaddeus, 8
Stillson, Henry L., 92, 141
Stone, William Leete, 97
Sunshine in Shadowed Lives (Martin), 83
Supreme Tribe of Ben-Hur, 5
Symbols: difficulty of interpreting, 13–14; as means to convey emotional meanings, 35–36, 144, 177*n*60; and tetragrammaton, 58, 148–49; and triangle, 58, 147–48; multivocalic character of, 62–63, 126–27, 149, 156–57; of light and darkness, 71, 89–90, 126; of death, 126, and point within a circle, 148. *See also* Fraternal ritual
System of Speculative Masonry, A (Town), 49

Tappan, Arthur, 73
Temperance societies, 7, 11. *See also* Good Templars
Tiger, Lionel, 202*n*35
Tocqueville, Alexis de, 2, 111
Tom Sawyer (Twain), 124
Tonawanda Reservation, 94, 96, 106
Town, Rev. Salem, 49, 97
Tricoche, George, 10–11
True Womanhood, 82–88 passim
Trumbell, Henry C., 155
Turner, Victor: on interpretation of rituals, 13, 177*n*60; on "liminal" rituals, 32–33, 156, 158; on "multivocalic" character of symbols, 63, 127
Twain, Mark, 124, 182*n*48
Typology: as used in fraternal ritual, 47

Uncle Tom's Cabin (Stowe), 73
Uniformed degrees, 141–43, 213*n*26
Union Veterans' Legion, 8
Unitarianism: Channing's views of, 50–51
United Confederate Veterans, 8
Upchurch, John J., 8–9

Valentinus, 147, 149
Veterans' organizations, 8; *See also* Grand Army of the Republic
Voice of Masonry, on stability of rituals, 28–29; on religion, 75, 76; name changed, 81; criticizes "Ladies' Degrees," 86–87; on ancient initiations, 117

Wallace, Anthony F. C., 31
Wallace, Lew, 5, 124–25
Watson, John, 155
Webb, Thomas Smith, 48–49
Weber, Max, 110
Weeks, Joseph, 35, 158, 193*n*33
Weld, Theodore, 73